Exemplarist Moral Theory

EXEMPLARIST
MORAL THEORY

LINDA TRINKAUS ZAGZEBSKI

OXFORD
UNIVERSITY PRESS

Oxford University Press is a department of the University of Oxford. It furthers
the University's objective of excellence in research, scholarship, and education
by publishing worldwide. Oxford is a registered trade mark of Oxford University
Press in the UK and certain other countries.

Published in the United States of America by Oxford University Press
198 Madison Avenue, New York, NY 10016, United States of America.

© Oxford University Press 2017

First issued as an Oxford University Press paperback, 2019

Library of Congress Cataloging-in-Publication Data
Names: Zagzebski, Linda Trinkaus, 1946– author.
Title: Exemplarist moral theory / Linda Zagzebski.
Description: New York : Oxford University Press, 2017.
Identifiers: LCCN 2016028873| ISBN 9780190655846 (hardcover : alk. paper) |
ISBN 9780190072254 (paperback : alk. paper) | ISBN 9780190655853 (online content)
Subjects: LCSH: Ethics. | Good and evil. | Heroes.
Classification: LCC BJ37 .Z34 2017 | DDC 171—dc23
LC record available at https://lccn.loc.gov/2016028873

Dedicated to the memory of my mother, Doris McTevia Trinkaus

Contents

Preface

THIS BOOK ORIGINATED about twenty years ago when I got the idea of creating a type of moral theory that arises out of direct reference to particular persons—not their traits of character, but the persons themselves. Eventually I developed this idea into a distinctively Christian form of ethics that I called *Divine Motivation Theory* in a book published in 2004. The basic idea of that book was that all value flows from God, the supreme exemplar, and it made the Incarnation both the theoretical and the practical focus of the theory. My primary intention was to give a new way to solve some puzzles in philosophical theology, but it contained the germ of the theory I now call exemplarist moral theory, or just exemplarism.

I pursued the idea of making exemplars the focus in defining a good life in a paper I called "The Admirable Life and the Desirable Life," first presented at a conference in Dundee, Scotland, at the invitation of Timothy Chappell, and subsequently published in *Values and Virtues*, edited by Timothy Chappell, Oxford University Press, 2006. Portions of that paper have become part of Chapter 6 of this book.

In June 2008 Heather Battaly invited me to give a paper at a conference on virtue and vice at California State University, Fullerton, which became the basis for Chapter 1. I gave the paper again at the invitation of Miguel Angel Fernandez Vargas at the National Autonomous University of Mexico, Mexico City, in November 2008. It was published as "Exemplarist Virtue Theory," *Metaphilosophy* 41:1–2, January 2010, pp. 41–57, and reprinted in *Virtue and Vice: Moral and Epistemic*, edited by Heather Battaly, Wiley-Blackwell, 2010.

After taking a few years to write a book in epistemology (*Epistemic Authority*, 2012), I returned to the exemplar project and presented a paper, "Moral Exemplars in Theory and Practice," at a symposium on the topic "Can virtue be taught?" at the School of Education, Stanford University,

October 2012, and then as a keynote address at the conference on virtues and values, Peking University, Bejing, China, November 2012. The paper was subsequently published in *Theory and Research in Education* 11:2 (July 2013), edited by Randall Curran.

In spring semester 2013 I was fortunate to receive a generous fellowship from the Wake Forest Character Project to work on the manuscript of "Exemplarist Virtue Theory," and I received another generous grant from the John Templeton Foundation in academic year 2013–14 to complete a draft of the manuscript. I am very grateful for both of those grants, in particular, to Craig Joseph, who encouraged the project, and to Christian Miller, who gave me very detailed and extremely helpful comments on the entire manuscript.

In fall 2014 I taught a graduate seminar on the book manuscript at the University of Oklahoma, and I want to thank the students in that seminar for invigorating discussions and many comments that improved the manuscript enormously. Their contributions to my thought both inside and outside the classroom are a source of deep satisfaction to me.

In September 2014 I was fortunate to be invited by the philosophy departments of St. Olaf College and Carleton College, Minnesota, to participate in a weekend retreat centered on the manuscript. The project was greatly improved by the discussions that weekend, and I am particularly grateful to Charles Taliaferro, chair of the St. Olaf Philosophy Department, for the invitation for a very enjoyable and profitable weekend.

While working on the manuscript I wrote two papers on admiration that became portions of Chapter 2. "Admiration and the Admirable" was published in *Proceedings of the Aristotelian Society* supplementary volume, 2015, and I am very grateful to Terence Irwin for his companion paper in the same volume. Both papers were written for the Joint Session of the Aristotelian Society and the Mind Association. The second paper, "Exemplarism and Admiration," has been published in *Character: New Directions from Philosophy, Psychology, and Theology*, edited by Christian Miller, Oxford University Press, 2015, and was supported by the grant from Wake Forest University.

In fall 2015 I gave five Gifford Lectures on exemplarism in St. Andrews, Scotland. I am very grateful to Louise Richardson, principal and vice-chancellor of the University of St. Andrews, for the invitation, and to the Divinity School, particularly to my gracious hosts, Professor Mark Elliott, head of school, and Professor Alan Torrance. I want to make special mention of the expert organization of my whole trip by Bethan Williams, who made my visit delightful. I was fortunate to share meals and lively conversation with many faculty and graduate students in the divinity school and the philosophy department at St. Andrews, including Sarah Broadie, Katherine Hawley, John Perry, and Eric Priest, as well as visitors who came for the lectures from other countries, particularly Benjamin and Michael Polansky from the United States, Maria Silvia Vaccarezza and Michel Croce from Italy, and Carsten Fogh Nielsen from Denmark. I want to give special thanks to students Sonia Blank and Wes Skolits for enjoyable conversation, meals, and sightseeing.

Tom Carson has been a special friend and supporter throughout this project, and I am grateful to his master's student, John Roselle, S.J., for his work on exemplarism. Tom's work on the exemplarity of Lincoln is apparent in several places in this book.

I owe a special debt of gratitude to my outstanding research assistants. David Spindle assisted me at the beginning of the project in 2012–13, and at the very end of the project in spring 2016. Benjamin Polansky was my research assistant in 2013–14, and Cody Weaver in 2014–15. Kevin Nordby gave me considerable assistance during fall 2015 while I was preparing and delivering the Gifford Lectures.

Finally, I want to thank my husband, Ken, and the University of Oklahoma for continuous support and encouragement in my life and in all of my work.

Norman, Oklahoma
May 7, 2016

1

Why Exemplarism?

1. Introduction

In every era and in every culture there have been supremely admirable persons who show us the upper reaches of human capability, and in doing so, inspire us to expect more from ourselves. These are the people I am calling exemplars. Most exemplars are not exemplary in every respect, although the Christian saint comes close, assuming that a saint is someone who is both spiritually and morally exemplary. A different kind of exemplar is the hero, a person who takes great risks to achieve a moral end, often the end of helping others in distress. Heroes have dramatic moral accomplishments in character and in action, but they might not be praiseworthy in every respect.

There are also persons who are admirable for something non-moral. Geniuses and the athletically or artistically gifted are admirable for a talent, but while they are inspirational, we cannot imitate their talent. Such people do not express an ideal that others can adopt for themselves. But it is significant that talented people do not usually attract our admiration unless they have also developed their talent through determination and hard work, and those are qualities we can imitate.

There is also the category of the sage, or wise person, whose admirable features include both moral and intellectual excellences, and sometimes spiritual excellences. The sage is an important figure in Confucianism and Stoicism, and there are variations of the idea of the sage in Hinduism, Sufism, Buddhism, the Rabbinic literature, and Native American literature.[1] Aristotle distinguished two kinds of wise persons: the *sophos*, or

---

1. Chief Plenty Coups, the last great chief of the Crow tribe, is an interesting example of a visionary sage who led his people at a time of radical disruption in their traditional way of life. I discuss him in Chapter 3. Rabbi Akiba ben Joseph, one of the most prominent of the

theoretically wise person, and the *phronimos*, or practically wise person. The latter can be used as a touchstone for moral decision making, whereas the former seeks goods above the human and is often useless in practical matters (*Nicomachean Ethics* [*NE*] 6 1141a 20–1141b 8). This division between two kinds of wisdom complicates the use of the sage as an exemplar for the purposes of moral theory, but I do not mind beginning with a notion of an exemplar that is somewhat broader than the idea of the *moral* exemplar as recognized in contemporary Western discourse. I have no firm view on the limits of the moral anyway, and I think it is helpful to let the historical literature frame the discussion, recognizing that cultural and historical inclusiveness pushes us in the direction of broadening the domain of the moral. For readers who have a more restricted view of morality, it should be relatively easy to modify the theory I propose in this book to suit their point of view.

I will begin, then, with a notion of the exemplar that includes the saint, the hero, and the sage, but it will not include the genius.[2] I assume that in-born talent is admirable, but in a sense that is non-moral even when the moral is broadly construed. I will, however, include the sage. Confucian ethics does not make sense without the sage, and I take it for granted that Confucian ethics is ethics.

Exemplars are not just good; they are supremely excellent. I said that they are supremely admirable. That is because I assume that there is something in us that detects the excellent, and that is the emotion of admiration. We identify the excellent with the admirable, and we detect the admirable by the experience of admiration. We can be mistaken in what we take to be admirable, and hence excellent, and that means that the emotion of admiration can be mistaken. It can mislead us. I will have more to say about admiration and its trustworthiness in Chapter 2, but I assume that the emotion of admiration is a universal human experience, and we recognize a connection between feeling admiration and seeing someone *as* admirable, as deserving of admiration. As we will see later, people sometimes resent the admirable, and this is one way in which judging that someone is admirable is not always associated with feeling

---

sages in the Mishnah, is a prime example from early Rabbinism. In Sufism, one might consider the India-born Hazrat Inayat Khan of the last century.

2. It is interesting that Max Scheler ([1933] 1987) includes the genius as a category of exemplars, along with the saint, the hero, the leading mind of a civilization, and a master in the art of living.

admiration, but I believe that the emotion of admiration is the primary way we identify exemplars.

My purpose in this book is to show how to use exemplars to construct a comprehensive ethical theory.[3] I will define all central terms in moral discourse, including "virtue," "right act," "duty," and "good life," by direct reference to exemplars, or persons *like that*, where *that* is the object of admiration. In each case, the idea is not to construct a conceptual relationship between the term to be defined and the *concept* of an exemplar. Rather, the idea is to begin the explanation of what these terms mean by referring directly to actual exemplars, identified through the experience of admiration. The theory is modeled on the theory of Direct Reference in the form in which Hilary Putnam (1975) and Saul Kripke (1980) used it in giving the semantics of natural kind terms, but I am not interested in natural kinds per se, and will not discuss subsequent work on natural kinds except when pertinent to the model I am proposing.

In constructing this theory, I have a number of aims, some of which are theoretical, and some of which are practical.

First, I have the philosophical purpose of creating a comprehensive ethical theory that serves the same purposes as deontological, consequentialist, and virtue theories. I will not present the theory in sufficient detail to be a fully developed alternative to these theories, but I will explain and defend the basic features of the theory. One of the ways in which the theory is unusual is that it is designed to be completed by other parts of our moral practices, including narratives and work in a number of fields outside of philosophy.

Second, I have the practical purpose of producing a theory that can be used to actually make persons moral by structuring the theory around a motivating emotion, the emotion of admiration. Moral educators have often been disappointed with philosophical ethics because there is so little connection between understanding ethics and being a morally good person. Of course, it should not be surprising that a theory is theoretical, not practical, and I will say more about my theory of moral theory in the next section, but it is an important advantage of an ethical theory if it is practically useful. By that I mean both that it gives us directions on what to do and how to live, and it can be used to make us want to do so.

---

3. Like many, but not all philosophers, I use the terms "ethical" and "moral" interchangeably.

Third, I want an ethical theory that tracks moral development. I consider it an advantage of a moral theory if it is not simply an abstract structure, but it also explains and justifies a genealogy of morals. The genealogy I have in mind is both the moral development of an individual person and the development of a cultural community that is capable of undergoing moral change, even the rare moral revolution. There are psychological conditions for moral development that we can identify. It often takes place in the telling and re-telling of narratives, and in the imitation of models. I aim at a theory that is responsive to these conditions for human moral development and can justify them.

Fourth, I aim to link the a priori side of ethics with research in psychology and neuroscience. Lately there has been a great deal of interest in integrating empirical work with moral philosophy. The theory I will present integrates empirical work in a strong sense. It is constructed in such a way that it gives empirical studies a central place in the body of the theory. This is one of the ways in which the theory I am presenting here is incomplete. Parts of the theory await the outcome of empirical work. Later I will refer to some of the work that has already been done to show the direction that I think should be pursued to fill in the substantive details of the theory.

Fifth, I aim at a theory that meets the need for different versions for different communities, including faith communities, but which is also useful in framing the discussion in cross-cultural discourse. This point applies both to discourse between radically different societies and discourse within a pluralistic society. I assume that we do not wish to require people to adopt as their sole moral vocabulary moral terms used and accepted by all members of a larger society. Certainly, deliberations and debates about public policy issues must attempt to reach as many persons as possible, but that is no reason to think that the detailed narratives and rich conceptual resources of individual communities must disappear from public debate. I aim to propose a theory that is sensitive to this problem. The structure of the theory does not require that the exemplars in all communities are exactly alike. The exemplarist approach permits different versions for communities that identify distinct but overlapping sets of exemplars while giving a natural way for members of different communities to find common ground. A central aspect of my theory is that there are linguistic conditions for finding common ground, and I discuss that in Chapter 7.

2. My Theory of Theory

Since the theory I propose is novel in several ways, I begin by describing my theory of moral theory. I think of a moral theory as an abstract structure that aims to simplify, systematize, and justify our moral beliefs and practices. Creating theories is included in the practice of morality. Since one of the aims of a moral theory is to simplify, it needs to leave out many subtleties and complexities in the practice of morality. But we would not construct theories unless we thought that there is something to be gained by simplifying. The limitations of the human mind prevent us from understanding a domain taken as a whole unless we ignore part of the domain we want to understand. The bigger and more complex the domain, the more we have to leave out if we want to understand it. The realm of the moral is enormous, involving almost every aspect of human life and, to some extent, non-human life. It is not surprising that we cannot get our minds around it without mentally stripping away much of interest in our moral practices. There is nothing wrong with that as long as we are not under the illusion that the features of moral practice left out of the theory disappear. We are simply not attending to them when we are engaged in theory building and discussion. They will reappear when we engage in some other part of the practice.

I think this is a general point about understanding that applies even to the understanding of something as simple as the layout of a city. If every feature of the city was on a city map, the map would be as complex in its layout as the city is, and the map would not help us understand it. So the map leaves out many things. It may also distort some things. For instance, the lines depicting roads are often straighter on the map than the roads actually are, and there is even greater distortion in the shape and relative size of countries near the poles on a two-dimensional map of the world. The map can be misleading, but a two-dimensional map is often more useful than a globe, even with the distortion. The distortion does no harm as long as we are aware of it.

In the same way, it is useful to conceptualize moral reality without certain things in it, but it is helpful to keep in mind that what we leave out is done by choice, and the choice can skew the result. For instance, most moral theorists believe that a good moral theory leaves out the identities of the persons in the practice. That is because we think that we get impartiality in our way of understanding morality if we do not mention

who is who. Since I am going to propose a kind of moral theory that identifies certain individuals, I think it is worth thinking about the fact that we
usually make the choice to leave out the identities of persons in a moral
theory, and the choice is made for a reason. As long as we are aware of the
reason for the choice, we might decide that it is not always an advantage
to make that choice.

Maps have different scales, and the same can be said for theories. If we
have a map of a large geographical area such as a continent, we expect to
be able to tell where maps of smaller regions fit on the map of the larger
region. So we should be able to tell where a city map fits on the map of the
continent. We imagine that if we zoomed into the dot on the larger map
indicating a city, we would see the city map. Likewise, if we zoomed into
a part of our moral map, we should be able to reveal theories of friendship, of rights, of duties to future generations, of fair distribution of resources, and all of the other aspects of moral practice that need theoretical
treatment to aid our understanding. In my theory, we should be able to
tell where all of our moral beliefs and practices fit on the map, including narratives, aphorisms, rules like the Ten Commandments, practices
of punishment, and so on. A theory cannot and should not have too many
details, but we should be able to tell where the details fit on the map as
they arise.

For the same reason, I think that an ideal moral theory should also
have a place for other theories, especially theories that are widely known
and adopted. That is because the creation of theories is part of the practices theory is intended to explain. If people sometimes use the principle
of utility or a principle that all persons ought to be treated with respect, a
good theory should include those principles. When philosophers produce
theoretical structures that attempt to justify those principles, their practice of producing the theory becomes a component of our moral practices
taken as a whole, and ideally, a theory should show us why these theories
develop, where they fit on our moral map, and how they might be justified.

I believe that a moral theory is not primarily a manual for decision
making, and it is not primarily constructed for that purpose. Again the
map analogy is helpful. A detailed street map will help us get around a
city, but many maps do not have a practical purpose. When we look at
maps in history books, or when we see maps of battlefields or weather patterns, our aim is not to get anywhere. Likewise, a map of the world is not
detailed enough to help us get from place to place, and it is not intended
to do so. A comprehensive moral theory is similar to a map of the world.

Theories of parts of morality are closer to street maps. But even a street map is not constructed with the sole purpose of guiding a person from place to place. If your primary purpose is to get from one point in a city to another, you might decide that a voice navigation system is a more efficient tool for helping you get around, and you might not use a map at all. But a navigation system cannot give you the understanding of the layout of the city that you get from a map. Similarly, if our main purpose was to get guidance in moral decision making, we would want a manual, not a theory.[4] But the manual would not give us understanding of the domain of morality as a whole.

I said that a moral theory is not a manual, but if a theory can give us directions while satisfying the other desiderata in a moral theory, so much the better. To do that, there has to be some way that a user of the theory can connect the theory to what the theory is about. When we are using a city map, it is only helpful if we can find something in the city that hooks it to the map—*that* intersection over there is *this* one on the map. A stationery map in a shopping mall or tourist area of a town will sometimes have a mark that says "You are here" in order to orient the user. It seems to me that a moral theory needs something that serves that purpose—something that tells her that *this* element of moral belief or practice is *that* element in the theory. Unlike a map of an imaginary city, a moral theory is like a map of an actual city, and a user needs to connect the map with actual moral practice if the map is to be any help in negotiating the practice. I suggest, then, that a moral theory needs a hook to connect it to the domain of moral practices of which it is a theory. Just as a city map is useless unless we can identify something on the map by reference to something in our environment, a moral theory is useless unless we can find a place where the theory connects to a part of the moral domain we can identify independent of the theory.

It is surprisingly easy to fail to get a hook or to have the wrong hook. For example, when Aristotle says at the beginning of the *Nicomachean Ethics* that everyone desires happiness (*eudaimonia*), and goes on to explain the relationship between happiness and virtue, a student may understand the theoretical relationship, but teachers often discover students who have no idea what Aristotle is talking about. They get off

---

4. What I have in mind here is the sort of manual that Catholic priests used to use for the purpose of counseling sinners in the sacrament of Reconciliation (Confession). They included a large catalogue of sins, classified under general moral principles. But priests were trained to understand the moral theology underwriting the manual.

the track on the first page when they encounter the idea of *eudaimonia*. Often they do not connect Aristotle's target with anything in their experience, or even worse, they make a connection, but they confuse *eudaimonia* with something else, usually happiness as a subjective feeling. That makes it very hard for them to track the rest of the work. They are like users of a map who can follow directions—from this point on the map turn right, go fifty yards, turn left, and so forth—but they started in the wrong place, and so they do not end up at the right destination. To avoid this problem, exemplarism is designed with the hook in mind. Exemplars are my hook.

When a map is intended to be used for navigation, it cannot serve its purpose unless there is a motive to follow it. My theory is intended to provide the motive for following the map. It might seem impossible that a theory can arise out of a motivating emotion—not the concept of an emotion, but an emotion itself, but that is what I am going to propose. The motivating element is at the root of the theory. Since admiration motivates emulation of admired persons, the theory is also useful for the purposes of moral education. I think it is a particular advantage of a theory if it can link up with narratives since narratives are one of the primary vehicles for the moral education of the young, and the basic way humans of any age develop and alter their moral sensibilities. Narratives capture the imagination and elicit emotions that motivate action.

I think it is important to keep in mind that our moral practices pre-exist theory. It is an illusion to think that moral theory can be constructed outside of the practices the theory is attempting to systematize and justify. This is not to deny that some parts of our moral practices should be revised, but there are elements of our pre-existing moral practices of which we are more certain than we are of any theory. However, sometimes a theory can lead us to alter our beliefs or practices in response to the theory. In this respect a moral theory is unlike the map of a city. I suppose that we can imagine a map that we liked so much that when the map and the layout of the streets did not coincide, we changed the streets, not the map. But assuming that we do not want to move the streets around, the point of a map is to give us understanding of the physical layout of a city that is already there and that will change for reasons that have nothing to do with the map. Moral theory is different because one of the purposes of the theory is to justify the practices that pre-exist the theory. We might find out that some element of the practice is not easily justified if it is related to other elements of the practice as given in the theory. That could lead us to change the practice in response to the theory. In contrast, a map does not seek to justify the layout of a geographical area, only to depict it.

Given my theory of theory, it is not clear whether moral theories are in competition with one another. Presumably, some theories are better than others, but it is not obvious that there cannot be two equally good theories that are strikingly different. Most of us would strongly hesitate to allow the possibility of two equally good moral manuals that give conflicting moral directions, but as I have said, a theory is not the same as a manual, and I am leaving open the possibility that there can be more than one equally good moral theory. If a theory aims to be comprehensive, it would be naive to think that it would not be compared to other theories that aim to be comprehensive, but if we return to the map analogy, I think we can see that since maps always leave something out, good maps can leave out different things. A topographical map often leaves out roads and political borders, whereas maps that indicate roads and borders typically lack indications of elevation and elevation contours. A map that has both is not necessarily a better map because too much information can be confusing. The map may be hard to read or understand. But when a map is designed to get you somewhere, multiple maps should get you to the same place. That is why different moral theories yield mostly the same moral verdicts about particular cases. When they do not, we know that one of them is faulty.

3. Direct Reference

The theory I propose is foundational in structure. By that I mean that the entire theory is constructed out of a single point of origin. Foundationalist theories have advantages of simplicity and elegance, but they are particularly vulnerable to skepticism about the proposed foundation. It is no accident that neo-Aristotelian theories that start from the concept of *eudaimonia*—happiness or flourishing—generate more discussion about the vagueness of the foundation and the difficulty in justifying it than the very rich and interesting derivative parts of the theory. The same point applies to the Kantian idea of the Good Will and the various forms of consequentialism. This problem need not be devastating to the theory, but if a theory begins with something that requires that important substantive issues have already been decided, it is bound to raise lots of questions before the theory gets going. I want to make the foundation of my theory something that most of us trust—the people we admire upon reflection. The structure is foundationalist, but instead of starting with a concept, the theory begins with exemplars of moral goodness identified directly by the emotion of admiration. The identity of exemplars is one of the dominant features of the moral practices that precede theory, and we are often more certain of the identities of exemplars than we are of any conceptual foundation. For instance, I think that we are more certain that Confucius, Jesus, and Socrates are admirable than we are of claims about the good of pleasure, or what human flourishing is, or the good of doing one's duty, or any of the other claims that are used to ground a moral theory. In fact, I think that we are more certain that they are admirable than we are of *what* is admirable about them. Of course we may disagree about which individuals are exemplars, but I think that as a community we can agree about a lot of them, and we do not need very many to get the theory going. This is an advantage of starting with exemplars.

My model for the foundational move in constructing a theory of this kind is the influential theory of Direct Reference, which was developed by Hilary Putnam (1975), and Saul Kripke (1980) in the 1970s and led to a revolution in semantics. Direct reference has been used in a completely different way from the one I propose in the well-known theory of Richard Boyd (1988). I agree with Boyd that close attention to the semantics of direct reference opens up a different kind of connection between the mind of the user of moral terms, on the one hand, and the user's linguistic community and the moral world the user seeks to understand or change, on the other. But I am going to proceed in a different direction. Let me begin with the traditional semantics direct reference sought to replace.

The dominant theory of meaning prior to Putnam's 1975 paper, "The Meaning of 'Meaning,'" was the descriptivist theory that went roughly as follows: Knowing the meaning of a word is being in the psychological state of grasping a descriptive concept that roughly corresponds to the meaning of the term as given in a dictionary, and a user of the term designates whatever satisfies the given description. For instance, the meaning of "hammer" is something like "heavy tool with a handle at a right angle to the head, used to drive in nails." A person who grasps the meaning of "hammer" (a) mentally grasps that description, and (b) refers to objects that satisfy that description when she uses the word. When she has beliefs about hammers, or makes assertions about hammers, or asks questions about hammers, she is thinking and talking about objects in the world that fit the description in her head.

Even if we find this account of meaning and reference plausible for terms such as "hammer" and other common nouns and adjectives such as "table," "book," "cupcake," "pretty," and "funny," it is not plausible for proper names, and it is not plausible for natural kind terms—terms for naturally occurring substances and species.[5] Take "water" as an example. The meaning of "water" cannot be "colorless, odorless liquid in the lakes and streams and falling from the sky," or any other description that we use in ordinary discourse to pick out water. That is because we can imagine that something other than water looked like water and fell from the sky and ran in the streams. Furthermore, we can succeed in referring to water even if we associate the wrong descriptions with "water."[6] What makes water *water* is that it is H_2O. But the meaning of "water" cannot be "H_2O" since people did not even have the concept of H_2O, much less use it in explaining the meaning of "water," until recent centuries, nor do we think that the discovery that water is H_2O was a change in the meaning of the word "water." We think that at some point in the early modern age human beings found out the nature of something that people had been talking about all along.

The theory of direct reference explains these features of "water" and other natural kind terms. Leaving aside some variations in the theory, the basic idea is that a natural kind term like "water" or "gold" or "human" refers to whatever is the same kind of thing or stuff as some indexically identified instance. Gold is, roughly, whatever is the same element as *that*, water is whatever is the same liquid as *that*, a human is whatever is a member of the same species as *that*, and so on, where in each case the demonstrative term "that" refers directly—in the simplest case, by pointing. This approach explains how it is that often we do not know the nature of the referent of a term, and yet we know how to use the term in a way that links up with that nature. Someone may not know the nature of gold—its deep structure—and for millennia nobody did, but that did not prevent people from successfully learning the word "gold" in a way that fixed the

---

5. As I mention below, Putnam (1975, 160) says that he has used natural kind terms as his examples, but he believes that his points about direct reference apply to the great majority of nouns, including artifact terms, and other parts of speech.

6. Perhaps the first person in the direct reference movement to point out that we can succeed in referring when we associate the wrong description with the term was Keith Donnellan (1966). He says he can succeed in referring to a certain man by calling him "the man drinking a martini" even when the intended referent is drinking something other than a martini.

reference of the term and continued to do so long after the discovery of what distinguishes gold from other elements. We now know something important about the nature of the same stuff of which people used to be ignorant. The theory of direct reference explains how "gold" referred to the same thing before and after the discovery of the molecular structure of gold. The descriptivist theory does not.

The theory of direct reference therefore maintained that speakers of the language can use certain kinds of terms to successfully refer to the right things without going through a descriptive meaning. It is not necessary for semantic success that every speaker be able to reliably identify instances of a kind like gold, nor need they be able to explain what distinguishes gold from other elements. However, in Putnam's version of the theory, the semantic success of ordinary speakers depends on their connection to other speakers in the community who can identify instances of gold, and who understand what makes gold the kind that it is. Ordinary users of the word "gold" can form beliefs and make statements about gold because they are semantically connected to gold through a linguistic network that privileges certain users—the experts. Putnam called this the Principle of the Division of Linguistic Labor (1975, 144–146).[7]

Direct reference leads to an important distinction between superficial features and deep features of a natural kind. If a natural kind is *that*, we can use superficial features of *that* to fix the reference of a kind term in order to examine it. For water, the superficial features are something like being an odorless, colorless liquid that flows in the streams and falls from the sky. We can only point to a few instances of water, but the superficial features permit us to identify other instances of water for examination. Similarly, for gold, the superficial features are something like being a golden colored metal with sufficient malleability to be made into jewelry. The superficial features do not give the meaning of a natural kind term, and they are not necessary and sufficient conditions for being a member of the kind. They are merely the easily observed features that permit us to identify enough other members of the kind that we can go on to discover what deep features instances of the kind have in common. We find out

---

7. Putnam (1975) emphasized the social dimension of meaning with deference to experts. In Kripke's (1980) version of the theory, a natural kind term refers in a way that he thought was analogous to proper names, causally linked to a historical baptism: "Water is that." Later speakers then refer to the same thing originally designated "water." I am not using a historical version of the theory here, although there is historical continuity in our use of moral terms.

what makes a substance or species what it is through empirical observation of the stuff we pick out through the superficial features. In this way we find out that water is H_2O, that gold is the element with atomic number 79, that tigers are the species with a certain biological structure, and so on.

The deep features of a kind are significant in two ways. First, we think that the deep structure (being H_2O, having atomic number 79, etc.) is what makes the kind the kind that it is. Being H_2O is what makes water *water*. And second, we think that the deep features explain the superficial features. Being H_2O explains why it is that water is a colorless, odorless liquid. This approach to the meaning of natural kind terms therefore smoothly connects semantics to science. The semantics tells you where to look. The science does the observation.

If we add some plausible assumptions to the theory of direct reference, we get the interesting consequence that there are necessary truths discovered empirically. Kripke thought that once the reference of a natural kind term like "water" is fixed by ostension, scientists then discovered the nature of water—what is necessary to it, by observation. Nathan Salmon argued ([1981] 2005) that we get Kripke's conclusion that "Water is H_2O" is necessary a posteriori provided that we know a priori that what makes water water is its deep physical structure.[8] So the idea is that we know a priori that whatever the basic structure of water is is essential to it, and we then discover by observation that the basic structure of water is H_2O. Under the assumption that something is known a posteriori just in case it cannot be known without observation, it follows that "Water is H_2O" is necessary a posteriori. We return to the possibility of necessary a posteriori truths in Chapter 8.

An important implication of the semantics of direct reference is that meaning is determined outside the mind of an individual speaker. Putnam argued that the contents of our thoughts and speech when we talk about water, gold, tigers, and other things is determined outside of our heads in two ways: (1) It is determined by the way the world is. The fact that we are thinking/talking about H_2O when we think or say "water" is determined

---

8. Keith Donnellan argued in unpublished work in the late 1970s that we do not get the conclusion that "Water is H_2O" is necessary a posteriori without additional arguments to those provided by Kripke or Putnam. See Donnellan's "Kripke and Putnam on Natural Kind Terms" in Donnellan (2012), and Erin Eaker (2012). Salmon (1981) refers to Donnellan's argument in his construction of the argument that "Water is H_2O" is necessary a posteriori. I discuss these works in Chapter 8.

by the fact that water is H_2O, not by an idea in our minds. (2) What we are talking about also depends upon a social linguistic network in which ordinary speakers defer to experts. I will use both of these ways in which kind terms are semantically externalist in this book.

How far does direct reference extend? Putnam (1975, 160) said that he believes it extends to artifact terms like "pencil," and to most adjectives and verbs, as well as the majority of common nouns. Each term has a hidden indexical element. "Pencil" is "an object like that—and we point to a pencil. "Jumps" means "an act like that"—and we point to someone jumping. Putnam was not claiming that an artifact or an act of jumping has a deep nature, so he was not claiming that all these terms function the same way as natural kind terms. But he thought that the indexical element is present in most terms. Semantic externalism spreads throughout language in a way that undermined the descriptivist theory of meaning across the board, not just for the special case of natural kind terms. The question I want to raise is how semantic externalism might be applied and defended for moral terms.

4. Direct Reference to Exemplars

When we look at the ways moral terms like "good person," "virtue," "courage," and "good life" are generally treated, I think we see the descriptivist theory Putnam and Kripke rejected. Moral philosophers have almost always attempted to identify the conceptual content of moral terms descriptively, and to identify the referents of the terms by the satisfaction of the given descriptions. Like my example of "hammer," it is assumed that a person who knows the meaning of these terms must grasp a description in her head that gives necessary and sufficient conditions for the application of the term, and when she forms thoughts or makes judgments using the term, she is thinking about or talking about whatever satisfies the description. This has led to no end of problems because of disputes about the descriptive content of moral concepts. What do we mean by a good life? What is the concept of a virtue? What do we mean by "wisdom" or "courage" or "justice?" For instance, I have heard people say that we could not continue a discussion of wisdom without first "defining wisdom," and they meant that we had to settle on a descriptive meaning of "wisdom"; otherwise, we would not be talking about the same thing. It is an important part of the theory of this book that this view is false.

Another problem is that even when there is some agreement about the descriptive content of a word like "virtue," this has led to skepticism that there is anything in the extension of the term "virtuous person" because almost nobody satisfies the description.[9] As I attempt to show, these problems can be avoided if we use the Putnam-Kripke theory of the semantics of natural kind terms in the construction of a moral theory.

I propose that basic moral terms are anchored in exemplars of moral goodness, direct reference to which are foundational in the theory. Good persons are persons *like that*, just as gold is stuff *like that*. Picking out exemplars fixes the reference of the term "good person" without the need for descriptive concepts. It is not necessary for ordinary people engaged in moral practice to know the nature of good persons—what makes them good. In fact, it is not necessary that anybody knows what makes a good person good in order to successfully refer to good persons, any more than it was necessary that anybody knew what makes water *water* in order to successfully refer to water before the advent of molecular theory. We need not associate a descriptive meaning with "good persons" that is sufficient to identify them, and users of our language can successfully refer to good persons even when they associate the wrong descriptions with the term "good person." Furthermore, like natural kind terms, it is not necessary that every individual be able to correctly pick out instances of good persons for reference to succeed. There must, however, be a socially recognized procedure for picking out instances of the relevant kind. For biological and chemical kinds, we have experts whose job includes identifying instances of the kind. For moral exemplars, we have different procedures embedded in our practices, particularly the telling and retelling of narratives.

We learn through narratives of fictional and non-fictional persons that some individuals are admirable and worth imitating, and the identification of these persons is one of the pre-theoretical aspects of our moral practices that theory must explain. Exemplars are those persons, the persons who are most imitable or most deserving of emulation. They are most imitable because they are most admirable. We identify admirable persons by the emotion of admiration, and that emotion is subject to education through reflection on further experience and the emotional reactions of other persons. In brief, I am proposing that the process of creating a highly abstract

9. Gilbert Harman (1999) and John Doris (2002) made skepticism about the existence of character traits in actual persons a topic of much discussion in the first decade or so of the present century. Christian Miller (2014) gives a good overview of the debate, along with his own theory of personality, and he discusses Harman and Doris in Chapter 8.

structure to simplify and justify our moral practices is rooted in one of the most important features of the pre-theoretical practices we want to explain—the practice of identifying exemplars, and in a kind of experience that most of us trust very much—the experience of admiration, shaped by narratives that are part of a common tradition.

This theory is compatible with the view that our identification of exemplars is revisable. Just as we can be mistaken in our judgment that some sample of what we call "water" is really water, we can also be mistaken in our judgment that some person we call paradigmatically "good" is really good. However, I do not think that we could be mistaken about most exemplars for the same reason that we cannot be mistaken that most of what we take to be water is water. That is because there is a connection in meaning between good persons and the individuals we identify as good: Good persons are persons like that, just as water is stuff like that.

According to Putnam's hypothesis of the Division of Linguistic Labor, natural kind terms are among those terms that are such that it is important that many people in the community acquire the word, but it is not necessary that every person acquires a method for recognizing precisely when the term applies. The conditions for membership in the extension of the term—for example, which things are gold—are present in the community considered as a collective body, but the community divides the "labor" of knowing and employing the methods of identifying the items in the extension. If Putnam's Principle of the Division of Linguistic Labor applies to the term "good person," then people who are members of the same linguistic community mean the same thing by "good person" even though not all of them are able to identify the features that make a good person good, just as only some members of the community can identify the physical properties that distinguish gold from fake gold. It is not necessary that every member of the community can distinguish gold from fake gold, and I suggest that similarly, it is not necessary that every member of the community can distinguish a genuine exemplar from a counterfeit. The difference is that most people in the community are willing to defer to experts in identifying natural substances and species, whereas most people consider themselves expert at identifying exemplars. Actually, conscientious reflection will tell us that we cannot be expert in isolation from others because our emotional reactions are subject to collective appraisal. This leads to some issues about the difference between referring indexically to what we admire, and referring indexically to a natural substance, and I address that in later chapters.

The direct reference approach has an interesting consequence for disagreement between communities and reveals a disanalogy between natural kind terms and moral terms. In Putnam's famous Twin Earth thought experiment, we imagine a planet just like Earth except that the liquid in the lakes and oceans and falling from the sky is a different substance from what it is on Earth. Say it is XYZ. We imagine that XYZ looks and tastes just like water does on Earth. Putnam says that if the Twin Earthians point to XYZ when they say "water," while we Earthians point to H_2O when we say "water," we are not disagreeing about the nature of water. We are talking about two different substances. In fact, Putnam thinks we *mean* something different by "water" from what they do.[10] The parallel situation would be one in which one group of humans routinely pointed to persons who are brutal, greedy, and envious when they say "good person," whereas others point to persons who are compassionate, generous, and sympathetic. If this happened, their disagreement would be more radical than a disagreement about which traits are good traits. They would disagree about what "good" means.[11] Fortunately, I think that such a situation cannot happen for beings like us who share the same nature, the same emotion dispositions, and at least roughly the same physical, psychological, and social needs. There are no differences between Putnam's Earthlings and Twin Earthlings. They refer to different substances when they say "water" solely because of a difference in the physical environment. In contrast, Twin Earthlings who admire the brutal and vicious would have to differ from ourselves in much more than physical environment. In fact, they would differ from us to such an extent that it is doubtful that they are in the same natural kind as ourselves. So we will not face a problem of disagreement as radical as I have described. Nonetheless, there are differences in admiration between individuals and

---

10. Putnam actually argues that either (1) the Twin Earthians mean something different by "water" from what we do, in which case "meaning ain't in the head" since what is in the Twin Earthians' heads is the same as what is in the Earthians' heads, or else (2) meaning (intension) does not determine reference (extension). Either way, the Earthians and Twin Earthians are not talking about the same thing when they say "water" (Putnam 1975, 139–144).

11. Thomas Kuhn (1969, 200–201) makes the parallel point about exemplars in scientific discourse. He says that terms such as "element," "mixture," "planet," and "unconstrained motion" are acquired from direct application to exemplars. When problems arise in the application of these terms, the problem is not one that can be resolved by applying to the dispute criteria accepted in a neutral language used by both sides and adequate to the statement of both theories.

between communities that will need to be acknowledged and discussed in later chapters.

One of the most interesting features of the Kripkean account of natural kinds is the way empirical investigation can reveal natures, and I think this also is a feature of exemplarism. If the concepts in a formal ethical theory are rooted in a person, then narratives and descriptions of that person are morally revealing. It is an open question what it is about the person that makes him or her good. For the same reason, when we say that a good person is a person like that, and we directly refer to St. Francis of Assisi, or to Confucius, or to Jesus, we are implicitly leaving open the question of what properties of Francis, Confucius, or Jesus are essential to their goodness. The exemplarist approach has the advantage that substantive matters about what makes a person good need not be settled at the outset. We need not start by assuming that certain traits are the virtues or that certain acts are right. But we do think in advance of investigation of particular exemplars that what makes good persons good is their deep psychological structure, just as we think in advance of investigation that what makes water *water* is its deep physical structure. Careful observation tells us what the psychological structure of a person is, just as careful observation tells us what the physical structure of water is. If we think that being H_2O is an essential property of water, we might also think that having certain properties such as compassion, justice, and wisdom are essential to being a good person. I think, then, that Kripke is right that deep and important, perhaps even necessary properties of the object class can be determined by empirical observation, although how we know what counts as deep and important is another question. Since narratives are a form of detailed observation of persons, exemplarism gives narrative a crucial place within the theory analogous to scientific investigation in the theory of natural kinds. I am leaving open the possibility that narratives reveal necessary features of value by uncovering the deep properties of a good person. In Chapter 8 I look at the possibility that there are necessary a posteriori truths about good persons.[12]

---

12. In Kripke and Putnam's theory of natural kind terms, it is important that that stuff is the same liquid in other possible worlds as it is in the actual world. In contrast, a supremely good person is not supremely good in every possible world in which that person exists. To use Kripke's terminology, "good person" is not a rigid designator of particular persons. I discuss this difference between natural kind terms and moral terms in Chapter 8 when I discuss the possibility of necessary a posteriori moral truths.

Perhaps we will find out that exemplars do not have a common deep psychological structure. Maybe there is nothing psychologically deep and important in common among the Dalai Lama, Jesus Christ, Confucius, the Stoic sage, the Greek heroes, and the exemplars I mention in later chapters. I do not want to prejudge the results of close observation of exemplars. After all, it could have turned out that the stuff in the lakes and streams and falling from the sky when it rains has no common physical structure. It could have turned out that "water" is like "tasty drink," which we classify as a kind only because of similarities in superficial qualities.[13] Maybe admirable persons do not have anything important in common other than being admired by us. A more plausible outcome is that "good person" is multiply realizable. Perhaps there is not a single essence of good personhood, but there is a set of interesting, yet distinct ways in which a person can be admirable.[14] It is also possible that the set of exemplars gradually changes over time, a possibility I discuss in Chapter 8. After a moral revolution such as the revolution in attitudes toward persons of different races, some, but by no means all, features of the persons we recognize as exemplars changed. I am suggesting that these are all testable hypotheses.

Once we identify exemplars, empirical research may reveal interesting features of their attitudes and behavior. In later chapters I refer to a number of different kinds of empirical research that directly bear on the theory I am proposing. For instance, there is a small amount of research on admiration, which I mention in Chapter 2. There is also a small but growing body of research in neuroscience on the features of exemplars, both real world exemplars and exemplars in laboratory games, which I describe in Chapter 3. I also know of research on the psychological features of at least two sets of exemplars—Holocaust rescuers and L'Arche caregivers, which I also summarize in Chapter 3. In addition, there is research on imitation and emulation, and I discuss some of that work in Chapter 5. One of my purposes in this book is to connect this research with a theoretical structure, but another purpose is to motivate researchers to connect these different bodies of empirical research with each other. There are many other potential empirical studies on exemplars that would be useful for identifying their moral traits and behavior dispositions.

---

13. Putnam mentions that this could have happened with the term "water" in Putnam (1975, 159).

14. I thank Catherine Elgin for this suggestion.

Let me summarize.

(1) What I mean by an exemplar is a paradigmatically excellent person. An exemplar is a person who is most admirable.

(2) We identify the admirable by the emotion of admiration. I do not assume that we always trust our emotion of admiration, and since the emotion is shaped by experience, beliefs, and the emotional responses of others, it gradually changes in response to similar phenomena. I discuss admiration and the need to have basic trust in it in Chapter 2.

(3) I propose that a person who is admirable in some respect is imitable in that respect. The feeling of admiration is a kind of attraction that carries the impetus to imitate or emulate with it. This is rough because there are many reasons we do not or cannot imitate those we admire. For instance, I admire Sir Robert Falcon Scott, who made an expedition to the South Pole in 1912 under very arduous circumstances, resulting in the death of the entire party, but I have no inclination to go to the South Pole myself, even if I were guaranteed I would not die. But there is a way in which my admiration *does* make me want to imitate Scott—not in any specific way, but in wanting to be the kind of person who would be capable of doing such a thing. So admiration is motivating, and my position is that admiration has the potential to give us both the theoretical resources needed to chart a map of moral terms and the desire to be like the exemplar in being a good person ourselves.

(4) The features of exemplars that make them admirable can be discovered through observation in the broad sense that includes the kind of observation that we get in narratives and the kind of observation that we get in the laboratory. It is also possible that we discover features essential to moral goodness by observation. It might turn out that something like "A good person is generous" is a necessary truth, not because being generous is part of the *concept* of a good person, but because it is the nature of good persons qua good to have such a trait, a trait that we can discover by observing them carefully.

(5) What a moral term means is determined outside the mind. The features of exemplars can be discovered through observation, and what moral terms mean is determined by those features. What ordinary persons mean is also determined by our connection to a linguistic network, and I argue in Chapter 7 that while the network does not have experts in the sense of scientific experts, the network does divide the labor of determining the extension of moral terms and other semantic features of these terms.

5. The Theoretical Structure

Although a moral map leaves out some things, I think there are some very basic terms that ought to have a place in the theory. These terms include "a good life," "a good motive," "a good end," "a virtue," "a right act," and "a duty." I do not insist that every good moral theory must have a place for all of these terms. For instance, Elizabeth Anscombe (1958) remarked over a half century ago that Aristotle's theory shows that it is possible to have a comprehensive ethical theory without the idea of duty, and many people would consider John Stuart Mill's classic version of utilitarianism comprehensive even though he ignores virtue. But I mention this series of terms because they play an important role in modern moral discourse, and I think that ideally, they should all be included in a comprehensive theory. However, as I have said, my aim is not to elucidate concepts. I offer my way to define "virtue," "good motive," and "good end" in Chapter 4; "good life" in Chapter 6; and "duty" and "right act" in Chapter 7.

The definitions of moral terms I propose are indexical, and they are all defined by reference to exemplars. When I say "definition," I want to reiterate that I am not giving the content of a concept, and it is not descriptive. Here I give a preview of the main definitions to show the shape of the theory.

(1) A *virtue* is a trait we admire in an exemplar. It is a trait that makes a person like that admirable in a certain respect.

(2) A *good motive* is a motive we admire in an exemplar. It is a motive of a person like that.

(3) A *good end* is a state of affairs that exemplars aim to bring about. It is the state of affairs at which persons like that aim.

(4) A *virtuous act* is an admirable act, an act we admire in a person like that.

(5) An *admirable life* is a life lived by an exemplar.

(6) A *desirable life* (a life of flourishing) is a life desired by an exemplar.

(7) A *right act* for person A in some set of circumstances C is what the admirable (more specifically, practically wise) person would take to be most favored by the balance of reasons for A in C.

(8) A *duty* in some set of circumstances C is an act an exemplar demands from both herself and others. She would feel guilty if she did not do it, and she would blame others if they do not do it.

The diagram in Figure 1.1 shows the basic structure of the map that follows in later chapters.

In each case, the term we want to place on our theoretical map is defined via indexical reference to a paradigmatically good person. So a virtue is a trait we admire in *that* person and in persons like that. A good end is a state of affairs at which persons like that aim. A good life is a life desired by persons like that. A right act is an act a person like that would take to be favored by the balance of reasons. A duty is what persons like that demand of themselves and others.

I have already said that these definitions are not intended to give the content of a series of concepts, but notice also that they are not intended to reveal the "deep" nature of virtue, right action, or a good life. They do not tell us what a virtue, a right act, or a good life *is*, but they give us directions for finding out. They are like defining "water" as "stuff like that," leaving the determination of the deep nature of water for investigation. The purpose of the definition is to identify the reference of the term to make investigation of it possible. Similarly, the purpose of the definitions I have given is to permit us to identify the reference of moral terms in such a way that we know what to investigate to find out what virtue, right action, and a good life are.

I think that Aristotle uses a definition similar to this pattern in the *Nicomachean Ethics* when he defines virtue as a mean between extremes "as a person with practical wisdom (*phronesis*) would determine it" (1106b35). It is possible that Aristotle thought that the *phronimos* can

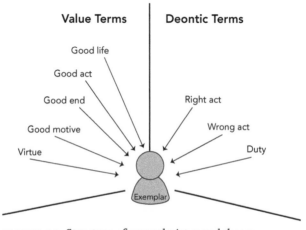

FIGURE 1.1 Structure of exemplarist moral theory

be picked out directly, in advance of specifying the properties that make someone a *phronimos*.[15] It also seems likely that Aristotle did not think that every competent Greek speaker must be able to identify *phronimoi* reliably as long as they are recognizable within the community. If so, that is another feature that makes "*phronimos*" like "water" in the theory of direct reference, but I am not suggesting that Aristotle intended to offer an exemplarist moral theory.

Confucius is a stronger historical example of exemplarism, according to Amy Olberding (2012), who argues that exemplarism is the key to interpreting the ethics of the *Analects*. Confucius treats the Duke of Zhou as an exemplar, and Confucius's students treat Confucius as an exemplar. In both cases, the ideas of a good human trait and the proper way to behave are determined by reference to the exemplar, and Olberding interprets the text in detail, using the theoretical structure of exemplarist ethics. I briefly discuss Olberding's treatment of the *Analects* in Chapters 3 and 4.

Christian ethics is a natural candidate for an exemplarist approach because of the centrality of the person of Jesus Christ as a moral exemplar in Christian teaching. Elsewhere I have proposed a Christian form of exemplarist moral theory, and then used the theory to show a way to resolve a series of problems in philosophical theology, including puzzles about divine goodness, and the problem of evil (Zagzebski 2004, 2002). A fuller version would interweave narratives from the Gospels and the lives of the saints into the pattern I have described, but that is a project for another time.

6. Some Initial Worries

I anticipate a few lines of objection that I would like to address here in a preliminary way.

First, there is the issue of whether we *can* emulate saints, heroes, and sages. In the late 1950s, J. O. Urmson published an influential paper, "Saints and Heroes," in which he argued that the current moral division of acts into duties, indifferent acts, and wrongdoing was inadequate, and he asked philosophers to theorize in a way that does not tacitly deny the

---

15. If Aristotle intended to define "*phronimos*" directly, he can be defended against the common charge that his definition is circular. This is the objection that Aristotle defines "virtue" by reference to the *phronimos*, but the *phronimos* is identified by the possession of virtue. The objection assumes that "*phronimos*" is defined descriptively, whereas I am suggesting that Aristotle may have intended it to be like "water" in direct reference theory.

moral importance of saintly and heroic acts (1958, 215). Some years later, A. I. Melden (1984) replied that saints are too far above us to be exemplars for us. The saint casts aside goods that make our own lives worthwhile—family, hobbies, special interests—in order to carry out his "astounding mission." We cannot emulate such a person because he is radically different from the rest of us. We can, however, emulate the person who takes risks to help another. For instance, Melden says that we can emulate the man who, while knowing the risks involves, assists refugees from El Salvador in entering the United States illegally in order to avoid torture and imprisonment in their home country. "For the man who does this sort of thing is one like ourselves in the very many sorts of interests he has, but is far better than the rest of us—one who sets an example for others to follow—in his sensitivity to the human rights of those El Salvadoreans who have fled from the terror in their homeland" (79). As for the saint, however, Melden says, "we can only regard him with awe" (77—78). If Melden is right, we cannot emulate the most admirable persons, at least not those in the category of saints. They are just too far above us.

In my experience, people who attempt to emulate saints can improve in the qualities that the saint expresses, including self-sacrifice and love for strangers, but unless they completely refocus their lives, they will never be very similar to Francis of Assisi or Mother Teresa or Thomas More, or any other famous saint. As Melden observes, those saints gave up goods most of us could not give up. St. Francis gave up his family and possessions; Thomas More gave up his life. However, we can do some of what they did, albeit in a less impressive way. If I watch Julia Child cook, I feel awe at a performance I could never adequately emulate, but I *can* partially emulate her, and under her inspiration, become a better cook. It is unlikely that any of us can bring out the best of our cooking ability without models of the peak of cooking expertise. It is similarly unlikely that we can know how far we can stretch ourselves morally without the experience of moral exemplars who show us how far human beings have gone in developing and expressing admirable human qualities. When I speak of emulating X, then, I mean taking X as my model, attempting to become more like X. I do not think of emulation in such a way that whenever A emulates X, it is possible for A to become as good as X, nor does it include A's belief that she can do so.

Melden's worry was that we cannot emulate exemplars. A related worry is that we should not even try because "The perfect is the enemy of the good." Recognizing the vast gulf between ourselves and perfection can be discouraging to all but the most morally hardy. Do we experience the exemplar as elevating, or do we experience her as deflating? Why shouldn't we just accept who we are and not try to become perfect? This raises a problem for our use of particular exemplars in our personal lives. Moral improvement comes in stages, and if we aim too high at the outset, we may set ourselves up for failure. Direct imitation of the exemplar may come only after a person has reached a certain level of moral development. Before that, we do better at imitating persons who are better than we are, but not so much better that we cannot clearly see the path to becoming like the exemplar. This issue shows us again why narratives are so important for the practical purpose of emulation. Narratives of exemplars generally do not start with the end of the story—the time when the exemplar is exemplary. Instead, they describe the process the person went through in becoming morally excellent. Sometimes, like St. Augustine, the person begins by living immorally. Sometimes, like St. Francis of Assisi, the person is not vicious, just irresponsible in the typical way of privileged youth. It is important to have many stories of exemplars because they follow so many different paths, and different persons need different models.

Another potential problem for exemplarism is the well-known issue of skepticism about the desirability of becoming the type of exemplar Susan Wolf calls a "moral saint." Wolf argues that the utilitarian saint and the Kantian saint are unappealing people, "dull-witted, humorless, and bland" (1982, 422). If that is true, then the people Wolf calls moral saints are not exemplars in the sense I mean because they are not admirable. But that is not the end of the matter because we may have the sneaking suspicion that we ought to admire them even though we do not, and that raises the issue of trust in our feeling of admiration, which I address in the next chapter. There is also the interesting possibility that the people Wolf has in mind are admirable, and we *do* admire them, but we do not like them. I will not name names, but some saints are just plain annoying. We would not want to emulate them, and we would not want our children to emulate them. More recently, Larissa MacFarquhar (2015) has identified a kind of admirable person who is pejoratively called a "do-gooder," a person whose unrelenting commitment to morality seems inhuman and for that reason, distasteful. As MacFarquhar describes these people, we cannot reject their admirability wholesale, yet admiration is mixed with a sense of dread. The same worry is expressed by George Orwell (1968) in his review of Gandhi's memoir.[16] Although Orwell clearly admired Gandhi, he rejected Gandhi's belief that exclusive loves detract from the impartial love of all humanity, and a seeker of goodness must give up such attachments. Orwell dislikes that kind of person, and says that to be human is not to seek perfection.

> It is too readily assumed ... that the ordinary man only rejects [saintliness] because it is too difficult: in other words, that the average human being is a failed saint. It is doubtful whether this is true. Many people genuinely do not wish to be saints, and it is probable that some who achieve or aspire to sainthood have never felt much temptation to be human beings. (Orwell 1968, 467).

If Orwell is right, there can be a disconnection between admiration and the urge to imitate. I find it interesting that this problem only arises for a certain class of putative exemplars. Heroes are not annoying, and they are quite clearly human. I imagine that that is why narratives of heroes make good movies, whereas narratives of saints rarely become films, and when they do, the story often comes across as didactic. Movies are rarely made about sages either, but that is probably because there is limited entertainment value in watching sages acting sagely, even though we admire them and may wish to emulate them. It is interesting that Wolf does not express skepticism about the desirability of being a hero or a sage parallel to her skepticism about the desirability of being a saint, and Orwell's objection to the saint is limited to the kind of saint who refuses to form personal attachments. However, the example of a saint I l describe in Chapter 3 is not that kind of saint at all.[17]

What about the moral or religious extremist? By an extremist, I do not mean a person who uses violent means that would eliminate him from the category of the admirable. I have in mind individuals like the Buddhist monks who set themselves afire as a form of protest against the Vietnam War, or the fifth-century ascetic stars of Syria, the most famous of whom was Simeon Stylites, who lived thirty-seven years on top of a pillar. I admire Simeon Stylites, but would anybody want to emulate him? What

---

16. "Reflections on Gandhi," originally published in *Partisan Review* (1949). The text can be found at http://www.online-literature.com/orwell/898/.

17. Larry Blum (1988) aptly argues in response to Wolf that exemplars of heroism such as Oskar Schindler and Magda Trocme are worthy of our highest admiration, and appropriately understood, our aspiration. Blum does not discuss the sage.

makes Simeon's story ironic is that he started living on a platform in an attempt to get away from all the people coming to him for advice, but his austerities made him even more famous. The pillar kept getting higher and higher, as the number of people who came to see him increased, and it reputedly reached fifteen meters. People who wanted to talk to him had to climb a high ladder. As Peter Brown (1971) describes him, Simeon was a man of power. He mediated disputes, could forgive debts, specified the interest rate that one party should pay another, performed exorcisms, and protected the oppressed guilds. Simeon did not advise people to live like he did; in fact, he advised them not to. This case suggests that we treat some admirable persons as models for ourselves, but we treat others as authorities. I believe that there is a connection between the authority of an exemplar and the exemplar as model for ourselves. I have argued extensively in another place (Zagzebski 2012) that this connection explains why authority is compatible with autonomy. I briefly discuss the objection that emulation is incompatible with autonomy in Chapter 5, but I do not discuss authority in this book.

Finally, I want to mention two opposite worries about emotion. On the one hand, those who are skeptical about emotion will think that admiration is a flimsy basis for a theory. As I have mentioned, I give a brief defense of the trustworthiness of emotions in general and admiration in particular in Chapter 2. From the other direction, it can be argued that given that we rightly trust the emotions relevant to moral judgment, there is no reason to make admiration the focus. Among the other emotions we trust are indignation, horror, sympathy, gratitude, love, compassion, disgust, and contempt. Perhaps some of these emotions are less trustworthy than others, but it is reasonable to think that if admiration is trustworthy, so are many other emotions. But some of these emotions give us a more direct path to moral judgment than admiration. For instance, if I feel indignant at an act and that leads me to judge that it is wrong, is it necessary to make my judgment dependent upon the judgment of an exemplar? If I feel gratitude at an act of kindness to me, do I judge that expressing gratitude is justified by the reactions of an admired other? Surely the answer is no.

I agree that it is not always necessary to explain and justify our moral judgments by reference to exemplars. The emotions mentioned above can be a sufficient basis for judgment in many cases, and the theory I propose does not suggest otherwise. I have proposed that a moral theory is designed to simplify, systematize, and justify our moral beliefs and practices, and we need to be aware that it may lead to some distortion. We already have moral beliefs and practices in advance of devising a theory, and we will continue to have those beliefs and practices after the theory is constructed. Unlike a map, a moral theory might lead us to revise something in our practices, but there are many items of our moral practices of which we are more confident that we are of the theory— any theory. This is not an objection to moral theory. It is simply an acknowledgment of the plain fact that many elements of moral practice are more trustworthy than any theory we devise to justify them. We rightly think that a strong feeling of indignation gives us a reason to believe that an act is wrong, independent of the verdict of a moral theory, and we might also trust that reason more than we trust the verdict of the theory, even when they coincide. Exemplarism gives a particular emotion, admiration, a primary function in a theoretical map, but that in no way implies that admiration is a more trustworthy emotion than indignation or many other emotions, nor does it imply that we should not attend to the moral judgments justified by those other emotions. I am using admiration to structure a theory for the purposes I have described. Other ways of structuring theories are possible, and I have said that I doubt that there is only one good moral theory anyway. I am drawing a map of the moral domain that is very different from other maps, and it has a number of advantages over other theories. But I want to repeat that what is not on the map is not being excluded from the domain, so it is fair to bring up any part of our moral practices as a way to test whether the structure is useful in giving us a way to navigate the domain. The theory must have a place for the moral judgments delivered by other moral emotions and the other features of our moral practices when it is filled out.

7. Conclusion

The theory of direct reference radically changed the philosophy of language and the philosophy of mind by introducing a new interpretation of the way we refer to objects in the world. It had important implications for the social construction of meaning, and it raised some important questions about the difference between the metaphysical distinction between the necessary and the contingent, and the epistemological distinction between the a priori and the a posteriori. I believe that some of these same issues arise for moral philosophy of language, moral philosophy of mind, and the metaphysics of morals. In the last chapter, I make some suggestions on the implications of exemplarist moral theory for meta-ethics, including a line of argument for stronger and weaker forms of moral realism. But in the next six chapters, I show how the theory can be developed, beginning with the foundation in the emotion of admiration.

2

Admiration

1. Introduction

There are two very different ways in which we can respond to things we call "good": we can *admire* them or we can *desire* them. We admire compassion and bravery; we desire health and long life. We desire friendship, but we admire the loyal and trusting relationship of some friends. We desire financial resources, but we admire the way some persons use those resources. Aristotle expressed this distinction as the difference between what is praised and what is prized. Praise is appropriate to virtue, he says, but "no one praises happiness (*eudaimonia*) as he does justice, but rather calls it blessed, as being something divine and better" (*NE* Bk 1.12).

This line from Aristotle suggests that the distinction between what we admire and what we desire applies to our response to human lives. Some lives are admirable, but not desirable. We admire a life of martyrdom or self-sacrifice, but other things equal, do not desire such a life. We would praise such a life, but would not call it blessed. Similarly, most of us desire a life that has all the goods of human well-being– health, love and friendship, characteristic human pleasures, financial security, political freedom, and purposeful work, but even if such a life was free from vice, we would not admire it as much as the more virtuous life that lacks some of the goods we prize.

I believe that there is nothing more basic than admiring and desiring in our attitudes toward what we call good, but the fact that there are two attitudes is puzzling. Surely, the admirable is not the same as the desirable, but if they are both good, we expect them to be related in some way. Of course, it could turn out that the term "good" has two unrelated meanings, but that does not follow simply from the fact that the admirable differs from the desirable. We shall have to look more deeply.

In addition to the evaluative terms "good" and "bad," there are the deontic terms "right," "wrong," and "duty," and a complete moral theory should also say what we mean by the terms in this category. Is there a connection between the right and the good? If there is, we will want to know whether the connection is between right and the admirable, or right and the desirable. Similarly, we will want to know whether wrong is connected with the undesirable, the contemptible, or neither one.

I am going to propose a moral theory based on the emotion of admiration. It is a map of the moral domain that derives the good in the sense of the desirable from the good in the sense of the admirable. It also derives what we mean by a right act, a wrong act, and a duty from the admirable. As I mentioned in Chapter 1, we have other emotions that reveal moral value besides admiration, and some of them can be the basis for moral judgments, but I will argue that admiration can serve the function of systematizing and harmonizing our moral judgments in a way that makes it potentially much more powerful for moral theory and practice than other moral emotions. Contempt, which I believe is the opposite emotion, may also have a foundational role in the formation of our moral concepts and in the development of moral character.[1] If admiration is a way to perceive moral value, contempt is presumably a way to perceive moral disvalue. A fully developed theory therefore ought to give attention to contempt and I will have a bit more to say about contempt later, but my theory is constructed primarily out of the positive emotion of admiration. I think it is easier to model ourselves on what we want to be like rather than on what we want to avoid. In any case, I feel more comfortable naming admirable persons than naming contemptible persons, and I imagine that empirical researchers prefer investigating exemplars rather than anti-exemplars for similar reasons.

In constructing a theory in which the admirable is more basic than the desirable, I am reversing the priority Aristotle gives in the *Nicomachean Ethics*. There he defines the good as the desirable—what everyone desires for its own sake (*NE* 1094a 18–20), and he identifies that with *eudaimonia*,

---

1. I am not sure that I have correctly identified contempt as the emotion opposed to admiration. Scorn and disdain are other possibilities, and perhaps admiration has no single contrary emotion. Furthermore, contempt may be opposed to other emotions besides admiration. Robert C. Roberts (2013, 149–150) makes the plausible point that contempt undermines civil relationships. If so, an argument can be made that it contrasts not only with admiration but also with respect. See Bell (2013) for a valuable book on the moral importance of contempt. However, Bell does not say contempt is the opposite of admiration, and in fact, says almost nothing about admiration in that book.

a life of well-being or flourishing. Aristotle defines virtues, or admirable traits, as constituents of a life of *eudaimonia* (e.g., Ackrill 1980), or on another interpretation, as means to such a life (e.g., Kraut 1989). Either way, the good in the sense of the desirable is basic, and the good in the sense of the admirable is derivative. In contrast, I propose that the good in the sense of the admirable is basic, and the good in the sense of the desirable is derivative. I think that an advantage of basing a theory on admiration rather than on desire is that we trust the connection between admiration and the admirable more than the connection between desire and the desirable. However, since I believe there can be more than one good moral theory, I give very little critique of other theories, and in any case, I have no intention of criticizing Aristotelian virtue theory.

2. What Is Admiration?

Admiration is an emotion, and so I begin with a brief account of my view of emotion in general. I try to make the features of emotion I identify as uncontroversial as possible since I aim to make exemplarism acceptable to a wide range of readers. It is my hope that if the reader disagrees with something I say about emotion in general or admiration in particular, it will not affect the basic thrust of the theory. I begin with a summary of my view of emotion in previously published work, and comment on a distinctive feature of my account that makes the close connection between the theoretical and practical sides of exemplarism more obvious. I do not describe how the theory can be modified for alternative theories of emotion, but in the last chapter I mention realist and non-realist versions of exemplarism arising from different positions on the relationship between the emotion of admiration and moral reality.

First, I assume that an emotion has an object. Having an intentional object is roughly what distinguishes an emotion from a sensation or a mood. We fear something, hope for something, pity someone, love someone, feel indignation at some state of affairs, feel sympathy with someone's plight, feel angry at someone, and so on. When I reflect, I can reasonably ask whether it is fitting or appropriate that anger is directed at the object of my anger, whether what I fear is really fearsome, whether the object of my indignation deserves that emotion, and so on. For some emotions we think that the issue of fit is relative to the subject. If I feel annoyed at someone, it is possibly fitting for me to feel annoyed even though annoyance would not be fitting for many other people. Even so, I might later judge that I should not have been annoyed, and that suggests that there is an issue of fit even when what counts as fitting varies from person to person. So in general, emotions can fit or not fit their objects, and we think that an emotion ought to fit its object. I do not assume that this feature applies to all emotions, but I will assume that it applies to admiration. Admiration has an object, and it may or may not fit its object. That is to say, what we admire may or may not be admirable.

Second, an emotion has an affective component. It has a characteristic feeling. It feels different to admire someone than it does to love her or to fear her or to be angry at her. Although there can be subconscious emotions, I think that we identify emotions in part by their characteristic feeling when they are conscious. I argue that there are at least two different kinds of admiration, and it is likely that they do not feel exactly the same way, but I assume that there is a general similarity in the feeling aspect of admiration in its various instances.

Third, I think that because an emotion has an affective aspect, it is potentially motivating. It can move us to respond by action or simply by expressing the emotion overtly. Admiration, like other emotions, moves us. In particular, I think that under appropriate conditions, admiration for a person moves us to emulate the admired person in the respect in which the person is admired.

I also believe that in a state of admiration, the object of admiration appears admirable, and I think this is a general feature of emotions. In a state of fear the object appears fearsome; in a state of pity the object appears pitiable. I am not suggesting that an emotion includes a judgment or belief. Something can appear fearsome to the agent when she does not judge that it is fearsome. In fact, she may judge that it is not fearsome. But if something appears fearsome to her when it is not, there is a misstep of some kind—a lack of fit between her faculties and her environment. The faculty or disposition through which something appears to her in her emotional state is misrepresenting the object. Similarly, if someone appears admirable when she is not, there is a misalignment between the world and the emotion disposition operating in that situation whether or not the emotion is accompanied by the judgment that she is admirable. This feature of appearance in emotion is one explanation for the first feature of emotion I identified: An emotion may or may not fit its object.

As an initial proposal, then, we can say that admiration is a state consisting of a characteristic feeling of admiring someone or something that appears admirable. Admiration need not include the judgment that the object of our admiration is admirable, but if we trust our emotion, we will be prepared to make that judgment. We tend not to make the judgment if we are skeptical of our emotion state, or if we wish to withhold judgment until we have been able to reflect or investigate the admired object further. The fact that we think we can critique our emotion is another reason to think that there is an issue of whether admiration in a given instance fits its object.

My theory of emotion includes another feature that I believe enhances the theory, but it is not essential for the purposes of exemplarism. I think that the feeling component of an emotion cannot be detached from the appearance. In a state of emotion, the object appears to fall under what I call a thick affective concept. *Pitiful, fearful, admirable,* and so on are thick affective concepts in the sense I mean. They are concepts that combine a descriptive part and an affective part in a way that cannot be pulled apart. These concepts are not understandable apart from the disposition to have a feeling of a certain kind, and on a particular occasion, we cannot see something *as* falling under a thick affective concept without the feeling that goes with it. So in a state of pity, someone is seen "as pitiable," and seeing someone as pitiable includes feeling pity for her. She cannot be seen as pitiable without the feeling of pity directed toward her, and the feeling of pity would not be *that* feeling were it not directed at someone who appears pitiable. Similarly, the feeling of fear would not be that feeling were it not directed at something that appears fearful, and the appearance of fearfulness includes the feeling of fear. If I am right about this feature of emotion, that would explain why an emotion is both a state that is directed toward an object that has a certain appearance, and it includes a feeling that is potentially motivating.

Given my view on the nature of thick affective concepts, it follows that the concept of the admirable is not understandable apart from the disposition to admire. In a state of admiration, one feels admiration for an object seen "as admirable." The feeling of admiration would not be *that* feeling were it not directed at something that appears admirable, and nothing can be seen as admirable without the admiring feeling attached to it. I believe that this proposal that the cognitive and feeling aspects of emotion cannot be detached solves some puzzles about the way we treat moral judgments as both cognitive and motivating.[2] In the case of admiration, it explains why a theory that begins with admiration can generate the conceptual apparatus desired in a theory, along with the motivations we want for the practical purpose of making us want to be moral. The cognitive side of admiration leads to the set of concepts that form the backbone of the theory—admirable person, admirable trait, admirable motive, admirable act, admirable life. The feeling side of admiration moves us. The theoretical framework of the admirable and moral motivation therefore arise from one and the same emotion.

In other places I have said that the object of admiration can be described most generally as the "imitably attractive" (Zagzebski 2006, 2010, 2012). A disadvantage of this way of describing the emotion of admiration is that it builds the typical response to the emotion—imitation, into the description of the emotion itself. I do not want to say that the urge to imitate or emulate is a necessary component of the feeling of admiration, but calling attention to the reactive response reminds us of what it feels like to have the emotion to which we typically respond in that way. Saying that in a state of admiration the object appears imitably attractive highlights two features of the feeling of admiration that I want to emphasize: (1) the object appears attractive, not repulsive or evaluatively neutral; (2) the way in which the object is attractive typically gives rise to the urge to imitate or emulate the object, assuming certain practical conditions are satisfied. I think we can also say that in standard cases, admiration is a positive emotion in another sense. It is not only directed at what appears good, but it feels good to have it. But admiration can feel bad, and I will return to that possibility later in this chapter.

3. Kinds of Admiration

We may get a clearer idea of what admiration is like by looking at similarities and differences among the objects of admiration. We admire a wide range of acts and personal qualities. In Chapter 1 I gave some examples of exemplars: St. Francis of Assisi, Confucius, Jesus, the Dalai Lama, Mother Teresa, Sir Robert Falcon Scott, Simeon Stylites, and Thomas More. This

---

2. In Zagzebski (2003) and (2004) I argue for the view of emotion I have mentioned here. In Zagzebski (2003) I argue that thick affective concepts are used in what I call ground level moral judgments. The "thinning" of these concepts explains why we find moral weakness simultaneously puzzling and common.

is already quite a diverse list, and it becomes even more diverse if I expand it to include many other persons I admire in very different ways, such as the following:

- Marie Sklodowska Curie, who won Nobel Prizes in both physics and chemistry for her pioneering work on radioactivity.
- The Trappist monks of Tibhurine, who refused to abandon their ministry amid danger in war-torn Algeria, and were subsequently kidnaped and murdered by rebels.[3]
- St. Catherine of Siena, a mystic and central figure in the affairs of fourteenth-century Europe, who stood up to more than one pope and managed to convince Pope Gregory XI to return to Rome from Avignon.
- Leopold Socha, a Polish sewer inspector and former criminal, who protected Jews hiding in the sewers of Lvov for fourteen months, first for money, then gradually out of compassion and at great personal risk.[4]
- Arthur Miles, the protagonist of C. P. Snow's novel, *The Search*. Miles is an ambitious scientist doing groundbreaking research in crystallography. At the point of making a major discovery, he finds counter-evidence that he is at first tempted to destroy, but then accepts it and reports that the hypothesis that would have made him famous is false.[5]
- Lorenzo Ghiberti, creator of the breathtaking Baptistry doors in Florence.
- Suzie Valadez, who devoted her life to ministering to the poorest people of Juarez following a religious awakening.[6]
- Brian Shaw, said to be the strongest man in the world.[7]
- A woman I know who is impeccably groomed and keeps her house always ready for company, while caring for her husband with Alzheimer's.
- Any man who can sing the last verse of "Walk the Line."

In spite of the wide diversity of the individuals on this list, I think they have something in common that elicits my admiration. Each has a human power in a high degree of excellence—intellectual or artistic genius, moral

---

3. See Kiser (2003), and Xavier Beauvois's film, *Of Gods and Men* (2010).

4. See Chiger (2008), Marshall (1990), and Agnieszka Holland's film, *In Darkness* (2011).

5. Discussed by Jason Baehr (2011, 142).

6. See Colby and Damon (1992, Chapter 3).

7. See Bilger (2012).

leadership, stalwart courage, compassion, open-mindedness and intellectual honesty, the virtues of a hostess and loving spouse, physical strength, the ability to sing as low as Johnny Cash. Obviously, some of these qualities are more important than others. Some of them do not have much to do with what makes a person the person that she is, whereas others are much deeper, integrated into the whole of the person's life, such as helping the poor is for Suzie Valadez. In contrast, the ability to sing low or to lift heavy weights is far from exhausting the qualities of a person, even a person who focuses most of his attention on developing that ability.

My hypothesis is that the main division among objects of admiration is natural versus acquired excellences. We admire both because both are ways in which humans are excellent, but the emotion directed toward native talents feels different from the emotion directed toward acquired excellence. A story about Lorenzo Ghiberti told by Vasari in his *Lives of the Artists* illustrates the difference. In 1400 there was a major competition in Florence to create bronze relief scenes for the Baptistry doors. Each competitor was to create a bronze panel depicting Abraham sacrificing Isaac. Among the six competitors were Brunelleschi and Donatello, who were already famous, and Lorenzo Ghiberti, a young man in his early twenties. Vasari tells us that Lorenzo Ghiberti's entry "was absolutely perfect in every detail: . . . [T]he scene was finished so carefully that it seemed to have been breathed into shape rather than cast and then polished with stone tools" (1991, 108–109). Brunelleschi and Donatello were reportedly so impressed that they recommended to the thirty-four judges of the Merchants Guild that the commission should go to Ghiberti rather than to one of them.

It seems to me that we admire all three of the artists in this story, but we admire Ghiberti differently from the way we admire Donatello and Brunellschi. I think that admiring artistic genius feels different from admiring generosity of spirit. There is also a difference in the way the two kinds of excellences can be emulated. I can imitate a person with an acquired excellence, but I cannot imitate a natural talent. It is not something I can hope to attain myself if I do not already have it. But it is significant that the people who excel in intellectual or artistic excellence or physical strength would rarely be noticed if they did not improve their talent with hard work, perseverance, determination, and courage, often making sacrifices to develop and express their gift. Lorenzo Ghiberti succeeded in creating his gorgeous panels for the Baptistry doors through perseverance as well as talent. Vasari tells us about that also. He says that Ghiberti's first bronze cast came out badly, "but without panicking or losing heart,

Lorenzo found out what had gone wrong and promptly made a fresh mould ... and it came out splendidly" (1991, 109). Brian Shaw was not born the strongest man in the world. It took a tremendous amount of hard work to achieve that goal. Marie Curie's indomitable spirit explains her Nobel prizes at least as much as her natural intellectual brilliance. I think, then, that persons with extraordinary natural gifts are admirable in one way because of the natural gift, and in another way because the level of excellence they achieve is partly due to effort and acquired traits that can be imitated. I am a person on the lower end of the scale of physical strength, but even I can lift weights. I do not have Ghiberti's artistic genius, but I can imitate the perseverance he needed for success. However, it is likely that the ability to sing low is mostly inborn. Either you can do it or you cannot. So my (testable) hypothesis is that there is a difference in the way it feels to admire natural excellence and the way it feels to admire acquired excellence, and a purely natural excellence or the natural part of an excellence cannot be imitated, but the acquired part can be. The object of admiration for a natural excellence is not imitably attractive.

A different way to look at the difference between admiration for talents or natural gifts, on the one hand, and admiration for acquired excellence, on the other, is to consider the opposite emotions. If we feel admiration for an acquired excellence like kindness, we feel contempt for an acquired defect like meanness. Meanness is not simply the absence of kindness. It is an acquired trait that is opposed to kindness. Meanness is a vice—an anti-virtue. But I doubt that there is any such thing as an anti-talent. There is, of course, such a thing as the lack of talent, but normally we do not feel contempt for it. In general, I doubt that we have any emotion at all toward a person who lacks a particular talent, although if someone is extraordinarily lacking in a normal human gift—is tone deaf, for instance, we might feel pity, but not contempt. I think, then, that admiration for inborn talent and admiration for acquired excellences are two different kinds of admiration. The latter kind of admiration has contempt as its contrary. That is the kind of admiration I am interested in for exemplarism.[8]

---

8. What if an excellence is a gift from the gods, and bypasses the agency of the person who has it? When Agamemnon and Achilles quarrel in the first book of the *Iliad*, Agamemnon says: "What if you are a great soldier? That's just a gift from god" (Homer 2.211). In other words, Achilles does not deserve credit since the gods made him that way. We do not deserve credit for natural talents and by the same reasoning, we do not deserve credit for a gift that falls from heaven. If so, the excellences that pertain to morality are neither natural talents nor unearned gifts. They must be acquired through the agency of the possessor. But

In Chapter 1 I said that what I mean by an exemplar for the purposes of this book will include the hero, the saint, and the sage, but not the genius. I propose now that the genius is admirable in a different way from the hero, saint, or sage, assuming that what we mean by genius is superb natural talent. Natural talent might also be a condition for sagehood since I surmise that being a sage requires greater than average natural intelligence, whereas being a saint or a hero does not. But that is another claim that can be tested. It suggests that the line between natural talent and acquired excellence is not easy to draw, and there are probably many mixed excellences. For instance, the Dalai Lama was chosen for a natural gift, but he is admired for acquired virtues. I do not think this is a serious problem, but it does affect the extent to which a given person can emulate certain kinds of exemplars. In Chapter 1 I mentioned Melden's view that the saint is too far above us to be imitated, and I disagreed with him about that. It might turn out that the sage is as far above us as the saint, and sagehood is as unattainable for most people as sainthood is according to Melden, but the unattainability of some form of exemplarity does not preclude exemplars from being models for moral improvement and education. I offer empirical evidence for this in the next section.

Although I think we admire natural intellectual talent differently from the way we admire moral virtues, I think we admire intellectual virtues in the same way we admire the moral virtues. The intellectual honesty and selfless open-mindedness of C. P. Snow's character, Arthur Miles, is admirable in the same way honesty is admirable, and it is admirable in the same way self-sacrificing virtue of any kind is admirable. I think also that closed-mindedness and intellectual dishonesty are contemptible. If so, the main division in admirable traits is not the division between intellectual and moral traits. It is the division between the natural and the acquired.

In this section I have proposed that admiration is directed at human excellence of all kinds, but the primary division in the range of the admirable is that between natural and acquired excellences. I propose that the two kinds of admiration feel different to the person experiencing them, they have different contrary emotions, and they differ also in the way in which we respond to them. We can imitate acquired excellence but not

---

a difficulty for this view in Christian moral theology is the idea that the theological virtues of faith, hope, and charity are infused by the Holy Spirit. If these gifts are no different from the gift of courage that Achilles got from the gods, then the same objection would be raised.

natural talent. These hypotheses can all be empirically tested. I am not suggesting that this division in the kinds of admiration and the admirable is something we know a priori. If the empirical results do not support my contentions, the way exemplarism is applied will need to be modified. If the contentions are correct, we can focus our attention in constructing the theory on admiration for acquired excellences.

Another hypothesis I proposed in this section is that intellectual virtues are among the acquired excellences, that they are admirable in the sense that is opposed to the contemptible, and that they belong to the class of traits relevant to exemplarism. A sage like Confucius is someone whose admirability blends the moral and the intellectual, and it is important to Confucian ethics that Confucius is intellectually virtuous. Readers who believe that an ethical theory should be restricted to the domain of traits and acts that are good in a distinctively moral way can easily adapt exemplarism to their viewpoint, but when we begin to identify those exemplars who are admirable in all or most morally relevant respects, I think it will turn out to be *morally* relevant that there are exemplars who have intellectual virtues.

4. Haidt on the Psychology of Admiration

There is very little work on admiration by psychologists, but an exception is a series of articles authored or co-authored by Jonathan Haidt.[9] Haidt calls admiration an "other-praising emotion," arising from witnessing the non-moral excellence of others. He invents the term "elevation" for the other-praising emotion that he says arises from witnessing the moral excellence of others that does not benefit the self.[10] Haidt says he got his idea for the features of elevation from a letter by Thomas Jefferson on the benefits of reading great works of fiction. Jefferson writes:

---

9. Haidt (2003a and 2003b), Algoe and Haidt (2009), Haidt and Seder (2009), and Vianello and Haidt (2010). See Onu, Kessler, and Smith (2016) for a helpful review of the literature on admiration.

10. Haidt says gratitude is the emotion directed toward the moral excellence of another that does benefit the self, and he places gratitude in the category of other-praising emotions. I do not discuss gratitude here, but it seems to me it is quite different from emotions focused on praise for another. We can be grateful for the ordinary things people do for us even though there is nothing particularly admirable about those things, and yet it is appropriate to feel grateful. I also think that what Haidt calls elevation can be felt even when the self is a beneficiary of a morally exemplary act, as I mention below.

When any ... act of charity or of gratitude, for instance, is presented either to our sights or to our imagination, we are deeply impressed with its beauty and feel a strong desire in ourselves of doing charitable and grateful acts also. On the contrary when we see or read of any atrocious deed, we are disgusted with its deformity and conceive an abhorrence of vice. Now every emotion of this kind is an exercise of our virtuous dispositions; and dispositions of the mind, like limbs of the body, acquire strength by exercise.

Jefferson goes on to say that fiction generates physical feelings as much as those caused by observing real persons:

[I ask whether] the fidelity of Nelson, the generosity of Blandford in Marmontel do not dilate [the reader's] breast, and elevate his sentiments as much as any similar incident which real history can furnish? Does he not in fact feel himself a better man while reading them, and privately covenant to copy the fair example?[11]

Haidt uses Jefferson as a basis for his proposal that "elevation" is the name of the emotion we direct toward moral exemplars. That emotion has features that he has confirmed in subsequent small research projects, including interviews in Japan and India. The main components he identifies are these:

a. It is elicited by acts of charity, gratitude, fidelity, generosity, or any other strong display of virtue.
b. It leads to distinctive physical feelings, including the feeling of dilation or opening in the chest, combined with the feeling that one has been uplifted or "elevated."
c. It gives rise to a specific motivation or action tendency: emulation, or the desire to perform the same kind of acts oneself.

As I have said, Haidt invents the term "elevation" for the emotion he describes, but I think "admiration" is a perfectly good term for our emotional responses to both morally and non-morally exemplary persons. Algoe and Haidt's studies indicate that both the emotion they call "elevation,"

---

11. Jefferson ([1771] 1975, 350); quoted in Haidt (2003); a portion also quoted in Algoe and Haidt (2009).

directed at exemplars of moral excellence, and the emotion they call "admiration," directed at exemplars of non-moral excellence such as skill and talent, motivate the subject to emulate the person at whom the emotion is directed in some way, with the difference that admiration for natural talent energizes people to work harder to succeed at their own goals, whereas elevation leads them to emulate the moral goals of the other.[12] I think, then, that in spite of our differences in terminology, Haidt's research shows us some interesting features of admiration in my sense, and confirms my hypothesis on the connection between admiration and emulation.

However, in addition to terminology, there are some differences between Haidt's view and mine that I want to note. Haidt's studies on elevation focus on acts of moral excellence that do not benefit the self. His examples include acts of charity, generosity, fidelity, and gratitude, "or any other strong display of virtue." But I can feel elevated by someone's virtuous acts even if I am a beneficiary, as when someone's generosity includes generosity to me. Jews rescued from the Nazis felt elevation for the courage of the rescuers even when they were the beneficiaries of the rescuers' courageous acts. Furthermore, there are intellectual virtues that have the features Haidt identifies in elevation. I think we feel as elevated by the self-sacrificing open-mindedness of Arthur Miles in the C. P. Snow novel I mentioned above as by displays of charity, fidelity, and generosity. In addition, there are intellectual virtues that are just like moral virtues except that they apply in the intellectual domain. There is no reason to think that intellectual humility, intellectual courage, and intellectual perseverance are less elevating than humility, courage, and perseverance in the practical domain. These intellectual virtues benefit others as well as the self, and they motivate us to emulate the person who displays these virtues.

I think, however, that the objections I have mentioned are not significant since I surmise that Algoe and Haidt's characterization of admiration and elevation is intentionally vague, and even if it is meant to apply to a narrower range of admirable traits and acts for the purpose of the studies they conducted, further research could show whether their conclusions apply to the broader sense of exemplarity I am using here.

Algoe and Haidt do make one claim that I think is importantly different from the view of admiration I am proposing. They suggest that the emotion that is the opposite of elevation is disgust, the feeling of moving down on what Haidt call the purity scale, and which is elicited

---

12. Algoe and Haidt (2009, 123–124). See esp. Table 5 and discussion of Study 3.

by witnessing vicious acts.[13] This idea seems to be suggested by the quotation from Jefferson that Haidt uses, where Jefferson says that "when we see or read of any atrocious deed, we are disgusted with its deformity and conceive an abhorrence of vice." Haidt thus subsumes the virtue-vice scale to the purity scale, with disgust at the lower end and elevation at the upper end. It seems to me, however, that the purity scale does not coincide with the virtue-vice scale, and I have already said that I think the emotion opposed to admiration (or elevation in Haidt's sense) is contempt (or possibly scorn or disdain), not disgust. A person who is brutal or unjust or stingy is contemptible. A person who has sex with a dead chicken (one of Haidt's well-known examples) or eats feces is disgusting. I would not deny that many acts are both contemptible and disgusting, but it seems to me that contempt is the emotion directed toward what we see as morally vicious.

Let me summarize what I think we can say about admiration so far:

(1) Admiration is the emotion of feeling a distinctive way toward a person seen as admirable. The emotion may or may not fit its object. That is, the object may or may not be admirable. But if we trust our emotion of admiration, other things equal, we will be prepared to judge that what we admire is admirable.

(2) Admiration for acquired human excellences differs from admiration for natural talents (supported by the Haidt studies mentioned above). Contempt is the emotion opposed to admiration in the first category, but not the second. The kind of admiration we want for exemplarism is admiration for acquired excellences. These excellences include intellectual virtues.

(3) Admiration for acquired traits is often associated with physical feelings, particularly feelings of being uplifted or elevated by witnessing or reading about something admirable (supported by the Haidt studies mentioned above).

(4) The admired person is imitably attractive. That is, admiration for acquired excellences gives rise to the motive to emulate the admired person in the way in which she is admired (also supported by the Haidt studies).[14]

---

13. Algoe and Haidt (2009, 106). The same features are identified in (Haidt 2003a, 280–281).

14. See also studies by Aquino et al. (2011), who argue that moral elevation and prosocial acts in response is stronger in people whose moral identity is "highly self-defining."

The emotion of admiration in the sense I have described is not the only emotion that is directed toward supremely good persons. Schindler et al. (2013) argue that adoration is a related emotion that is directed toward the divine and leads to a network of religious practices as well as moral acts. They explore the commonalities and differences between the emotions of admiration and adoration and argue that both emotions contribute to the formation of ideals and identities, but differ in that admiration leads to the internalization and emulation of the admired person, whereas adoration leads to adherence to the teachings and expectations of a divine or superhuman meaning maker. In my vocabulary, "adoration" is the name of a form of behavior rather than an emotion, but I think it is clear that the emotion they call "adoration" exists, and deserves scholarly attention.[15]

Another emotion related to admiration yet distinct, is awe, an emotion that Kristján Kristjánsson (unpublished) argues is necessary to explain our attraction to transpersonal ideals—moral goodness itself, aesthetic beauty, the elevation we feel when faced with overpowering truth. We see each of these ideals exemplified in particular persons and circumstances, but the emotion to which he refers is directed toward the abstract ideal itself, not the particular instantiation of it. In this book I am taking admiration as the focal emotion for exemplarism, but I think that a fuller development of the theory would require an account of a series of emotions of appreciation—the emotion directed toward natural talents, the emotion directed toward products of great moral insight, such as the US Constitution, the emotion directed toward the ideals abstracted from their personal exemplifications, and the emotions directed toward God.

5. Trusting Admiration

We know that admiration can go wrong. Can it be trusted? I have recently discussed the issue of trusting our emotions at some length, and I begin this section with a brief summary of my argument that basic trust in our emotion dispositions is both inescapable and rational. I then mention some ways admiration can go awry that have been discussed in the

---

15. Schindler (2014) has also developed a new measure of admiration and adoration and has looked at the connection between these emotions and other emotions, both positive and negative.

psychological literature, as well as the problem of emotion disagreement—the problem that there are differences among those admired by different groups of people. A more serious problem, I believe, is a general cynicism about the admirable that leads to a reluctance to admire anybody. I conclude the chapter with a brief interpretive genealogy of the psychological path leading from admiration to envy to resentment of admirable persons to the denial that the admirable is admirable. I think that this general cultural phenomenon is more threatening than disagreement about the set of exemplars.

In my recent book *Epistemic Authority* (2012), I argued that we face a problem of psychic circularity that is a generalization of the well-known problem of epistemic circularity. The problem of epistemic circularity is a problem about the way we can tell that our belief-forming faculties get us the truth. We can never find out that any given belief we have is true without relying on our belief-forming faculties as a whole, but we cannot tell that our belief-forming faculties are reliable as a whole without relying on the truth of particular beliefs. I think that this problem can be broadened to include not only our perceptual and belief states, but also states of emotion. Any reason we have to think that a state fits its object—that a belief is true, a memory veridical, a perception accurate, an emotion fitting—is that it fits, and continues to fit, our other psychic states taken as a whole. That includes states of belief about the beliefs or emotions of other persons trust in whom survives reflection. The best we can do to be confident an emotion is fitting is the same as the best we can do to be confident that a belief is true: we find that it survives reflection over time on our total set of psychic states when we are using them the best we can to make them fit their objects. That is what I mean by conscientious self-reflection.[16]

Although I think that the basic way we test the fittingness of our emotions is the same as the way we test the truth of our beliefs, we need to admit that experience shows us that many kinds of emotion are less likely to pass the test than many classes of beliefs. Romantic love, anger, and certain forms of fear often do not survive reflection. Presumably emotions

---

16. I argue for the rationality and inescapability of epistemic self-trust in Zagzebski (2012) Chapter 2, and give the parallel defense of the rationality of emotional self-trust in Chapter 4. I explain and defend what I mean by conscientious self-reflection in Chapter 2, and argue in Chapter 3 that consistent epistemic self-trust requires us to have basic epistemic trust in others. The parallel argument that consistent emotional self-trust requires us to have basic emotional trust in others is given in Chapter 4.

like hate, envy, jealousy, and feelings of vengeance are often, perhaps usually, unfitting. Lately some writers have raised doubts about the trustworthiness of disgust.[17] Nonetheless, there are many emotions we trust, and our ability to act morally would be crippled if we were not able to place basic trust in these emotions. In this category I would place sympathy, compassion, and indignation. It is hard to imagine a functional moral life without trust in these emotions, and I think that admiration is in this category. Admiration is both the basis for many moral judgments, and the basis for other moral responses, such as imitative behavior.

This does not yet show that we ought to trust admiration, only that we are strongly inclined to trust it and often use it as the basis for the way we behave. Clearly, we sometimes make mistakes in admiration, even from our own point of view, as when we change our mind about someone's admirability. That happened to many people when Nelson Mandela was put on a US terrorism watch list in the 1980s and remained on the list while he was in prison, but subsequently became a universally admired hero in America. We also can lose our admiration for a person or admire him less when we find out more about him. We find out that Martin Luther King Jr. was a serial adulterer, or that Abraham Lincoln was a non-attentive parent, if not a negligent one.[18] This often means that the person is admirable in one respect, but not another, and in Chapter 4 I discuss the way close observation of exemplars and attention to our responses of admiration and dis-admiration can permit us to chart the individual virtues. But this is not a problem for the trustworthiness of admiration. It just means that we need to be attentive to our responses of admiration or the lack of admiration in a variety of situations.

We also know that individuals and communities disagree about what they admire. Some individuals admire persons whom others find

---

17. The appropriateness of the emotion of disgust has received some attention in the recent literature. The research of Jonathan Haidt et al. (1993) indicates that people who refer to disgust as a reason not to do something often cannot justify their judgment any further than the experience of disgust itself. Martha Nussbaum (2004) has given an extended argument that disgust should be irrelevant to the law, but she clearly thinks that disgust is often an inappropriate response to a situation quite apart from its legal ramifications. Do moral exemplars feel disgust? I think that their reactions are relevant to the trustworthiness of the emotion and deserve further study. I return to the connection between the emotions of exemplars and their reasons for making moral judgments in Chapter 5.

18. See Donald (1995). Apparently Lincoln was away for much of the childhood of his eldest son, Robert, and had a strained relationship with him. Lincoln was evidently warm and attentive toward his other sons who died in childhood.

dis-admirable or even contemptible. What should we say about the fact that contemporary adolescents admire pop singers and sports stars? Many cultures have admired brutal warriors. Nazis admired Hitler. I said at the beginning of this chapter that I am not comfortable naming names of contemptible persons, but it is always a safe bet to mention Hitler. What should we say about the fact that he was admired by thousands? Should those persons have trusted their emotion? Should we respond to their failure by losing trust in our own emotion of admiration?

In Claudia Koonz's (2003) interesting study of the moral conscience of the Nazis, she finds a wide correspondence between the people we admire and the people the Nazis admired. Apparently they recognized most of the same virtues in exemplars that we recognize. The problem, in Koonz's view, is that human beings have the capacity to rule out of the moral community whole classes of persons, and many groups of people in history have exercised that capacity, leading to genocide and other heinous crimes. The biggest moral revolution of modern times is the attack on the exercise of that capacity, an attack that was led by moral exemplars, widely admired for qualities that, as Koonz notes, even Nazis recognized as admirable. I cannot say with certainty that self-reflective Nazis could have figured out that there was something wrong with Hitler by comparing him with other persons they admired, but that is my hypothesis. A Nazi who is conscientious in my sense would reflect upon his admiration for Hitler, compare Hitler with other persons he admires, and compare his reaction to Hitler with the emotions of others he trusts. Inconsistencies in his disposition to admiration should have been revealed by that process if Koonz is right that the Nazi conscience in most ways did not differ from that of the rest of us.

But whether or not the Nazis could have figured out that Hitler was not admirable, hardly anybody reacts to the Nazi admiration for Hitler by saying that maybe the Nazis were right and we are wrong. And the same point applies to the adolescent admiration for pop stars. We trust our dispositions to feel admiration and contempt when they survive reflection over time, and I think we are right to do so. But the Nazi experience is reason to investigate the causes of glaring errors in admiration, not just out of a questionable desire to blame but because the regulation of our emotions requires attentiveness to those causes.

Hopefully, most of our mistakes are not as extreme as the mistakes of the Nazis, but we are all subject to biases that can be countered by reflection. For instance, there is evidence that people are more inclined to admire good-looking people.[19] Adam Smith argued that people have a tendency to admire persons because of their high social status,[20] although some recent empirical studies suggest that admiration often functions instead to regulate the social hierarchy.[21] In any case, the most admired persons in the annual Gallup Poll are usually persons of high status. In this poll Americans are asked "What man that you have heard or read about, living today in any part of the world, do you admire most? What woman that you have heard or read about, living today in any part of the world, do you admire most?" The top man and woman are usually US presidents or First Ladies, and often a single individual is named by as many as 15 percent of the people polled. But it is not clear that the Gallup polls give us evidence that people admire others because they have high status. Obviously, nobody can be named by 15 percent of the people polled unless at least 15 percent of the people polled have

---

19. Becker and Luthar (2007) say: "Universally agreed upon in the literature is the prominent role played by physical attractiveness and athletic ability in relation to peer status among adolescents from diverse backgrounds. . . . Among all students, physical attractiveness was linked with perceived admiration. Among suburban girls, links were especially strong. . . . Indeed, findings for the significant value of suburban girls' attractiveness were rather unsettling." An interesting incident involving physical attractiveness occurs in the Hebrew Scriptures in the passage in which Samuel is told by God to anoint a new king from among the sons of Jesse. When Samuel sees Eliab, God says, "Do not consider his appearance or his height, for I have rejected him. The Lord does not look at the things people look at. People look at the outward appearance, but the Lord looks at the heart" (1 Samuel 16:7). The Lord seems to be reminding Samuel that people are inclined to admire those who are tall and good-looking, but they may not be admirable. Still, when Jesse's youngest son, David, stands before Samuel and the Lord says to anoint him, the Scripture describes David as handsome in appearance.

20. Terrence Irwin (2015) discusses this viewpoint in Adam Smith. Smith says: "That wealth and greatness are often regarded with the respect and admiration which are due only to wisdom and virtue; and that the contempt, of which vice and folly are the only proper objects, is often most unjustly bestowed upon poverty and weakness, has been the complaint of moralists in all ages" (i 3.3.1, pp. 61–62). However, it is not clear to me that Smith is talking about the same kind of admiration I am addressing here since he says, "Our obsequiousness to our superiors more frequently arises from our admiration for the advantages of their situation, than from any private expectations of benefit from their good-will," (i 3.2.3, p. 52).

21. Joseph Sweetman et al. (2013) write: "Philosophers . . . and psychologists . . . have proposed that admiration plays an important functional role in the maintenance of social hierarchy. More specifically, admiration is thought to carry with it a tendency for the subject of the emotion to defer to the target of the emotion. . . . In this sense, admiration can be seen as maintaining social hierarchy. A key point of departure between the present approach and previous theorizing on admiration is that we suggest that admiration does not only act to maintain the social order. Rather it can also, depending on the object of admiration, serve as a means of engendering behavior that challenges the social hierarchy or inhibits behavior that would maintain it. Put simply, we suggest that admiration's role in regulating social hierarchy depends on the object of the emotion (Iyer and Leach 2008)" (p. 534).

heard of that person, and it is statistically impossible that little-known admirable people will be named by a large percentage of people polled. Furthermore, it seems to me that the question on the poll can easily be interpreted as asking for the name of a well-known person. Nobody is going to name his grandmother in an answer on a Gallup Poll. If so, the poll does not necessarily show that people are more likely to admire persons of high status than persons of low status, but that they interpret the poll to be asking them which among the persons of high status they admire the most.

Jeremy A. Frimer and colleagues (2012) have done a fascinating series of studies of recent history's most influential figures in an attempt to identify which ones personified moral excellence and to examine their motives. I return to this study in Chapter 4, but for this chapter, I want to point out an interesting detail in the admirability ranking of the long list of individuals they studied. Participants were faculty "experts" sampled from graduate-level Canadian universities. A list of 105 influential persons was taken from *Time* Magazine's annual lists of the world's most influential persons, and participants were asked to rate them on the criteria of principled/virtuous, consistent, brave, inspiring, and humble. The results were tabulated and the 105 figures ranked. The results had some curious anomalies, but the most striking to me was that George W. Bush ranked slightly lower than Hitler. I think this mean that we need an effective way to correct for political bias in judgments of admirability. (It no doubt also means that university professors are not the best participants for such studies.)

Reflection about our disposition to admiration can help to counter bias that favors good-looking people and those with high status, and bias that is politically based. However, I think the fact that someone else is admired by others *is* relevant to whether I should take him or her to be admirable. I have argued elsewhere (Zagzebski 2012, Chapter 4) that the trustworthiness of any instance of an emotion, including admiration, entails that I have reason to trust the same disposition in others when it satisfies the conditions for trusting my own emotion. To the extent that I conscientiously believe that certain other persons have the same quality of conscientious self-reflection that grounds my trust in my disposition to feel admiration, it follows from the principle that I ought to treat like cases alike that I ought to trust the emotion disposition of these other persons. This test rules out trusting the Nazi's admiration for Hitler, but if I believe that Katherine is as trustworthy as I am in her disposition to feel admiration, and Katherine feels admiration for Ben, I have a reason to admire Ben. Of course, emotion has a feeling component, and coming to believe that someone else has a given emotion is rarely sufficient to cause me to have the same emotion, but the question is whether I have a reason to judge that Ben is admirable. I think that roughly, the answer is yes. I have a prima facie reason to think that Katherine's emotion fits its object, and so I have a prima facie reason to judge that Ben is admirable even if I do not feel admiration for him. That also means that if someone scores high on admirability in the Gallup Poll, I have a prima facie reason to believe the person is admirable.

This result has the consequence that emotion disagreement is a problem for the conscientious person for the same reason that disagreement in belief is a problem. In my experience, we are much less likely to trust the emotions of others than to trust their beliefs, and I find that curious. In cases in which we trust our own disposition to have a certain emotion, we do not generally extend the same trust to the emotions of other persons, even when we have the same grounds for trusting the other as ourselves, and there are no relevant differences in our circumstances, and we agree on the relevant descriptive facts. But at the same time, we often unconsciously adopt the emotions of others, particularly those we trust and admire. There is plenty of empirical evidence of the way we pick up emotions, including admiration, from other persons (e.g., Walden 1991, Thompson 2006, Hills et al. 2010). If we already do it unreflectively, it seems to me to be better to do it reflectively. Admiration that survives conscientious reflection is justified, and it reduces the chances that we will be subject to the biases to which we are prone when we admire unreflectively. So my argument in this section has a dual purpose: to defend admiration against emotion skeptics who say we are not justified in trusting the disposition to admiration, and to suggest a framework for the critique of admiration.

6. Painful Admiration and Resentment of the Admirable

Reflection on admiration clearly will need to include reflection on the psychological and cultural forces that distort it. We are subject to mistakes of many kinds, and I have mentioned some empirically confirmed biases and the problem of emotion disagreement, but there is a different kind of mistake that I think is a particular threat to moral understanding and moral development. It begins with a reluctance to emulate admirable persons, and when pressed far enough, it leads to the refusal to admire the admirable, and even the rejection of the admirable as a moral category. I suspect that this psychology explains more of the skepticism about admiration in our culture than disagreement about who the exemplars are and our tendency to admire influential and good-looking people.

The story of the move from admiration to envy to rejection of the admirable as a cultural phenomenon can begin with the Greeks. T. H. Irwin (2015) has argued that the precursor to admiration in Greek literature is *thaumazein,* which means wonder or amazement, and in Homer its objects include anything marvelous—the shield of Achilles, Achilles' single-mindedness, the pride of Ajax. Moral goodness is among the marvels of the world, but there are many wondrous things. Irwin proposes that *thaumazein* becomes admiration when it is directed at human goods.[22] I interpret *thaumazein* as a precursor to admiration. Wonder or amazement is akin to elevation in Haidt's sense, but what is missing is the motive to emulate the admirable quality. I think that what distinguishes the feeling of marveling at a good and the feeling of admiring with the urge to emulate is a sense of a self that can become like an ideal by one's own choice. Achilles' god-like strength is a marvel to behold, but we cannot emulate it any more than we can emulate his marvelous shield.

Thaumazein has the uplifting component of admiration, but not the component of emulation. In the *Rhetoric,* Aristotle describes an emotion that has the emulation component, but not the uplifting aspect. He calls it *zēlos,* usually translated "emulation." As Aristotle describes it, *zēlos* is painful, and I think that its painfulness is a connecting element in an interesting deviant psychological path from admiration to envy to *ressentiment.* Aristotle writes:

> Emulation (*zēlos*) is [defined as] a kind of distress at the apparent presence among others like him by nature of things honored and possible for a person to acquire, [with the distress arising] not from the fact that another has them but that the emulator does not. Thus emulation is a good thing and characteristic of good people, while

---

22. In this paper, Irwin examines my claim that Plato and Aristotle neglected admiration, and gives a wide-ranging and impressive historical treatment of admiration in response. In addition to Homer, Irwin discusses its treatment in Herodotus, Plato, Aristotle, Cicero, and Adam Smith. My paper (Zagzebski 2015) and Irwin's paper were written for a symposium at the Joint Session of the Aristotelian Society and the Mind Association, 2015.

envy is bad and characteristic of the bad; for the former, through emulation, is making an effort to attain good things for himself, while the latter, through envy, tries to prevent his neighbor from having them. (1388a 30–36)

Aristotle then goes on to mention the objects of emulation, saying that moral goodness in all its forms is among the objects of emulation (1388b 10), as well as what is serviceable and useful to others, such as wealth and beauty (1138a 11–14). Some persons are objects of emulation; persons of the contrary sort are objects of contempt (*kataphronesis*) (1388b 21).

As I use the word "emulation," it is a term for a form of behavior, not an emotion, but I assume that what Aristotle means by *zēlos* is close to what I mean by admiration, although the objects of *zēlos* he mentions cover a broader range of goods than I have mentioned, including not only moral traits and natural talents, but also wealth and beauty. I want to focus on a more important difference, however. Aristotle treats *zēlos* as painful, whereas I have been treating admiration as a positive feeling. The source of the difference seems to be that Aristotle makes the focus of attention in *zēlos* one's own *lack* of certain goods, whereas I am interpreting admiration as focusing on the possession of good in the other person and the possibility that I can acquire it myself.

If, as Aristotle says, we feel pained when we see that somebody else exceeds us in some good, we can see why the emotion Aristotle describes can be mistaken for envy, and why he feels it necessary to distinguish them. Kristján Kristjánsson (2006) points out that the word "envy" is sometimes used in a way that includes both an admiring kind and a spiteful kind. In admiring envy we do not wish to deprive the admired person of the good we also want to have, whereas in spiteful envy we do wish to deprive the other of the good, and we do so without any good moral reason. Kristjánnson argues that this difference is important enough that it is inadvisable to classify admiring envy as a form of envy, and he judges that Aristotle was right to treat emulation and envy as distinct emotions.

There are at least two issues here. One is whether the reaction to the admired person feels positive or negative. If two persons witness the same act of superb generosity, perhaps one would feel the elevation Jefferson described whereas the other would feel pained at his own lack of generosity. It is possible that both would be moved to emulate the admired person, but that would need to be investigated. The second issue is the connection between admiration and envy. What leads one person to want to emulate the admired person, and another person to want to deprive her of her admired features?

So we have at least three reactions to an admired person:

(a) a positive feeling that leads to emulation,
(b) a negative (painful) feeling that leads to emulation,
(c) a negative (painful) feeling that leads to wanting to deprive the admired person of his admired features.

Reaction (a) is what I have been calling admiration. Reaction (c) is envy. Reaction (b) is what Aristotle calls *zēlos*, translated "emulation." Is (b) a form of admiration or a form of envy? Kristjánsson argues that Aristotle was right to deny that (b) is envy.

In a very helpful and extensive review of the psychological literature on envy, Smith and Kim (2007) take a similar position. They say that people sometimes use the term "envy" to refer to a benign state, envy without any hostile feelings, but they think that this state is closer to admiration than to envy.

> This type of envy may be more common than envy proper and may often bring about constructive, emulative actions rather than ill will and its possible destructive consequences. Yet the acceptance of a benign form of envy may obscure the nature of envy. The absence of hostile feelings in benign envy may render the emotion fundamentally different from envy proper both in terms of the felt experience and in terms of its likely consequences.... In our view, benign envy is envy sanitized ... and lacks a core ingredient of the emotion, namely, some form of ill will. (47)

Although Smith and Kim do not mention Aristotelian *zēlos*, I take it that they would agree with Aristotle and Kristjánsson that it is not a form of envy.

I have not found much work on benign envy.[23] The majority of the scholarly work on envy is on the hostile form of envy, or what Smith and

---

23. However, van de Ven et al. (2011) have argued that benign envy outperforms admiration in leading subjects to study harder, provided that the subjects believe that self-improvement is possible.

Kim call envy proper. There are a couple of noteworthy features of hostile envy. First, although Smith and Kim say that envy proper includes some form of ill will, they do not say it is necessarily spiteful. That is, they do not say that it includes the desire to deprive the envied person of the desired good. The focus of the emotion seems to be on the inequality between the envier and the envied person. So if Jones envies Smith's new Maserati, does the envy disappear once Jones gets his own Maserati? If it does, the desire to deprive Smith of his Maserati was not an essential feature of his envy. What makes Jones hostile is the fact that Smith has something Jones wants and Jones does not have. The envy disappears if *either* Smith loses his Maserati or Jones gets one too. If I am right about that, the spiteful desire to deprive the envied person of his good is not a necessary component of envy, and so Aristotle and Kristjánsson's description of envy will need to be modified.

The second interesting feature of the scholarly work on envy is that virtually all of the cases of envy that have been empirically studied are directed at non-moral goods and advantages. But I wonder if there is a benign form of envy directed toward another person's moral traits. Aristotle seems to think so, but I do not know of any studies of it. What about true envy of a person for his moral trait—envy with hostile feelings? Smith and Kim say that envy occurs when the envied person is similar to the envier in the relevant characteristics but has an advantage relative to the envier, and the envier is not likely to obtain the desired good (2007, 60–61). But the second and third features of envy do not seem appropriate when the object of envy is a moral trait. If the perceived advantage is moral, there is no reason the envier cannot obtain the good in question, and it is not even clear that the term "advantage" is appropriate when the good is a moral quality like bravery rather than something like wealth or honors. Moral traits may give a person an advantage in reputation, and one can envy the reputation, as Aquinas remarks in a comment on Aristotle, but that is not the same thing as envying the person for having the moral trait.[24] There is a difference between envying someone's honors and envying her amazing courage.

---

24. In answering the question "Whether envy is a kind of sorrow," Aquinas says: "a man may regard another's good as his own evil when it diminishes his renown or excellence. Then envy is discontent over another's good. Consequently men are especially envious of those goods where glory lies, goods which bring honour and esteem, as Aristotle says [*Rhet.* 2.10]." (*ST* II-II, q 36, a. 1, corpus, 1972)

My hypothesis is that true envy for a morally admirable person is pos-sible when the envious person cares more about how he measures up to the other person than about acquiring the good the other person has. Whether or not Jim can become as courageous (kind, just) as some other person, Mary, he knows he is now inferior morally in that respect. If he really hates to be morally inferior to someone else, he can feel envy of a moral quality as much as for the neighbor's new car—in fact, more so if he thinks that rating high on the moral scale is a measure of how he rates as a person. Can he feel envy without spite, as he can when he is envious of his neighbor's automobile? My conjecture is that envying someone for having a virtue prevents, or at least inhibits, the acquisition of the virtue. If I envy someone's automobile, that does not prevent me from getting one too, but envying someone's courage counteracts the motives that would lead me to become courageous because it makes emulation of a courageous person impossible. I cannot emulate someone if I have hostile feelings toward that person. If Jim has true envy of Mary for her courage, he cannot attempt to become courageous—that is, to become like Mary. But if he envies Mary her courage and cannot get it himself, he can become equal to Mary only if she loses her courage, or even better, if he can tell himself a story according to which she never had it. If I am right that courage is the kind of good one cannot acquire when it is the object of envy, it follows that envy of a moral quality is always accompa-nied by spite.

Let us now return to my summary of the different kinds of responses to admirable persons. Admiration essentially involves an awareness of a superior good in another person. If the focus of the emotion is the per-son's possession of the admired good itself, the admiring person will feel uplifted, and she will attempt to emulate the admired person, as Haidt's studies suggest. The admired person in this case is not a competitor, but is more like an ideal self.[25] If instead, she focuses on her own lack of the ad-mired good, she will feel pained, as Aristotle says, but as long as she sees the good as something she can acquire, she will be inclined to emulate the admired person. This is *zēlos*, and it is sometimes called envy of a benign

---

25. David Velleman (2002) describes the emulation of an admired person as an ideal self. If an admired person is seen as an ideal for oneself, that presumably prevents the aberration of moving from admiration to envy, although Velleman does not discuss envy in that paper. I return to this paper in Chapter 5.

sort. I agree with Aristotle (and Kristjánsson) that it is not true envy but a form of admiration.

Envy occurs when we add another feature to the admiring person: His desire for equality with the admired person is stronger than his admiration. Equality can be gained either by depriving the admired person of her trait or by acquiring it himself. But if, as I have conjectured, envy of a virtue prevents the acquisition of the virtue, he will feel spite as well as envy. Notice, however, that whether or not envy includes spite, it cannot exist unless the envier values the good possessed by the envied person. Jones does desire a Maserati, and the morally envious person does admire someone's courage. Nobody can be brought down unless she is first thought to be high on some scale of value. Smith has an object Jones desires, and Mary has a trait Jim admires. Envy over a moral trait does not make sense without admiration. So I propose three emotional responses to a person who possesses an *admired* good: (a) true admiration, (b) Aristotelian *zēlos*, (c) envy with spite. The psychology of envy of an admirable trait requires both that the envied trait be admired, and that such envy be accompanied by spite. This suggests that spiteful envy of an admirable trait is an aberration of admiration that we can detect by examining the psychological process that generates it.

Kierkegaard, who was one of the most perceptive writers on envy, interprets it as a distortion of admiration in *The Sickness unto Death*:

> Envy is concealed admiration. An admirer who feels that he cannot be happy by surrendering himself elects to become envious of that which he admires. So he speaks another language, and in that language of his the thing which he really admires is called a stupid, insipid, and queer sort of thing. Admiration is happy self-surrender; envy is unhappy self-assertion. (1954, 217)

I cannot tell whether Kierkegaard means that the envious person denies that the virtuous person is virtuous, or whether he means that the envious person denies that their virtues are virtues.[26] The latter interpretation is closer to Nietzsche, who made the concept of *ressentiment* famous in *The Genealogy of Morals*, where he theorizes that *ressentiment* leads to an inversion of value, explaining the rise of Slave Morality in Western culture.

---

26. I have also checked the translations by Howard and Edna Hong and the English translation of the German edition edited by H. O. Lange, and I am still unable to tell which interpretation is correct.

In another work, Kierkegaard argued that envy is a constant temptation for people who feel admiration, and some ages handle it better than others.

It is a fundamental truth of human nature that man is incapable of remaining permanently on the heights, of continuing to admire anything. Human nature needs variety. Even in the most enthusiastic ages people have always liked to joke enviously about their superiors. That is perfectly in order and is entirely justifiable so long as after having laughed at the great they can once again look upon them with admiration; otherwise the game is not worth the candle.... In Greece, for example, the form envy [*misundelse*][27] took was ostracism, a self-defensive effort, as it were, on the part of the masses to preserve their equilibrium in the face of the outstanding qualities of the eminent. The outstanding man was exiled, but everyone understood how dialectical the relationship was, ostracism being a mark of distinction.... The man who told Aristides that he had voted for his exile "because he could not bear hearing Aristides called the only just man" did not deny Aristides' eminence, but admitted something about himself. He admitted that his relation to the distinction was the unhappy one of envy, instead of the happy one of admiration, but he did not try to belittle his distinction. (1962, 49)

I find Kierkegaard's mention of exile as a response to admiration rather amusing. If we cannot bear being around admirable persons, we can always send them away. That is more honest than denying that the admirable is admirable. But we see lots of examples of the latter in the delight people get in seeing admired persons revealed as having secret vices or unmasked as hypocrites.[28] There is a gleeful pleasure in finding out that someone is not an exemplar after all. Many books are written debunking moral exemplars

---

27. Kierkegaard's word in Danish was "*misundelse*," but some English translations give rise to an interesting confusion. Alexander Dru (Kierkegaard 1962) made the decision to translate the Danish word into English as "*ressentiment*," suggesting that Kierkegaard and Nietzsche were offering diagnoses of the same moral disease. But to Kierkegaard, *misundelse* has its roots in the secular world, whereas Nietzsche traces the roots of *ressentiment* to Christianity and even further back, to the Hebrew Scriptures.

28. See Shklar (1985), Chapter 2, "Let Us Not Be Hypocritical." Shklar focuses on the psychology of people who can't stand hypocrites but see them everywhere.

or persons admirable in other ways.[29] If we perceive the exemplar as a reproach, a demand made upon us by our own feeling of admiration, we will, indeed, find our emotion painful, as Aristotle maintained. There is more than one way to remove the pain. Emulating the exemplar is one way—the way of Aristotle's *zēlos*. But I have surmised that once admiration turns to envy, emulation is no longer psychologically feasible. Denigrating the exemplar is the only option. In the above passage, Kierkegaard noticed something Nietzsche later made famous: the ingenious ways in which the envious person can deprive the envied person of the good she possesses. These ways can become entrenched in a whole culture and affect the language we adopt in describing admirable persons. The phenomenon Nietzsche called *ressentiment* is not only a refusal to admire morally superior persons but is also a refusal to call their admirable qualities virtues. Of course, Nietzsche believed that there are admirable qualities, just different ones. I worry that our culture is suspicious of admired persons, and consequently, the vocabulary we use in describing them has been stunted.[30] I will return to the disappearance of terms for moral virtues in Chapter 7.

In summary, I think that reflection on admiration should include a critical awareness of a predictable line of deviation from

(a) admiration, a positive feeling with the desire to emulate, to

(b) Aristotle's *zēlos*, a painful feeling with the desire to emulate, to

(c) envy, a painful feeling without the desire to emulate, to

(d) spite, a painful feeling with the desire to deprive the object of the good he possesses, to

(e) *ressentiment*, a pervasive rejection of the admirable, particularly, the morally admirable.

---

29. A possible excuse for the proliferation of books denigrating admired persons is that nobody wants to read a book revealing that someone generally taken to be admirable is, in fact, admirable. That would be boring. Why take the trouble to read a book that tells you something you already knew? That is a partial explanation for the large number of books and articles allegedly unmasking heroes and saints. But if the desire to reveal the unexpected were the motive, there should also be many books revealing that the person perceived to be contemptible is actually admirable. But of course there are not. I suggest that people tend to find it more pleasant to learn that the reputedly good person is bad than to find out that the reputedly bad person is good. It is revealing that in the story of the Good Samaritan in Luke's Gospel, the purportedly contemptible person is the only one who shows mercy, but the people Jesus was addressing did not enjoy the story.

30. Although Nietzsche blames *ressentiment* on Christianity, Max Scheler (1987) (written before 1917) finds the source of *ressentiment* in a kind of egalitarianism that refuses to acknowledge the morally superior person, and which functions as a protest against the virtues.

I have offered the hypothesis that admiration turns to envy when equality is the main motivating value, and I have conjectured that since learning virtue requires emulation of persons who have it, emulation is incompatible with envy. So when the envied good is a virtue, the envier becomes spiteful; he aims at depriving the envied person of his good. Human beings are very clever at figuring out ways to perceive the admirable person as not admirable. But doing so requires suppressing the normal human emotion of admiration. At the extreme, the admirable as a category slips from public view.

Envy or resentment of the admirable is a complex and subtle phenomenon, and it requires sensitivity in the way my theory is applied. I have tried to be alert to this problem in what follows. I do not think that the exemplars I have chosen as exhibits in the next chapter are likely to produce hostile feelings or are controversial in other ways, but it would be interesting to find out which exemplars do produce such feelings, and how we ought to respond to that in social interactions and in education.

I began this chapter by saying that admiration is one of the two most basic attitudes we have toward what we call "good." We either admire it or we desire it. I think that the admirable is good in a different sense from the desirable, and I argue in Chapter 6 that the admirable is more basic in that we can explain a desirable life in terms of an admirable life, but can do the reverse only with great difficulty. But even if I am mistaken in my view that the admirable is the most basic sense of good, it clearly is an important sense, one that deserves attention from both philosophers and psychologists. I hope that there will be more empirical research on the psychology of admiration, and more attention from philosophers on the connection between admiration and our moral judgments. In this book admiration serves a dual role. It is the basis for moral learning by emulation, a process that does not require any theoretical beliefs, and it is the basis for an ethical theory. In the next chapter I begin looking at the kinds of persons we admire, persons whom I believe can serve both the theoretical and practical purposes of this project.

3

Exemplars

1. Where Are the Exemplars?

It is a good thing that there are people whose moral beauty attracts us. We are usually drawn to them initially because we admire something easily observable about them—typically, their acts, although it could also be something about their physical bearing or speech. Suppose we admire an act of courage or kindness. I think we can admire a courageous act or a kind act in advance of having the *concept* of courage or kindness. I do not know how that could be tested, but it seems to me pretty clearly true. We can also admire a person's trait of courage or kindness, and we can admire a person's trait in advance of having the concept of a trait of character, which in any case is a contested concept. But what we certainly can do is to say we admire *that*, and we point to a sequence of acts or a single extraordinary act, where what we mean to be designating is not the acts themselves but whatever it is about the person that leads her to do such acts. We might not know exactly what it is we are admiring, only that it is something in the psychology of the person that is expressed in observable acts. In Western philosophy that has been called a trait of character, but what a trait includes is also discovered by observation. All we need know at the outset is that there is something admirable about the person, something deep enough to be expressible in acts on many different occasions, and that is what we mean to be pointing to when we say we admire *that*. At some point we form hypotheses about the object of our admiration, and we may give it a name. We call it "courage" or "kindness." Of course, we learn these words from other persons who have their own hypotheses about the psychological source of similar forms of behavior. If we have studied ethics, we might go further and have an account of the constituents of these traits, but most of us have no such account, even if we have studied philosophy. We are like the ordinary users of "gold" who have

forgotten their chemistry or never studied it. We believe, or at least suspect, that there is more to gold than meets the eye. It has a deeper physical
structure worth studying, and that physical structure is what makes gold
gold. Gold is the stuff with that structure. Similarly, I think we believe that
the deeper psychological structure of a person who does admirable acts is
what makes the person admirable. From our own psychology we may get
the idea that observable behavior arises out of a structure that includes
perceptions, emotion dispositions, and aims, and we probably form some
hypotheses about the sources of behavior from our own case, but I also
think that we are vague about what that is, even in our own case.

I have said we assume that what makes a person admirable is something in her psychology that leads to acts we admire. That follows from
our response to cases in which we find out that an admirable act does
not have an internal psychological source but is largely caused by external
circumstances. To the extent that we believe or come to find out that the
source of an admirable act is something independent of the agency of the
person, we admire the person less or not at all. For instance, if we found
out that an act of apparent compassion was required by law and anyone
who did not do it would be punished, we would not admire the person
who did it. I am told that Israeli law requires bystanders to give assistance
to persons in obvious distress. I postulate that the coercive force of the law
takes away, or at least reduces, admiration for the Good Samaritan, and so
it reduces admirability.[1]

What we look for in the psychology of the person who does admirable
acts is not natural temperament. I proposed in the last chapter that we
admire natural talents differently from the way we admire acquired excellences. I think that for the same reason we admire natural temperament
in a different way than we do acquired traits. Some persons are inborn
extraverts and we may admire their sociality at a party or in the workplace,
but I think we admire them differently from the way we admire a person
who is generous or kind. I doubt that it is possible to be born generous
or kind, but if it is, I propose that we do not admire the inborn trait the
same way we admire the acquired one. That can, of course, be tested,

---

1. There are in-between cases. Suppose one's church requires that a certain amount of
money be donated to the poor. Membership in the church is voluntary, but given that one is
a member, the donation is not voluntary. My hypothesis here is that other things equal, our
degree of admiration for the act as one of generosity tracks what we believe to be the degree
of voluntariness of the act. This is a rough approximation because it will probably turn out
that there is a degree of luck in admirability.

and exemplarism is compatible with either result, but I am proposing hypotheses that guide us in our investigation of the sources of admirable behavior based on my interpretation of what we admire on reflection. So I suggest that we admire the person for performing admirable acts when we believe that the source of the act is something internal to the person's psychology, and it is acquired rather than inborn.

Does it matter how the trait was acquired? For instance, does it affect our admiration if the trait is the result of childhood training and parental attitudes? In section 3 I mention evidence of the influence of parents on persons who risked their lives to save Jews from the Nazis. In these cases the influences have been assimilated into the rescuer's motivational structure, and I do not admire someone less because of the parental influence. I assume that others are like me in this respect, but that also can be tested.

Opportunity is a different kind of external factor in admirable behavior. Opportunity is a necessary condition for the behavior, and we probably all agree that the persons we consider exemplars would not be recognized as exemplary had their circumstances not given them the opportunity to rise to moral heights. But that does not affect our judgment that they are exemplars. It just means that there are probably other admirable persons who do not have the opportunity to express their admirable qualities in external acts. So maybe there are some invisible exemplars. But it seems to me that the fact that opportunity is a necessary condition for acting admirably does not reduce our admiration for either the act or the person who performs the act.[2]

What if it turns out that the internal psychological source of someone's admirable acts is not a disposition that leads to consistently admirable behavior in relevantly similar circumstances? Someone may act kindly or compassionately on some occasions but not others. There is evidence that individuals who are honest in some domains of their lives are not necessarily honest in other domains.[3] Possibly most

---

2. The fact that opportunity affects moral praiseworthiness and blameworthiness is well known from Thomas Nagel's (1979) discussion of moral luck.

3. The classic study is Hartshorne and May (1928). For an important criticism of the interpretation of the results, see Rushton (1984). Rushton says that the 1928 study actually shows that there are stable traits like honesty, and that other people were able to identify them. For an extensive discussion of the psychological research on honesty and cheating, see Miller (2013) and Miller (2014). In the latter, Christian Miller uses honesty and cheating as the model for his "mixed-trait" framework, in which character traits in real life are combinations of positive and negative qualities.

people have situation-specific traits in that way. They are generous in some domains and not others, fair in some domains and not others, and so on. This issue does not arise for the exemplars I discuss in this chapter, who are obviously consistent in their behavior in the domain of their exemplarity,[4] but it reveals something interesting about what we admire in a person. If we witness two persons performing a similar act of kindness, we would presumably be inclined to admire their acts in the same way and to the same degree, but if we later discover that one of the persons routinely performs such acts, whereas the other one does not, we would probably infer from that that kindness is deeper in the psychology of the former than in the latter. I think that we would then admire the former more as a person than the latter, other things equal. The depth and persistence of the tendency to act kindly is a feature of the classical Aristotelian notion of virtue as a trait of character, and I propose that the root of the idea of a trait of character is in our disposition to admiration. We admire persons who have a strong and consistent disposition to act admirably more than persons who act admirably inconsistently. My point here is not the obvious one that the one person performs more admirable acts than the other, but that the degree of admirability of the person who performs the acts is greater when the acts arise from deep features of the person's psychology. If most people do not act consistently, it follows that most people are not exemplars.

Since reflective admiration is the test for exemplarity, we will be able to restrict the class of exemplars further once we begin investigating the motivations for admirable acts. Here I think the major division is between acts motivated by self-interest—desire for money, fame, or other external rewards, and acts motivated by concern for others. We admire a person who rescued Jews from the Nazis out of humanitarian concern much more than a person who did it for money. We will see an example of that difference in section 3.

---

4. Holocaust rescuers devoted themselves to their rescuing activities continuously for a long period of time, sometimes years. Such a large portion of their lives was involved with rescuing that even if they occasionally passed up an opportunity to rescue someone in a different situation of need, that hardly counts as being inconsistent. Similarly, as I describe below, the volunteers in L'Arche communities devote themselves full time to caring for the mentally disabled. Some live there for months, even years. They do not simply care for the disabled now and then.

I have proposed three hypotheses about what we reflectively admire about persons that guide us in our identification of exemplars and the task of observing them carefully:

(1) We admire psychological sources of admired behavior, not external causes that bypass the person's agency. To the extent that we find out that the admired behavior has external causes, we admire the person less. That does not rule out acts that are influenced by other persons as long as the external influences are integrated into the person's motivational structure.

(2) Within the category of psychological features, we admire acquired features in a different way than we admire natural temperament. We are interested in the former for the purposes of a moral theory. So we are attempting to identify acquired psychological features of the person that are the sources of acts we admire.

(3) Within the category of acquired psychological features that are the sources of acts we admire, we admire motives of concern for others more than motives of self-interest.

It is important for my theory that we do not need a defense of (1)–(3) other than what we reflectively admire. It is not necessary to defend the greater admirability of persons who act for the benefit of others rather than the self, nor is it necessary to defend the greater admirability of acts that have internal rather than external causes, nor the particular relevance to ethics of psychological features that are acquired rather than inborn. It is enough that these hypotheses are supported by what we admire upon reflection. Since (1)–(3) are hypotheses, they can be revised. The test of whether someone is admirable is always that we admire her on reflection and continue to admire her after we obtain more information about her and reflect on our emotion and the emotions of those we trust. If the test of reflective admiration shows that some of these hypotheses need to be revised, then that will change the way we go about identifying exemplars. A more likely and desirable outcome is that empirical research will permit us to make the hypotheses more precise. It can tell us the structure and components of the psychological sources of acts, and it can tell us which components affect admirability and which do not.

In discussing the theory of direct reference in Chapter 1, I mentioned the issue of how we distinguish between what we know about a natural kind through observation and what we know in advance of observation.

Do we know in advance of observation that what makes something the same substance as this stuff is that it has the same deep physical structure? The parallel question for exemplarism is whether we know in advance of observation that being an admirable person consists in having the same deep psychological structure as these exemplars. It follows from what I have said that whether or not we know a priori that sameness of substance is sameness of deep physical structure, we do not know a priori that sameness of admirability is sameness of deep psychological structure as the exemplars we have identified. Or to be more cautious, it is not wholly a priori. The identity of exemplars is determined by our reflective admiration, and that can change with new information about the exemplars. By observing exemplars, we find out what it is we admire about them. If we find out something that leads us to cease admiring them, then we cease identifying them as exemplars. I will return to the way in which we know that being admirable consists in having the same deep psychological structure as the exemplars in Chapter 8.

2. Three Ways to Observe Exemplars

What I mean by exemplars are those persons whom we see, on close observation and with reflection, to be admirable in all or most of their acquired traits. I do not mean that exemplars must be admirable in the highest degree in every one of their acquired traits. It is highly unlikely that there is anyone like that. For instance, we know that some saints are so committed to their moral project that they become demanding of other people. They cannot see why others do not join their cause. There are also highly caring individuals who neglect their children.[5] A harder kind of case is a person who is highly admirable for some trait, but is contemptible in some other respect, such as heroes who lack temperance or sexual restraint.[6] These persons are exemplars of a certain trait—courage, compassion, justice, but they are not exemplars all things considered. They are still useful as exemplars in the sense I want for exemplarism,

---

5. I mentioned in Chapter 2 that Abraham Lincoln was often away from home during the childhood of his oldest son and they had a strained relationship. Many people would consider Franklin Roosevelt an exemplar, but he was apparently a distant parent. Conversely, brutal Mafia boss Bernardo Provenzano was reputedly a doting father. (See the interview with his son in *Wall Street Journal* June 22, 2015, 1).

6. Blum (1986, 70–72) discusses the sexual infidelity of Oskar Schindler, concluding that it makes him less of a moral paragon but not less of a moral hero.

but since they are not exemplars without qualification, we need to keep the qualifications in mind in the way we use them for both theoretical and practical purposes. I believe, however, that there are persons who are admirable in most of their acquired traits. Whether there are such persons is something we can investigate by careful attention to people we admire in some way. Sometimes the more we observe someone, the less we admire her, but sometimes we admire her even more. We might have the good fortune to know individuals like that personally, but the primary cultural mode of transmitting observations about exemplars is through narratives.

I have identified three classes of exemplars for special treatment in this book: the hero, the saint, and the sage. In each category I focus on a particular person to exhibit the way the methodology of exemplarism can be applied. Although I think that all of the exemplars I discuss are admirable all things considered, each one is exemplary in a different way, and I believe that that is why it is important to separate the kinds of exemplars for investigation.

The exemplars I discuss are real persons, but I think that fictional exemplars are just as important. One of the advantages of fictional exemplars is that we get to see them in circumstances in which we would not be able to observe a person in real life, and we can have a window into their consciousness in a way that we rarely can do with actual persons.[7] What exemplars do for us and our moral conceptions is largely irrelevant to their actual existence. For instance, it did not matter if Ajax was an actual person to be an exemplar for the ancient Greeks. Besides, there is often a fine line between an actual historical figure and the legend we have inherited. Surely that is the case with Confucius. The Confucius of the *Analects* is an exemplar whether or not the actual Confucius is accurately depicted in that work, and of course New Testament scholars debate the historical Jesus in the same way.

Exemplars in life have the advantage that different types of narration can be used in observing the same person. The narrator's point of view can be that of a third person as the report of an observer, second person in the form of an interview, or first person as a story told by the person herself. All narratives are selective observations. Clearly, the narrator's values, interests, and psychological hypotheses shape the narrative. If the narrator is

---

7. See Chris Tweedt (unpublished) for a defense of the importance of fictional exemplars for exemplarist moral theory.

writing about herself, the image she wants to project affects the narrative. Most persons want to project an image of themselves that is better than they really are, but I assume that that is not admirable, and the kind of person I am considering an exemplar does not portray himself as better than he is. In fact, exemplars often project an image of themselves that hides some of their most admirable features, either intentionally or unintentionally.[8] Third person narratives distort as well. One type of distortion occurs when the narrator puts the narrative in a larger framework in which she is defending a certain set of values, and the narrative is governed by the end of promoting that set of values. Think of Plato's narratives about Socrates, or the use of edifying narratives about George Washington and other historical figures to shape the values of children. Even when the narrator does not consciously construct the narrative with the intention of promoting a particular value perspective, her perspective inevitably affects her selection of pieces of the narrative and the vocabulary she uses in creating it. A similar point applies to the interview. The interviewer selects the questions, and the person interviewed answers in the first person, but each is affected by the verbal and emotional responses of the other. So we need to keep in mind that narratives of any kind are never pure observations from which we select the acts, motives, and traits we admire.

I think this means that we need to handle narratives with a healthy critical eye, thinking of the persons who tell us narratives as contributors to the joint human project of figuring out what is admirable and what is contemptible, a project to which we also contribute. The narrator's hypotheses about the admirable and the contemptible will necessarily shape what he passes down to us as data from which we are to respond. Narratives can be controlled by the political, religious, or educational authorities and the media, and our responses will be affected by the way they tell the narratives. But there are ways we can exercise critical judgment. For one thing, our personal responses are tests of the narrator's point of view. In addition, there is often much more in a narrative than the narrator can

---

8. Benjamin Polansky (2014) argues that exemplars often practice irony, when they intentionally hide admirable features of themselves. He says he sees that in Socrates, Jesus, and Confucius. As we will see later in this chapter, Holocaust rescuers almost always deny they are exemplars, not because they are being ironic but because they have a type of humility that requires that they do not engage in judging themselves and show no signs of admiring themselves. They think they did no more than the obvious thing to do. Both the "ironic" exemplars and the "humble" exemplars raise interesting issues about emulating persons who do not fully reveal their admirability, as Polansky argues.

consciously or unconsciously distort, and that serves as a partial test of the elements highlighted in the narrative. People can even read the same story at different times, and different features of it strike their attention. The story is partly interpreted as it is constructed, but it is also partly interpreted as it is read or seen on the screen.

A second way of observing exemplars is through personal experience. Personal observation has both advantages and disadvantages over narratives in books and films. The obvious disadvantage is that personal experience is very limited in scope. Few people have had personal interactions with a Mother Teresa or a Pope Francis, much less with someone on the caliber of Confucius or Jesus. Still, the individuals we know personally can affect us in a much more direct way than the exemplars of other people's stories. We can decide questions to ask the exemplar and do not have to depend on the narrator or interviewer to get the admired person to reveal what we want to know about her. More important, if we have a personal relationship with the exemplar, our story can take the form of a dialogue that gives us knowledge of who the person is, not just what the person is like. Extended personal contact also makes it very difficult for anything relevant to be hidden. Personal experience is a check on any narrative that comes to us filtered through the emotional responses of other persons. The emotional responses of other persons is also a check on our own emotions, so the checking goes both ways.

A third kind of observation of exemplars is controlled empirical studies. As far as I know, these studies have begun only in the last few years. The range of the studies is necessarily limited by the nature of the methodology of empirical science and the fact that exemplars have to be identified by easily observed external features. Nonetheless, the kind of control that sophisticated empirical studies can employ is a healthy check on narratives and personal observation. Sometimes empirical investigation confirms the judgments we make based on personal observation or the observations of others passed on to us in stories, but sometimes the findings are surprising. Moreover, some questions we would like answered for moral theory are not easy to answer based on the kinds of experience we get from personal contact or in the narratives that shape the moral point of view of our culture. For instance, we might guess what an exemplar would do in a given set of circumstances, but controlled experiments can put persons designated as exemplars in circumstances of a certain kind to see what they do. We will see an example of that in section 3.3.

A prior question that can be empirically tested is whether there are persons who are consistently exemplary in some respect. Nobody yet has figured out a way to empirically study persons who are exemplary, all things considered, but consistency in giving and in rescuing has been identified in laboratory studies. For instance, M. J. Gill et al. (2013) have recently studied persons they call "consistent contributors." When deciding between keeping a resource for themselves or giving it to the collective good, these people *always* give to the collective good, even when they cannot get anything in return. The HABITVS research group (2010, 2013) has undertaken a series of studies on the psychology of exemplars, both real-world exemplars who work in L'Arche communities, and laboratory exemplars, and they have found interesting evidence of regularities in giving and rescuing.[9] Another series of projects on exemplars that has just been started as of this writing is the Moral Beacons program.[10] All of these research programs are important because psychological studies on virtue usually have the quite different aim of understanding what the average person will do in a given set of circumstances and finding out how consistent those people are at acting virtuously at other times.

A newer form of empirical study is investigation into the biological substructure of human emotion and behavior. The HABITVS group has observed brain activations of virtuous exemplars during participation in the experiments described below. This is a contribution to the study of the biological differences between laboratory exemplars and control groups, and they are currently attempting to learn whether there are any genetic differences. There is evidence that practice and habituation of moral behavior (e.g., compassion training) alters the brain, and the HABITVS research can confirm whether that is also the case with the behavior they are observing.[11] I discuss the work of the HABITVS project below.

---

9. "HABITVS" stands for "Human Archetypes: Biology, Intersubjectivity, and Transcendence in Virtue Science." The group was initiated by Michael Spezio, Warren Brown, Kevin Reimer, James Van Slyke, and Gregory Peterson. Subsequently Dirk Schumann, Steven Quartz, and Jan Glascher have joined the group. I mention their current studies below.

10. See the website for the Moral Beacons project at http://www.moralbeacons.org/. It is directed by William Fleeson and Michael Furr at Wake Forest University with a grant from the Templeton Religion Trust.

11. See Weng et al. (2013). This article notes the differential neural recruitment associated with people who receive compassion training, suggesting that practice and habituation in virtue alters our physiology in ways we are just beginning to understand.

One of the aims of this book is to show how we might integrate psychological studies, narratives from literature and history, neurological information,[12] and personal experience in a multi-disciplinary approach to observing moral exemplars, and creating a map of the moral domain within which these observations can be imbedded. In the next three sections I illustrate the methodology with three kinds of exemplars. I begin each section with a short narrative of an exemplar of a certain kind, followed by a summary of some recent psychological studies on exemplars of the relevant kind. I refer to these exemplars from time to time when I present the structure of the theory in Chapters 4 and 6.

3. Leopold Socha and the Holocaust Rescuers

3.1. The Story of Leopold Socha

On the last day of May 1943, the Nazis liquidated the Jewish ghetto in the Polish city of Lvov, now in Ukraine, which they had set up after the German invasion in 1941. During the day and all night long, Jews were shot, homes burned, and all surviving Jews were rounded up by the Germans and the Ukrainian militia and sent to their deaths in cattle trucks. A group of Jews with their families hid in the sewers beneath the city for fourteen months. They lived amid raw sewage and thousands of rats, in almost total darkness, battling dysentery, injury, and sometimes each other. They could not have survived without the aid of a Polish sewer inspector and former thief, Leopold Socha, who repeatedly risked his life to take care of them, using his ingenuity to bring them food, medicine, games, prayer books, candles for the Sabbath light, and providing them with crucial information about the outside world. Socha had the full cooperation of his wife and a friend and co-worker, Stefan Wroblewski, who helped Socha from the beginning. A journal was kept by Ignacy Chiger, a member of the group who hid in the sewers, and that journal, together with a book written by his daughter and interviews with other survivors, give us a picture of the man from the perspective of the people he was helping.

At the beginning, Socha was paid to hide the Chigers and a few others, but the group grew on the night of the terror when it became obvious that

---

12. The HABITVS group has found some fascinating information on the brain activations of the participants in their studies, but as a cautionary warning, Weisberg et al. (2008) show that people judge explanations of psychological phenomena as more satisfying when they contain neuroscience information, even when the information is irrelevant.

FIGURE 3.1 Leopold Socha

all of them had to either go into the sewers or die. The survivors say that their relationship with Socha was the cornerstone of the ordeal and its success for ten of them. Chiger says that Socha liked to tell the story of seeing Paulina Chiger for the first time. "When I squeezed through the shaft, into the little cellar, you were sitting there with Krysia and Pawel under each arm. Like a mother kite and her chicks. It was at that moment, when you were sitting there with the children, at that moment I decided to save you."

For hundreds of years, Lvov had been a center for Western culture and commerce on the eastern edge of the Austro-Hungarian empire, and Socha had the vague anti-Semitic attitude of most of the Poles and Ukrainians in Lvov. In a short time his motives evolved from anti-Semitism to a desire to protect the Jews from the Nazis, making greater and greater personal sacrifices, motivated first by money, and then, after their money ran out, out of care for them as individuals. He protected them from harms that had nothing to do with the Nazis. At some point he began to love them. When a man died, he and Wroblewski took great risks to give the man a proper burial. When a woman secretly gave birth to a baby, he ran off to find someone to care for the child, but sadly, when he returned with a plan, the mother had already smothered her infant, and they buried the baby. When hostility arose between Chiger and Weiss, the original leader of the group, Socha acted as keeper of the peace. When there was a violent storm and waters flooded the sewers, Socha ran into the sewer in a panic, terrified that the people had drowned, finding that the waters had stopped rising just as it reached their chins.

Ignacy Chiger became the leader of the group after Weiss attempted to escape and was shot. He says that Socha's relationship with him was based on mutual respect and trust. When Chiger gave Socha money, both men knew that Socha could have easily pocketed the money and then handed them over to the authorities and claimed a reward. No one ever thought he would do that. Socha liked to ask Chiger's advice about his own problems, and he told them accounts of his past life as a thief and his remorse over what he had done. He was a deeply religious man, and in speaking of his work to shelter the group, he told Chiger, "This is my mission. I have been called to do it, to atone" (Marshall 1990, 132).

The Russian army entered Lvov on July 26, 1944. Chiger's daughter, Krystyna, writes in her memoir (Chiger and Paisner 2008) that Socha had everything organized for them for their life after they left the sewers. He had found a building that could be divided into apartments, and prepared a home for each of the families with furnishings, clothes, and bedding (252). On July 28, 1944, the ten surviving Jews emerged from the sewers to the astonishment of a group of people who gathered to watch. Leopold Socha looked at the people and said proudly, "These are my Jews" (Chiger and Paisner 2008, 251; Marshall 1990, 187).

Socha died in the act of rescue, but it was not the rescue for which he thought he might die. On May 12, 1946, Leopold and his twelve-year old daughter, Stefcia, were riding their bicycles through a narrow street when a Soviet army truck careened toward them directly in the path of Stefcia, who was riding ahead. Leopold desperately pedaled forward and knocked her safely out of the way, but was crushed to death by the truck (Marshall 1990, 194).

In 1978 Leopold and Magdalena Socha were recognized as "Righteous among the Nations" by Yad Vashem.[13] Stefan Wroblewski and his wife were given the same honor in 1981.

---

13. Yad Vashem is a memorial commission in Jerusalem established by law in 1953. Its purpose is to commemorate the millions of Jews who died at the hands of the Nazis, and to honor those "Righteous among Nations" who risked their lives to save Jews.

3.2. Psychological Studies of Holocaust Rescuers

Many stories have been told about Holocaust rescuers, some in the first person, many in the third person, some in the form of interviews, some dramatized on stage or screen,[14] some interwoven with commentary. Most rely on the reader or viewer to interpret the events. Empirical studies of Holocaust rescuers have also been done in the last two or three decades, and usually the studies are designed to answer questions about the rescuers that are difficult to detect in an ordinary narrative. If we want to know what makes rescuers different from non-rescuers, it is not enough to read the story of one rescuer even though a well-told story of a rescuer like Leopold Socha can be more informative in some ways than an empirical study. One way of finding out the motives of these people is to listen to them talk about their lives, but another way is to compare rescuers with non-rescuers on the factors that might seem to explain their behavior.

Oliner and Oliner (1988) attempted to identify the sociopsychological factors that contributed to the behavior of rescuers, based on their interviews with 682 people—406 rescuers, 126 non-rescuers, and 150 rescued survivors.[15] Their detailed questionnaire and data collection yielded a large amount of data, the main purpose of which was to answer two questions: (1) Was rescue a matter of external circumstances that facilitated the rescue, and if so, what circumstances? (2) Was rescue a matter of personal attributes, and if so, which ones? The Oliners defined an "altruistic act of rescue" by four criteria: (1) it involved a high risk to the rescuer, (2) it was accompanied by no external rewards, (3) it was voluntary, and (4) it was directed toward helping a Jewish person (261). The reason for the last criterion was that Yad Vashem already had a list which the Oliners could use as representative of a subclass of altruistic rescuers, whereas it would have been almost impossible to identify a representative sample of the total population of rescuers from the Nazis.

Rescuers and non-rescuers were compared on a host of factors, including parental religiosity and political affiliation, parental attitudes toward Jews, their own politics and attitudes toward Jews, attitudes toward Nazis, occupational status before the war, general knowledge of events during the war, and sheltering potential. They were also compared on personal motives such as religion, patriotism, hatred of Nazis, desire for equity,

---

14. The story of Leopold Socha was made into the movie, *In Darkness*, directed by Agnieszka Holland (2011). It was nominated for Best Foreign Language Film at the 84th Academy Awards.

15. Oliner and Oliner describe their methodology in their Appendix A, 261ff.

and caring about the plight of the Jews. Oliner and Oliner concluded, "Rescuers did not simply happen on opportunities for rescue; they actively created, sought, or recognized them where others did not. Their participation was not determined by circumstances, but their own personal qualities. Chance sometimes provided rescuers ... with an opportunity to help, but it was the values learned from their parents which prompted and sustained their involvement" (1988, 142). The Oliners identify "values of caring" as the dominant cause for rescue, with honesty, truthfulness, and respect often revealed in interviews. In addition, rescuers were much more likely than non-rescuers to think of ethical values as applying universally, extended to all human beings (165, Table 6.7, 292).

Obviously the distinguishing features of rescuers identified by the Oliners track questions on their questionnaire, and although their questionnaire was enormous (see their Appendix C, 331–356), there are many features of the emotion dispositions, aims, and values of the rescuers that the Oliners could not discover. For instance, for theoretical purposes we would want to know whether the rescuers were caring and compassionate in other areas of their lives, and whether they were more likely than the non-rescuers to have other virtues. Nonetheless, many interesting things emerge from the Oliner study that are relevant to exemplarism. One is the importance of role-modeling in the lives of the rescuers, particularly parents and grandparents. Another is that rescuers felt a connection with Jews; some felt connected through close personal contacts, whereas others felt a sense of responsibility for the welfare of society or a sense of identification with all of humankind. Many of the rescuers interviewed by the Oliners had a strong sense of control over their lives rather than seeing the outcome of events during the Nazi occupation as determined by other people. A large subset of the rescuers identified by the Oliners had strong family bonds and religious commitments.[16]

---

16. The Oliners identify four general groups of rescuers. One group had strong, cohesive family bonds, religious commitments, and a childhood in which they felt potent, decisive, and independent (184–185). This group was highly aware of Jews but did not necessarily have personal contacts with them. A second group had consistently close personal contacts with Jews, and Jewish friends were an integral part of their lives. A third group had a strong sense of responsibility for the welfare of society, but not necessarily any close contact with Jews. The fourth group were people who identified with all of humankind, rejected ethnocentrism, and felt themselves to be similar to outgroups (e.g., Turks and Gypsies as well as Jews). Notice that as the Oliners interpret these rescuers, three of the four groups were marked by a sense of connectedness to Jews, although some felt more personally connected, and others felt connected through their humanity.

Although the Oliners could not interview Socha, we can tell how he would have answered some of the questions in their study. Socha began with anti-Semitic feelings and a motive of monetary again, but his motives changed partly because of the close personal connection he developed with Jews he was hiding, and partly because he saw rescue as a way to redeem his past life. Socha showed a very strong sense of personal control over his life, like a large percentage of the rescuers interviewed by the Oliners. Also, like a large subset of the rescuers in the Oliner study, he had strong family bonds and was deeply religious.

It seems to me that none of these features really goes to the heart of the matter, although the Oliner study permits us to rule out certain hypotheses on the motives for rescue. The sense of being in control of one's life rather than a helpless victim of circumstances may be an important psychological condition for rescue, but it is not a motive. To get closer to the motivational core of admirable persons, Colby and Damon (1992) did a study of about two dozen moral exemplars in an attempt to find out what sustains the depth of moral commitment that some people maintain over an extended period of time. They suggest that the way to answer that question is to look at the life history of these people through their own eyes:

> We believe that the best source is an autobiographical statement systematically structured around questions about how the individual's moral commitment originated, grew, and was sustained. The account is founded upon the person's own recollections and beliefs. The recollections are prodded and focused by a sympathetic interviewer, the beliefs are explored and challenged, and the resulting interpretations are negotiated between investigator and subject. To this end, we arrived at what some have called an "assisted autobiography" method of case study. (8)

Colby and Damon say that one of their aims is to demystify moral commitment since they believe that the popular culture tends to turn moral heroism into a "magical fantasy." Unfortunately, they say, the popular movie image of heroism can discourage ordinary people from identifying with moral excellence and aspiring to attain it. But Colby and Damon think that exploring the developmental roots of moral excellence "in a less remote and forbidding light" reveals its connections to the possibilities of moral growth inherent in everyone (4).

Colby and Damon's primary finding is that moral exemplars differ from other people, not because of a difference in moral beliefs or professed values but in the degree to which these values are integrated into the exemplar's sense of self. This insight was used in Kristen Renwick Monroe's (2004) intensive study of five persons who rescued Jews during the Holocaust. Monroe's method is quite different from that of Colby and Damon. She presents transcripts of minimally edited interviews conducted between 1988 and 1999 which she says enable her to convey the rich complexity of the psychology of each person interviewed (xii). But like Colby and Damon, Monroe concludes that the sense of identity is a powerful moral motivator, and the rescuers' choices were determined by their sense of self, which developed along with their personal understanding of their life story. This seems to be the case with Socha, although we do not have the advantage of an interview with him like the interviews Monroe conducted.

Observations of witnesses have one kind of objectivity because a witness will see things the rescuer might be too humble or embarrassed to mention, as well as things the rescuer might want to forget. On the other hand, the witness does not know what is really moving the rescuer, how rescuing fits into the narrative of her life. Most rescuers say that rescuing for them was the obvious thing to do, and first person narratives permit us to see how that can be true even though the witness sees the rescue as extraordinary. We need to see both points of view to understand what exemplars are like.

The second person method can give us knowledge of exemplars we cannot get any other way: a knowledge of what a person is like in relation to me, the interviewer. The interviewer poses the questions and poses new questions in response to the answers. The person interviewed gives answers *for* a particular person, where the relationship between them affects what is revealed, not just in terms of information passed along, but because there is a distinctive kind of knowledge one person has of another through personal interaction.[17] A good interviewer gets this knowledge for herself, but she is also a proxy for the readers of the book to the extent that they identify with the interviewer. Of course, somebody else's interview is not as illuminating for me as my own dialogue with the rescuer would be, but it is as close as we can get if we do not know the exemplar.

---

17. See Eleonore Stump (2010), Chapter 4, for a penetrating discussion of second person knowledge as a distinctive form of knowledge.

3.3 Rescuers in the Laboratory

A more recent kind of empirical study is one in which putative exemplars and control groups are placed in a controlled situation to investigate their behavior. In these studies very specific behaviors can be compared in highly artificial circumstances, but they are circumstances that can be made identical for all participants. The members of the HABITVS research group have undertaken a series of studies in which they have begun to study virtuous exemplars in a laboratory context and to compare them with virtuous exemplars in the real world. In addition, they have used neuroimaging of putative laboratory exemplars and controls while the participants make decisions about giving or helping someone in need.[18] In their experiments, the HABITVS group builds on the well-known "public goods game," designed to test participants' allocation of personal resources for the public good.[19] Previous studies (Bardsley and Moffat 2007) reveal that a small percentage of people consistently give, regardless of the behavior of others in the group. The HABITVS group calls these people behavioral paradigm exemplars (BPEs), with the assumption that their behavior in the laboratory game is exemplary in respect to giving.[20] They then designed experiments to determine whether the BPEs are "virtuous" in other contexts, and to use neuroimaging to see whether the brain activity of laboratory exemplars differs from that of controls.

In one study, the group invented a rescuer game that was intended to capture the situation of persons who must decide whether to put themselves at risk to save another person who is being victimized. In the rescuer paradigm (RP), each participant is an observer who witnesses a series of interactions between a perpetrator and a victim. At the beginning of each trial, the observer is given an amount of money (e.g., $300) that is twice as much as the victim has (e.g., $150). On each of the fifteen trials, the perpetrator steals money from the victim while the observer watches. (The game is in words alone. Participants do not see either the perpetrator or the victim). The amounts stolen vary randomly from $10 to $30. Following the theft, the observer is asked whether she wants to keep her money or to give her own money to the victim. If the observer keeps

---

18. See their paper, "Empirical Approaches to Virtue Science: Observing Exemplarity in the Lab," in Van Slyke (2013). My summary is largely based on that paper and personal communications. The group is continuing studies of the same kind.

19. See Ledyard (1993) for a summary of studies of the public goods game.

20. It would be interesting to see a study of the percentage of people who admire the BPEs.

her money, there is no financial penalty and the experiment continues. If the observer chooses to give, then the amount the perpetrator has stolen from the victim is deducted from the observer's account and given to the victim. However, participants are informed that they begin each round without being known to the perpetrator, but each time they decide to give to the victim, the chances of being discovered by the perpetrator increase slightly. If they are discovered, the perpetrator takes all the money for that session. In that case, the participant may continue to observe the interactions for the rest of the session and may even choose to continue to give to the victim. If she does that, her funds will become negative. Participants are told that the only way they can safely keep their money is never to give anything to the victim. At this point in the study several of the control participants asked something like, "Why should there be any reason to give to the victim?" BPEs never asked this question or anything similar to it.

The results showed (1) there are laboratory rescuer exemplars, and (2) a majority of the BPEs identified in the public goods game gave to the victim in a significantly greater proportion than the control group. In fact, 100 percent of the BPEs gave to the victims in a high degree, and few of the non-BPEs gave in the rescuer paradigm. In addition, no BPE who was discovered by the perpetrator stopped giving to the victim, and 7 out of 10 BPEs continued rescuing to the end and ended up with negative amounts. In contrast, the controls averaged 3 percent giving, with most controls not giving at all. Interestingly, the rescuer game experiments were conducted several years after the exemplars in the public goods game were identified, suggesting that the giving and rescuing behavior expressed continuity of character in those respects. Neuroimaging of the brains of participants was conducted during the rescuer paradigm study.

There are obviously questions about the extent to which the laboratory rescuer game models rescuers like Leopold Socha and the rescuers interviewed by Monroe and those by Colby and Damon. In the rescuer game, subjects never see the victim. Compare that with Socha's remark that the moment he saw Paulina Chiger with her children, he knew he would attempt to save them. However, many of the rescuers in the Oliners' study had no previous contact with Jews and seemed to be motivated by more abstract ideals than personal relationships. Another difference is that the studies by Colby and Damon and Kristen Monroe revealed the significant role of rescuing Jews in the life narratives of the rescuers, whereas it is highly doubtful that a life narrative has much to do with a subject's decision to give money to an unseen laboratory victim who has lost a few dollars to a laboratory thief. Moreover, Holocaust rescuers were responding to one of the most diabolical and systematically brutal projects in human history, whereas not much is at stake in the laboratory rescuer game.

But in spite of the obvious ways in which a controlled study cannot model Holocaust rescuing, the results of the studies by the HABITVS group reveal differences between people who rescue and people who do not, including differences in their brain activity during rescue. If we want to know what makes someone an exemplar, we will want to know whether there are any similarities between one kind of exemplar and another, and how exemplars differ from non-exemplars. In section 4, I return to some other studies by members of HABITVS in comparing real-life exemplars with laboratory givers, laboratory rescuers, and controls. So far the quantity of information we have is meager in comparison to the enormous number of questions we will have about exemplars. But I think it is worth remembering that altruism was not even a topic for serious study in the social sciences until recent decades. Skepticism that anybody is altruistic in a deep way pervaded the field of psychology and related fields, greatly limiting the history of these studies. The study of Holocaust rescuers by Oliner and Oliner was a breakthrough, and it was published fewer than thirty years ago. The use of fMRI technology is more recent and time will tell whether we can get important information from it.

The methodology I am proposing for exemplarism weaves together all the ways we can closely observe exemplars. We want studies that go beyond observations of overt behavior, and neuroimaging might give us one kind of window into the emotions that motivate exemplary behavior.[21] Combining this information with first person and third person narratives and interviews can give us a multi-layered approach to revealing the features of exemplars that make them admirable.

---

21. Mary Helen Immordino-Yang presented research participants with true stories of situations, some of which exhibited unusual generosity or selflessness. Participants were videotaped as they described how the stories made them feel, and then later underwent an fMRI while being reminded of the story and how they felt. This research shows us neuro correlates of certain emotions that can be useful in identifying emotions that motivate virtuous behavior. See a brief discussion of the importance of her work in Damon and Colby (2015, 80)

4. Jean Vanier and the L'Arche Communities

4.1. The Story of Jean Vanier

In 1964, Jean Vanier, a philosophy professor and former naval officer, bought a small house in Trosly-Breuil, a village north of Paris, and invited two men with mental disabilities to make their home with him. He called their community L'Arche, after Noah's Ark. The aim of Vanier and the other volunteer "assistants" was to live in a community inspired by the Beatitudes and to create a family life for the mentally infirm. The communities multiplied, and quickly became an interfaith and intercultural movement. By 2008 there were more than 130 L'Arche communities on every continent of the globe, including sixteen in the United States.

Vanier was born in Geneva where his father was a distinguished soldier and later governor general of Canada. His family escaped Paris ahead of the advancing German army in World War II, and Vanier spent most of the war in an English naval academy, subsequently joining the Royal Navy and then the Royal Canadian Navy. In 1950 he resigned his

FIGURE 3.2 Jean Vanier

commission, knowing that he needed to find another path. For a time Vanier studied for the priesthood in Quebec, but changed his mind and spent a few years searching, attempting to find the right kind of community. While he was in the navy, he had visited Friendship House in New York, a Catholic interracial apostolate founded in the early 1930s by Catherine de Hueck, and it touched him deeply. In Paris, while he pursued studies in philosophy and theology, he joined a small Christian community of students where everyone worked manually and prayed together. In 1962 Vanier earned his Ph.D. at the Institut Catholique de Paris with a dissertation on happiness in Aristotle. In 1963 his mentor and former philosophy professor, the saintly Père Thomas Philippe, inspired him to adopt a vocation to the intellectually disabled. Père Thomas was a scholar and a visionary whose mission focused on the "little" people, particularly people who had mental disabilities. When Vanier helped his friend refurbish a place to live and minister to these people, he felt a vocation to follow Père Thomas, yet he did not at first feel at ease with the mentally impaired. In January 1964, he went to the University of Toronto, where he had been invited to teach philosophy. At the end of the term he was offered a permanent position, but he decided to return to Europe and began visiting institutions for the mentally disabled. These places were horrifying, yet Vanier later said that he saw "something of God" in them that led him to decide that his true vocation was to bring about a gentle revolution:

> The idea of living together was there from day one, the idea of living happily together, of celebrating and laughing a lot, came very quickly and spontaneously. When the idea of the poor educating us came, I don't know exactly. The words of St. Vincent de Paul, "The poor are our masters," were always there, but when they became a reality is uncertain. (Spink 2003, 63)

Vanier's religious vision was never clear at the beginning, and he probably did not realize that he was creating a new kind of community. All he knew was that he had made an irrevocable decision to live with two disabled men, Raphael and Philippe, for the rest of their lives or his. Gradually more people came and more communities were formed: a community for women, a community for both men and women, and eventually, they began welcoming people with more severe and multiple disabilities. Some of these people had such severe disabilities that they appeared to be beyond reach—for example, blind, autistic Claudia, who had never known love, and whose inner pain made her seem totally mad, screaming day and night, and spreading excrement on the walls.[22] Vanier describes her transformation into a sweet, loving person under the guidance of her faithful caregiver, Nadine, and in story after story, we see the transformative power of those who can see the humanity in persons whom no one believed in and letting it blossom. The stories always include the transformative power on the caregiver as well—hence, the title of one of Vanier's most gripping books *Becoming Human*. Vanier's moral genius was in being able to create a revolutionary kind of human community, one that had never before been thought possible.

What the caregivers actually do is both extraordinarily simple and extraordinarily effective. More than forty years after L'Arche was founded, when it had spread to many countries, Kathleen Berken, an American woman assistant in a L'Arche community in Iowa, vividly described their daily life:

> I believe that we live as family despite roadblocks of anger, violence, and pain. Caring for our core members' needs while helping them be independent is staggering. We do most everything: cook; shop; bathe; brush teeth; wipe butts; handle expenses; drive them to medical appointments; spend weekends at Special Olympics; write letters; do paperwork; communicate with family, guardians, and case managers; accompany them to church; plan outings; go to dances, the park, restaurants. But more, we hope to be friends. Yet hope can slam you in the face when, without warning, an angry core member threatens to kill you. That makes it challenging to be friends. (Berken 2008, 14)

The mystery is that Kathleen Berken and the other L'Arche assistants can live as she describes, yet L'Arche keeps growing and the assistants keep coming, some staying for many years. Jean Vanier says at the end of his book, *Becoming Human* (1998), "We do not have to be saviours of the world! We are simply human beings, enfolded in weakness and in hope, called together to change our world one heart at a time" (163).

---

22. See Vanier (1998, 20–26) for Claudia's story. I return to Claudia in Chapter 4.

4.2. Psychological Studies of L'Arche Caregivers

What makes people go to L'Arche and devote their lives to the disabled? Psychologist Kevin Reimer (2009) was the first academic to be given access to L'Arche communities. During his two-year study, he visited eight communities in the United States, where he conducted semi-structured interviews with the inhabitants, asking them what happens in their community, why they think it is important, and what motivates them to keep going. Reimer wrote that the wide spectrum of mental abilities in L'Arche made it impossible to create standardized interview questions comprehensible to everyone, so the main focus of the interviews was on the caregivers, supplemented by talks with core members and direct observations of community life (9).

The volunteers in L'Arche are the leaders, and they get the primary credit for keeping the community together, but when Reimer talks about the "saints" who work in L'Arche, he stresses their fallibility, which he says is as psychologically interesting as their remarkable capacity for compassionate love (78). Like the core members, they are riddled with insecurities and problems. Everyone in the community needs meaningful relationships; the core members because they have experienced personal rejection, and the assistants for all the ordinary reasons—divorce, career failure, frustrations with life, sickness, depression. We might think of people who are extraordinarily giving as extraordinarily strong, but they often are not. It is important for the emulation of exemplars to know that they are ordinary in so many ways, a point stressed by Colby and Damon mentioned earlier. Reimer discovered that often the L'Arche caregivers emulate the disabled core members' ability to have their suffering "redeemed" by living in L'Arche. Both the caregivers and the core members are exemplars, but they are exemplars of different things, and their exemplarity is important for people with different life experiences. In Chapter 6 I return to the importance of having exemplars for developing a life narrative.

For the purposes of using exemplars in a comprehensive theory, it would be helpful to have some other information. We want to find out if L'Arche volunteers are similar to other kinds of exemplars, such as the rescuers, and whether there is a connection between these groups and the laboratory exemplars. In a recent study, the HABITVS research group compared the laboratory exemplars (BPEs) discussed in section 3 with longtime volunteers in L'Arche communities. The group used identical self-narrative interviews with four groups: (1) L'Arche volunteers who had served in the community for more than three years, (2) L'Arche volunteers who had served in the community for less than one year, (3) the laboratory exemplars identified in the earlier studies, and (4) a control group. Using latent semantical analysis, they analyzed the way these people related moral traits to their sense of self, future expectations, and expectations in interpersonal relationships. The results supported greater virtue-related semantic information in the interview narratives of long-term L'Arche assistants than for the shorter-term assistants, and significantly greater virtue information than that for the control group (Brown et al. 2013, 17). The virtue terms highlighted included terms for being just, courageous, loving or caring, and terms with religious or spiritual content. Interestingly, among the four semantic categories, religiousness was the least strongly represented in both long-term and novice caregivers, in spite of the religious inspiration of L'Arche communities. Virtue concepts dominated their narratives (18). Moreover, the same result was revealed in the narratives of BPEs, and a comparable study on Holocaust rescuers (Reimer et al. 2012) yielded similar results.

I have been told by these researchers that they interpret the results as early evidence of a similarity between rescuers, the long-term caregivers, and the laboratory exemplars. The studies give us some evidence of a connection between instances of real-life exemplars and laboratory exemplars, evidence of a connection between the self-understanding of Holocaust rescuers and L'Arche caregivers, and evidence of a growth in reflectiveness about virtue in concepts of the self with increasing experience. Together with the studies mentioned in section 3.3, there is beginning to be a body of research on the links between distinct virtuous character traits, and the links between those traits and measurable laboratory behavior. These studies are only at the beginning stages, but we may hope that the data will be useful in constructing psychological profiles that will help us make more sophisticated identifications of exemplars and their traits.

5. Confucius and Exemplars of Wisdom

5.1 The Sage and the Analects

Not all exemplars perform stunning acts of self-sacrifice or courage. Some are known for their wisdom. As I have said, I do not think that means

FIGURE 3.3 Confucius

that we have a concept of wisdom that we use to identify wise persons or sages. Rather, I think that in our natural moral development we learn what wisdom is by observing or reading about the persons who attract us in the way wise persons attract us. Wisdom is the quality that *that* person has. Unlike saints and heroes, we typically do not identify sages primarily by admirable overt acts, and we generally do not speak of "wise acts," although we might refer to "words of wisdom," and in retrospect, we may speak of "wise decisions." Wise persons may also attract our attention because they convey a sense of serenity and emotional tranquility, perhaps holiness. They have the harmony of soul that few of us have attained, and we can see that harmony in their outward demeanor. That was the case with Confucius.

Confucius is by far the earliest of the exemplars I mention in this book (b. 551 BC). Arguably he had the same pivotal role in the creation of Chinese philosophy that Socrates had for Western philosophy. Although Confucius himself showed no interest in building a theory in my sense of theory, Amy Olberding interprets the *Analects* within the framework of exemplarism, arguing that the moral theory of that work begins with identification of exemplary figures and careful observation of them, and then moves to increasingly refined and abstract moral concepts and rules derived from those observations. Confucius treats the Duke of Zhou as an exemplar, and Confucius's students treat Confucius as an exemplar. Olberding says, "The reasoning of the *Analects* begins with people and ends in theory. Its governing imperative is that we ought to seek to be like our exemplars, and its generalized accounts of the virtues reflect efforts to assay, in an organized and careful fashion, what emulation of exemplars entails and requires" (Olberding 2012, 13).

I said at the beginning of this chapter that we are initially attracted to exemplars because of something easily observed about them, usually their acts, and we then seek to identify the psychological source of those acts. In the *Analects*, moral character is revealed in more than acts. A person's physical bearing, movement, and manner of speaking are expressions of his moral character, and Olberding suggests that the way Confucius looks and moves, and the style of his speech get considerable attention in the *Analects* because of the way they reveal his exemplarity (Chapter 5, 110ff). Other people admire the graceful and devoted way in which Confucius performs the *li*, or rituals which, Olberding says, "can be understood to formalize characteristic responses of exemplars into a code of behavior and demeanor keyed to recurrent patterns of circumstance" (118). There is something striking in Confucius's sensitive performance of the *li* that makes him widely admired. There is a deep accord between his inclinations and the requirements of the *li*, yet because he has mastered it so perfectly, he can allow himself to improvise to great effect. Olberding proposes that Confucius was admired because his contemporaries and the readers of the *Analects* are able to see the way his motivations, emotions and behavior fit the circumstances. Moreover, Confucius is "uncommonly transparent" in the way he communicates the interior through the exterior. "His personal style . . . allows others to borrow a felt sense of his grace and ease in responding to the world as he finds it" (135).

The fundamental Confucian virtue is *ren*, which Olberding notes is variously translated "benevolence," "goodness," "authoritative conduct," "human excellence," or "virtue" (Olberding, 68). Olberding hypothesizes that the reason *ren* is so elusive is that it is the sort of quality that cannot be precisely defined, but Confucius recognizes it when he sees it, and Confucius's disciples see it in him (71ff). It is intended to pick out what makes people *like that* good. Confucius himself speaks of *ren* when he has in mind exemplars whose goodness he believes no concept or combination of concepts can explain (72). For Confucius, "*ren* is *that*," and we can trace his various abstract claims about *ren* to a person whose features are discoverable. Likewise, the authors of the *Analects* do not attempt to present an abstract conception of *ren* but offer Confucius as the primary exemplar of *ren*. Olberding concludes,

> Thus, on my reading, the images of Confucius proffered in the *Analects* do not simply heroicize a deeply admired teacher, nor do they simply propose him as another model for emulation. Rather, they indicate that *ren* will be in some measure sourced in understanding him. Such is to say that while the *Analects'* conceptual discussion of *ren* is thin in its particulars, the text nonetheless speaks volumes in its finely drawn portrait of Confucius himself. (74)

Olberding's use of the exemplar methodology raises some interesting questions about the use of historical figures about whom we have little knowledge and the observations of whom often come down to us through the lens of adoring followers. As I mentioned earlier, we face the same problem when we attempt to identify the historical Jesus. Damon and Colby, who use the method to great effect (2015, 1992), nonetheless consider this a defect in the method. They point out that accounts of persons from the distant past are "replete with inaccuracy and even outright invention," and the distortion is apt to be even greater when the actions described are moral (2015, xvi). I do not consider this a defect in the method I am describing in this book. I am proposing that we identify admirable persons directly through the emotion of reflective admiration, and close examination of these persons reveals what it is about them that elicits our admiration. For most of the purposes of the method, it does not matter if the person who elicits our admiration is accurately described or even if he or she is fictional. I have said that I think we should be content with fictional exemplars, and exemplars who are partly fictional are acceptable for the same reason. If it turned out that no real human being could be or do what the fictional exemplars do, that would be an important piece of information for the use of exemplars as models for our own moral development, but insofar as exemplars reveal the admirable to us, fictional exemplars can serve that purpose as well as the exemplars who actually lived, and as I have said, there are even some advantages in fiction over fact for this purpose.

Sagehood as an ideal continued throughout the era of neo-Confucianism, lasting until the twentieth century.[23] Recently, Stephen Angle (2009) has argued that we ought to take this ideal seriously in contemporary Western ethics. There are many different ways we could follow Angle's advice, and I am offering one way in this book. I think it is particularly important for exemplarism that the sage is an exemplar in the sense we want for both the task of mapping the moral domain and the task of emulating exemplars, and I return to the function of the sage for moral theory in Chapter 7. If that means broadening the domain of the moral beyond that commonly recognized in contemporary ethics, I have said that I think we ought to accept that. Angle makes a similar remark about the difference between Chinese and Western views on the scope of the moral (91–92), tracing the difference to the Western emphasis on a distinction between morality and prudence, a distinction that does not arise in Confucian ethics, where everything appropriate to a good life matters. Moreover, I think it is just as important that in Western philosophy there arose the distinction between moral and intellectual virtues, which Aristotle thought operated in different parts of the soul, and that eventually led to a narrowing of the domain of the moral in the West to those acts and traits of a person that pertain to the will rather than to the intellect.[24] But as Angle says, the features of a sage in the classical period of China included intelligence, broad skill or even omnicompetence, keen perception, creativity, and political authority, as well as supreme moral virtue (Angle, 14–15).[25]

---

23. The Chinese system of civil service exams that led a millennium of students to study the Confucian classics ended in 1905, and there are no longer public Confucian institutions, although Confucianism as an academic subject still exists. See Angle (2009, 223ff) for a discussion of the future of Confucianism.

24. Aristotle divided the moral and the intellectual virtues in the *Nicomachean Ethics*, but as previously noted, he closely tied the intellectual virtue of *phronesis*, or practical wisdom, with moral virtue. In subsequent moral philosophy in the West, the role of perception and intellect in virtue was de-emphasized, probably because of the close connection between acts deemed to be immoral and moral blame. The range of moral responsibility became narrower, eventually leading to the emphasis on the will as the ultimate bearer of moral properties.

25. Angle gives a fine example of the importance of intellectual creativity in the sage. The ancient Chinese philosopher Master Xun says that the early sages' brilliance enabled them to find a solution to the problem of endless competition for scarce resources, namely, the establishment of rites (14). Angle refers to the classic text Xunzi 19 and to Xun's account of sagely intelligence in Xunzi 21. Angle also refers to the discussion by Wang (1993, 287–288).

I think, then, that we have at least three reasons to broaden the range of the moral beyond the domain of the traditional moral virtues. In *Virtues of the Mind* (1996) I argued that intellectual virtues have the same structure as moral virtues and are acquired in the same way. In Chapter 2 of this book I argued that we admire intellectual virtues in the same way that we admire moral virtues. In this section we see an important historical reason to include intellectual virtues in the same class as moral virtues, and perhaps to include certain skills of competence, perception, and leadership as well: The sage is a moral exemplar. We need to let our observations of the features of sages that we admire dictate the contours of sagehood. If there is a connection between the sage's moral wisdom and his practical skills and intellectual virtues, we should be able to see that in contemporary sages as well as in the ancient Chinese sages.

Chief Plenty Coups (1848–1932), the last hereditary chief of the Crow Nation, is a fascinating example of a modern sage who combined visionary wisdom with practical skills. Plenty Coups led his people during the period when the wars over Native American lands were being waged. This was a period of rapid cultural change with the possibility of complete cultural collapse. It was not clear that the traditional moral categories even made sense any more, and the chief was forced to invent new ways to keep his people together with their traditional way of life, including collaborating with whites against other tribes. The outcome was that the Crow was the only Indian nation able to retain a portion of its ancestral lands. In his old age Plenty Coups told the moving story of his life to Frank B. Linderman (1962), the writer of American Westerns who had befriended him. Recently, his story has been told by Jonathan Lear (2008) in a book that uses history, anthropology, philosophy, and psychoanalytic theory in a penetrating depiction of Chief Plenty Coups as an exemplar of Aristotelian virtue.

Lear's book is more than a resource for the methodology of exemplarist moral theory; it is an application of the method I am advocating. Lear does not just tell a story; he uncovers the traits of character that made Plenty Coups admirable. What is surprising for me is to realize that in the context of the story that unfolds, certain things that I would not otherwise find admirable are admirable, and I would never have recognized some of them without a detailed narrative. Plenty Coups was a member of a warrior honor culture. His status was achieved by touching many enemies with his coup stick or taking away their weapons, thereby earning him many "coups." He and his tribe believed that he was destined to greatness because of a visionary dream he had as a child. It meant that he had to invent forms of courage, honor, loyalty, and justice in order to follow that dream. In Lear's interpretation, his most outstanding quality was hope, a virtue that appears in a different form in the hope of the L'Arche caregivers. I discuss this virtue more in the next chapter.

Narratives and other texts that give biographical descriptions can be used in exemplarism in different ways. Some narratives are stories that do not aim to highlight the admirable features of exemplars. They might aim primarily at supporting a historical thesis or a political position, or they might aim merely at entertainment. Nonetheless, these stories can show us exemplars whose admirable features we can draw out by careful attention to the story and to our emotional responses. Other stories do some of the theoretical work of the theory I am describing. Lear's book, *Radical Hope*, is like that. A work such as Olberding's book on the *Analects* goes even further in connecting the narrative with the semantics of exemplarism. These examples illustrate just some of the possible uses of the narrative riches that already exist for the theoretical structure of exemplarism. As I said in Chapter 1, my task is to construct the theoretical scaffolding. We can obtain the content from other parts of our moral practices. Written narratives and narratives on the screen exist in abundance, and I am proposing that we use them and our disposition to admiration and contempt for the purposes of obtaining the data we need to construct exemplarism.

5.2. Empirical Studies of Wisdom

Controlled studies of Holocaust rescuers and L'Arche caregivers have an obvious target. We know who they are, we admire them, and we can observe them to find out more about them. We encounter problems of vagueness when we say we are interested in persons *like that* and point to Holocaust rescuers, but at least we have a group from which we can generalize. The situation is harder with empirical studies of wise persons because we do not have a well-demarcated set of individuals that can form our core group for study. As I have mentioned, wise persons do not routinely engage in "wise acts" that get public attention. If they did, the situation for investigators would be easier, but that is not the way it is. In my opinion, the hardest part of studying wisdom is that we need a reliable way to find wise persons before we can study them.

Again, our situation can be compared to that of investigators of natural kinds. There must be features of water or gold or tigers that allow us to fix the reference of "water" or "gold," so that we know what to investigate when we say water or gold is stuff like that. Water has superficial qualities of taste and appearance that we use in identifying water, so when we say water is "stuff like that" we mean to say that water is the stuff that is like the stuff that is odorless, tasteless, flows in streams, falls from the sky, and so on. A central point of the semantics of direct reference is that these superficial qualities do not make water *water*, and they do not constitute a descriptive meaning of the word "water." We identify water by its superficial qualities, but what makes water water is that it is H_2O. Similarly, we need to have easily identifiable qualities of wise persons that enable us to fix the reference of "wise person" so that we can undertake an investigation of the features of them that make them wise. The deep properties of wisdom should explain the superficial properties that fix the reference of "wise person" in the same way that being H_2O explains the properties of being a colorless, tasteless, liquid. Just as we aim to figure out the physical structure of water, we will want to figure out the psychological structure of wise persons in virtue of which they have wisdom, and if there are neurological differences between wise persons and the rest of us, we would be interested in discovering that also.

So we need to distinguish two levels of properties of wise persons for the purpose of empirical investigation of them: (1) We need properties that make them easily identifiable, and (2) we need to find out by further study of them what it is about them that makes them wise. We want to distinguish their superficial features from their deep features, the way we do with natural kinds and the other categories of exemplars, as we see in Table 3.1. We ought to keep this distinction in mind in looking at empirical research on wisdom and wise persons. Perhaps wise persons elicit a different kind of admiration from that elicited by heroes or saints. That is, maybe admiring a sage feels different from admiring a hero or a saint. I think that we also use the reactions of other persons as a way to identify wise persons. Wise persons are admired in the area of practical judgment; they are often consulted by other persons who want advice; and they may be asked to settle disputes. Their advice turns out to be correct in retrospect. Perhaps it is even life changing. Often they display emotional equanimity and serenity. So we know some of the features of wise persons that allow us to identify them. But neither the fact that someone is the object of a distinctive type of admiration, nor that she appears serene,

Table 3.1

Kind term	Superficial properties that fix the reference	Deep properties of the kind
"Water"	Colorless, odorless, tasteless, flows in streams	H_2O
"Cat"	Looks like a cat	Has the biological structure of the species of cat
"Hero"	Performs observable acts we call heroic, e.g., Holocaust rescuers	Motivational structure of courageous persons (revealed in narratives, interviews, empirical studies)
"Saint"	Performs observable acts we call saintly, e.g., St. Francis, L'Arche caregivers	Motivational structure of saintly exemplars (revealed as above)
"Sage"	How do we find the target class?	What are the deep properties of the target class?

nor that she is asked to mediate disputes, nor that she is nominated as wise by others is a constituent of wisdom. These are simply features that we can use to find wise persons in advance of investigating them. The features that make them wise will presumably be deeper features that explain the easily observable features. What is it about them that allows them to give reliable and life-changing advice? What is it about them that makes them appear calm and serene? What is it about them that attracts us to them in a distinctive way? What is it about them that leads people to ask them to mediate disputes? In some cases, we know the answer. For instance, Eleanor Roosevelt was often asked to mediate labor disputes because she was known to be fair, impartial, and open-minded (Damon and Colby 2015, 117). Mother Teresa appeared calm and serene because of her awareness of a divine presence. Chief Plenty Coups was regarded as wise by the Crow because of his guidance by a dream that enabled him to make decisions they endorsed in retrospect.

Some researchers have proposed a scale to measure wisdom. Judith Glück et al. (2013) compared four established measures of wisdom with forty-seven wisdom nominees and a control group.[26] They then proposed

---

26. The four that were examined are the Self-Assessed Wisdom Scale (Webster 2007), the Three-Dimensional Wisdom Scale (Ardelt 2003), the Adult Self-Transcendence Inventory (Levenson et al. 2005), and the Berlin Wisdom Paradigm (Baltes and Staudinger 2000).

a Brief Wisdom Screening Scale (BWSS) that contains twenty items that were most highly correlated with performance across the scales. The BWSS is a self-screening scale that is intended to identify such features as self-transcendence, emotional regulation, reflectiveness, openness, humor about themselves, and critical life experience as features of exemplars. Some of these features, particularly critical life experience, do not seem to me to be components of wisdom but are at best predictors of wisdom. So my worry is that the wisdom scale conflates the superficial properties we use in identifying wise persons with the components of wisdom. However, the direct investigation of wisdom nominees is the method I am proposing. It has an advantage that is the same as an advantage of direct reference discussed in Chapter 1: It is not necessary to have a conceptual definition of "wisdom" before proceeding. As Glück et al. note in their study, the four scales they compared use different definitions of wisdom. Most researchers think that getting a definition is important, even critical. But if I am right in my proposal that we can identify exemplars of wisdom directly, it is not necessary to have such a definition at the outset.

I think, however, that it would be helpful to include in the target set of wise persons sages in history as well as contemporaries.[27] Obviously the former cannot fill out a questionnaire, but we can guess how they would do so to some extent, and at the least, we can identify questions on the scale that are culturally limited. For instance, one of the statements on the BWSS screening is, "I don't worry about other people's opinions of me." An affirmation of that statement is intended to be positively correlated with wisdom, but wise persons in an honor culture would disagree. The statement, "I am very curious about other religious/philosophical belief systems" is also intended to be positively correlated with wisdom. Perhaps wise persons in most contemporary cultures would affirm the statement, but that may be due to the particular requirements of the modern world, and it is unlikely that many wise persons of the past would have said anything comparable. I also suspect that there are some statements to which Confucius in particular would not react as predicted. I imagine he would disagree with the statements,

---

27. See Westrake et al. (2016) for a new series of studies on wisdom using an exemplar and prototype approach, including iconic cultural-historical figures.

"I can accept the impermanence of things,"[28] and "I have a sense of oneness with nature,"[29] both of which are supposed to be endorsed by wise persons.

It appears that ordinary people already have beliefs about the components of wisdom, although I do not know whether people consciously distinguish superficial from deeper properties. The folk theory discussed by Tiberius and Swartwood (2011) seems to aim at deeper features. They identify four components of wisdom as used by ordinary people: (1) deep understanding, (2) reflective capacities, (3) problem-solving capacities, and (4) the motivation to choose well and to help others choose well. Tiberius and Swartwood then suggest that given the desirability of greater theoretical precision and compatibility with empirical research, these components can be refined by the method of wide reflective equilibrium. As a result, they propose that wise persons cultivate policies of epistemic humility and open-mindedness to reduce the biases that affect decision making. Their method supports my position on the moral importance of intellectual virtues. If these traits are confirmed in direct studies of wise persons, then that would mean that there is an important class of *moral* exemplars whose exemplarity partly consists in having *intellectual* virtues.

A further piece of evidence of the place of intellectual virtue in moral exemplarity is the work of Colby and Damon (1992), who observed a common trait of intellectual humility in their comparison of twenty-three moral exemplars, and in their most recent book, they have made the same observation in their study of moral leaders (2015, 115–116). They say that the exemplars they examined were all characterized by moral certainty—"an unwavering conviction about moral principles and clear sense of responsibility to act"—but also by open-mindedness toward different perspectives. In fact, they conclude that open-mindedness is what distinguishes exemplars from moral fanatics.

I would like to offer my own hypotheses about the characteristics of wise persons. Some of these are implied by the results of empirical

---

28. Consider Confucius's unwillingness to let the old traditions disappear; on the contrary, he tried to resurrect them. Consider also his insistence on the importance of the mourning rituals for parents, and especially his mourning at the death of his favorite pupil, Yan Hui. These do not seem to be the actions of someone who has accepted the impermanence of things.

29. I am not sure about this one, but it does seem to me significant that Confucius rails against nature when his favorite student dies young.

studies, but I am not suggesting that my proposals here directly coincide with the conclusions of empirical researchers:

- They have insight and deep understanding as well as broad general knowledge (suggested by Tiberius and Sartwood 2011).
- They are reflective without being neurotic (suggested by Tiberius and Sartwood).
- They have impressive self-discipline.[30]
- They have emotional equanimity and serenity. They are not given to outbursts or other emotional extremes.
- They are good at mind-reading and rarely make emotional mistakes. (For instance, they would not inadvertently say something that hurts someone else or makes her angry.)
- They have the ability to see and appreciate other points of view (Damon and Colby, 2015).
- They have strong moral convictions (Damon and Colby 2015).
- They are intellectually humble, intellectually fair, and open-minded (suggested by Tiberius and Sartwood).
- They grasp values in proportion, by which I mean that they know better than others what to do when values conflict, and for this reason they are sometimes asked to adjudicate disputes.
- They are creative in solving problems and integrating complex practical considerations into a single course of action (suggested by Tiberius and Sartwood).
- They have mastered all the conventions that adults in a society should know, but they understand the proper place of "conventional wisdom" and how to adapt it to unique circumstances (suggested by Olberding's discussion of Confucius).
- They have strong religious sensibilities and are often guided by a sense of being called by God (suggested by Aikman 2003, xiii).[31]

---

30. David Aikman (2003) has done a detailed study of six "great souls": Billy Graham, Nelson Mandela, Aleksandr Solzhenitsyn, Mother Teresa, Pope John Paul II, and Elie Wiesel. Aikman says that each of them demonstrated phenomenal self-discipline from childhood throughout his or her life. These exemplars are not necessarily exemplary for wisdom in particular, but I find it enlightening that self-discipline from an early age is one of their common traits, and I am suggesting here that it is a common trait of wise persons. "My child, from your youth choose discipline, and when you have gray hair you will still find wisdom" [Sirach/Ecclus. 6:18] [tr. *New Revised Standard Bible* 1989].

31. Aikman says that the exception is Elie Wiesel, whose faith was sorely tested by the Holocaust.

I do not know which among these traits are essential elements of wisdom, but I think that some of these traits explain why other people admire those who possess them in the way sages are admired, and they explain why, given the right conditions, others go to these people for advice. But we still need an explanation for the fact that the above properties, or some alternative list of properties, make a person someone whom others trust for good counsel. There is a need for much more theoretical and empirical work on the way the distinct components of wisdom connect with each other, and I am hopeful that ongoing research from such programs as the Wisdom Research Network at the University of Chicago (www.wisdomresearch.org) will go a long way toward helping us answer these questions.

6. Conclusion: The Hero, the Saint, and the Sage

I have been treating the hero, the saint, and the sage as distinct classes of exemplars, and I want now to offer the conjecture that each type is dominated by a particular virtue. The saint is dominated by charity; the hero, courage; the sage, wisdom. There may be other classes of exemplars that each have a different dominant virtue. For instance, spiritual exemplars might have the dominant virtue of faith, or the virtue of reverence. Of course, exemplars have other virtues, but I am suggesting that the other virtues are accompaniments to the dominant virtue, perhaps necessary accompaniments. Clearly, the hero often lacks other virtues, and I surmise that that is because courage does not require many other virtues for its exercise. In contrast, the saint is supposed to have all the virtues, and that is what we would expect if charity underlies all moral virtue, as St. Paul said (1Cor 13:1–13). Whether the sage has all the moral virtues is an interesting question. I think it is important that Aristotle connected *phronesis*, or practical wisdom, with the possession of all the moral virtues, but I am leaving that issue open.

Another interesting point about the three classes of exemplars is that each only makes sense within a certain cultural context. Leo Strauss (1953) proposed that the character of a society is expressed by a certain type of person who is most admirable in that regime.[32] Persons of that kind set the tone for the whole commonwealth. I cannot say whether Strauss's

---

32. Strauss says, "The character, or tone, of a society depends on what society regards as most respectable or most worthy of admiration. But by regarding certain habits or attitudes as most respectable, a society admits the superiority, the superior dignity, of those human beings who most perfectly embody the habits or attitudes in question" (1953, 137).

view is right, but it does seem to me that different kinds of exemplars dominate different cultures. Ancient China is incomprehensible without the sage, and ancient Greece makes no sense without the hero. Arguably, the saint arose with Christianity, and the ideal of the saint in Western culture partially drove out the other ideals. Heroic cultures are disappearing, and there are so few sages in Western societies today that even the idea of a sage is in danger of disappearing. In the parts of the world that consider themselves post-Christian, the saint is disappearing too. There are not many kinds of exemplars that have a rich cultural identity and wide acceptance in Western Europe and the United States. A longing to believe that there are exemplars probably still exists, but it coexists with the suspicion that is characteristic of our age.

In Chapter 2 I referred to *ressentiment* as a motive for the denial of exemplarity. But a healthier motive is the desire to recognize exemplars we could realistically emulate. It is very hard and might even be counterproductive to try to emulate anybody who is too far above us morally. Recall that A. I. Melden claimed we should not even try to emulate a saint. But Kevin Reimer's L'Arche saints are weak and fallible. His emphasis on weakness in the exemplar is important for moral cultivation, but it is not very helpful for mapping the domain of positive moral concepts. Conversely, abstracting the exemplar's most admirable qualities and acts out of a complete narrative in order to identify the qualities and acts we deem admirable requires that weaknesses be ignored. Overlooking defects in such a context is not naïve; it is just doing what theory requires, as I understand it. In my theory of theory, a theory leaves out many things relevant to moral practice and belief, and it distorts some of what is left in. In Chapter 1 I said that I do not think of that as a problem as long as we are aware of the distortion and what is left out reappears in other contexts. That means that our exemplars need not be "pure" exemplars to serve the purpose of exemplarist moral theory. There are exemplars who are admirable all things considered, but we can safely be a bit vague about what that entails. It is more common to find persons whom we admire for certain kinds of acts, and when we investigate them, we find that their admirability is limited to a certain domain or context of action. Near the beginning of this chapter I proposed that there are many persons who are exemplars for a particular trait, such as compassion or courage. As I said, we need not identify the trait in advance of finding these persons admirable, and indeed, the identification of the trait is a hypothesis about the source of their admirability. We might decide on further observation that what makes them admirable is limited to whatever causes a certain range of acts, and that they are not admirable in other respects. That need not be a problem for exemplarism, but it complicates the procedure whereby we use exemplars as a touchstone for determining the moral properties of acts all things considered. I mention that issue again when I begin constructing the theory in the next chapter.

4

Virtue

1. The Primary Moral Terms

Putnam argues that the traditional view of meaning is mistaken because it assigns two incompatible roles to a meaning. A term's meaning allegedly (a) is a descriptive concept grasped by a competent user of the term, and (b) determines the reference (extension) of the term. Thought experiments such as his famous Twin Earth example, mentioned in Chapter 1, show that this view is mistaken, at least about natural kind terms. There is no reference-determining descriptive concept grasped by ordinary users of a natural kind term. In fact, Putnam goes on to say that although natural kind terms make good examples of his point about meaning, he thinks the same arguments apply to the great majority of nouns and other parts of speech (1975, 160). A meaning can do either (a) or (b), but it cannot do both. Putnam opts for the reference-determining role of meaning, in which case it follows that a meaning is not a descriptive concept in the head. To think so is to leave out two important contributions to the determination of reference—the social contribution, and the contribution of the world (164). The Earthians and Twin Earthians mean different things by "water," even though they have the same description in their heads, because their worlds are different. In contrast, two Earthians succeed in meaning the same thing by "water" even if they differ greatly in their understanding of what water is because they are connected by a cooperative social network for determining reference that does not require of most speakers more than minimal competence in the use of the term.

For ease of discussion, I will take the liberty of saying that when we use an expression such as "Water is whatever is the same liquid as that," we are giving the meaning of "water," or that we are "defining 'water,'" although Putnam thinks of a meaning as more complicated than that.[1] Given what I have said, it should be clear that when I say I am defining the fundamental terms in the theory, I do not mean that I am capturing the content of a concept.

I have proposed that the meaning of "good person" is determined by something outside the mind—exemplars, or the most admirable persons—to whom we refer directly through the emotion of admiration and by socially constructed networks for linking speakers in the community to exemplars. The meaning of the other terms of most relevance to the moral life are determined by the features of moral exemplars. That includes value terms such as "virtue," "good motive," "good end," "a good life," and deontic terms, such as "right act," "wrong act," and "duty." I discuss the value terms in this chapter and Chapter 6, and the deontic terms in Chapter 7. My purpose in these chapters is give the semantical structure of the primary terms that appear on standard maps of the moral domain, and to show how we can use narratives and empirical data to find out what virtues, right acts, duties, and so on *are*. The first task is comparable to saying that "water" means "stuff like that." The second task is comparable to showing how we find out that water is H_2O.

Before beginning the construction of the theory, I want to briefly address two prior questions. First, there is the matter of identifying the fundamental terms in theoretical ethics. Many people, even the philosophers among us, may wonder why the set of terms above deserve focal attention in a map of the moral domain. Who decided that these are the most important terms? Second, we will need to revisit the purpose of moral theory, given that the set of exemplars I have discussed in the last two chapters includes more than persons who are admirable in a distinctively moral way. The inclusion of a broad range of exemplars does not affect the shape of the theory, but it affects its substance, and I want to look again at the way theory aims to simplify and justify our moral practices.

The short answer to the first question is historical authority and the conventions of contemporary ethics. The terms I have listed are the ones that have attracted sustained attention from philosophers for many centuries, and the terms that dominate contemporary ethics are from the above list. However, it is interesting that many moral philosophers ignore

---

1. Putnam (1975, 165) proposes that we should identify a meaning with an ordered pair of entities: one is the extension of the term and the other is meaning vectors. The social component is included in the latter.

some of these terms while putting a great deal of emphasis on others. The idea of a duty and the idea of a wrong act have dominated moral philosophy since the beginning of the modern period, yet as I remarked in Chapter 1, Aristotle arguably ignores duty and has a view of wrong acts that is imprecise at best. It is hard to fault Aristotle for this since he simply lacks the modern zeal for creating a catalogue of right and wrong acts. Similarly, many modern moral theorists lack Aristotle's interest in giving a catalogue of the virtues. I will propose a way to define all of the above terms, but it would be naïve to think that critics will give the definitions equal attention. Philosophers have their favorite terms, and the legalistic terms "right," "wrong," and "duty" still dominate moral discourse.[2] I argue in Chapter 7 that the deontic terms have a different function in moral discourse from that of the value terms, yet they also can be defined via exemplars.

Focusing on exemplars allows us to highlight other important features of the moral life in addition to the central terms used in moral discourse. Narratives of exemplars reveal what they hope for, what they dread, what (if anything) they worry about, what they aim for, how they organize their lives around other persons and projects, how much they care about non-moral goods such as aesthetic values and physical health, how much they enjoy life, and what, in particular, they enjoy. Obviously, exemplars will differ in these respects, but if we include these features, we will have a richer and more complete theory than one that leaves these features out of the theory altogether, as most theories do. So my answer to the first question is that I will include definitions of the terms that get the most attention in contemporary and historically important ethical theories, but since many other terms can be defined by direct reference to exemplars, the methodology permits us to give attention to a much broader range of terms than is usual in moral theory.

This brings me to my other preliminary question. What do we need in a moral theory? In giving my theory of theory in Chapter 1, I proposed that a moral theory is an abstract structure that aims to simplify, systematize, and justify our moral beliefs and practices. The abstract structure will be

---

2. One term that I mention only briefly (in Chapter 6) is the term "good for" a human being. Thomas Hurka (1987) argues that "good for" should be "banished from moral philosophy," and replaced with the idea of good, period. Recently, Richard Kraut (2011) has taken the opposite position, arguing that the idea of good simpliciter should be eliminated from practical thinking and replaced with the idea of good *for* someone. See Sarah Stroud's (2013) discussion in a book symposium on Kraut's book (459–466) and Kraut's reply (483–488).

a pattern linking the main terms in moral discourse with each other; it must do that in order to simplify and systematize. The structure must also connect to the beliefs and practices the theory is explaining and justifying; otherwise, it will not be a theory of the right thing. It will not have a "hook" to our beliefs and practices. The greater the degree to which the elements of moral practices fit into the structure of the theory, the more complete it is. My aim is to have the most complete theory compatible with the simplest structure.

My principle of simplification is admiration. I am letting the emotion of admiration determine the scope of the moral for the purposes of the theory, and I am letting admiration determine the contours of the terms to be defined in the theory. I have hypothesized that there is more than one kind of admiration, and that admiration for natural talents and temperament differs in the way it feels and in its typical behavioral response from admiration for acquired traits. I have said that it is the latter kind of admiration that I am using for this theory. The approach permits the inclusion of sages in the class of moral exemplars, and it includes intellectual virtues in the same domain as moral virtues. The test, however, is always admiration—what we admire upon reflection. If I am mistaken in my judgment that we admire intellectual traits like open-mindedness and intellectual honesty and courage the same way we admire moral virtues, then the theory would need to be modified. Similarly, my hypothesis that we admire sages in a way suitable for inclusion in a moral theory can also be tested, and the theory can be modified if I am mistaken. I have already mentioned that one reason for including sages in the domain of exemplars is historical precedent. I also think it will turn out that we can incorporate more elements of our moral practices into the theory if we include sages. For instance, some exemplars are imitable mostly for their emotions, aims, and acts, whereas others are imitable for their moral judgments. The sage is important for the latter.

I have also hypothesized that some persons are exemplary in certain respects and not others. This is particularly noticeable with heroes, less so with saints and sages. In developing the structure of the theory, once we have a way to identify virtues we will be able to designate certain persons as exemplars for a particular virtue. But I will start with the simplest structure and make it more complex as necessary to do justice to our observations.

One of my guiding principles in constructing the definitions of this chapter is that we are more certain of the identities of certain exemplars than we are of the terms to be defined. So I think that we are more certain of the fact that Leopold Socha, Jean Vanier, and Confucius are exemplars than we are of the definitions of "virtue," "wrong act," "good end," and so on. I do not mean that we are more sure of the identities of these exemplars than we are of any particular moral judgment. If we see a helpless person being abused, we may be at least as sure that *that* act is wrong as we are of the fact that Vanier is admirable. We are at least as sure that Leopold Socha's act of sheltering Jews was admirable as we are of the fact that he is an admirable person. But I think that we are more certain of the admirability of Socha and Vanier than we are of the definitions of "courage" and "compassion," and we are much more certain of the admirability of these exemplars than we are of the definitions of "virtue," "right act," "duty," and so on. I think that in general we are more certain of particulars—which acts are admirable, which persons are admirable, which acts are wrong. What I am proposing is a series of definitions of central moral terms that link them to something of which we are more certain than we are of the putative descriptive content associated with those terms.

2. Defining Value Terms

Exemplarism is a theory with a non-conceptual foundation—a collection of exemplars of admirability. Exemplars differ from water samples in an obvious way. All samples of water are alike except for impurities. It does not matter which sample we designate as "water" for the purposes of studying water. In contrast, individual exemplars differ from each other in many ways, some of which are relevant to their exemplarity. To find out all the ways persons can be admirable, we need to investigate many of them. One paradigm is not enough. In this respect "good person" is more like the name of a biological species than a chemical kind. There are different kinds of exemplars, but there are also different subspecies of tigers—Bengal tigers, Siberian tigers, Malayan tigers, and others.

There is another possibility that I pursue further in Chapter 8. If the species Tiger gradually changes through evolution, perhaps good person-hood gradually undergoes changes as the body of exemplars changes over time. Kripke thought that a natural kind term refers to an abstract object— a species or substance. "Tiger" does not refer severally to individual tigers or to collections of tigers, but to the species *Tiger*. There are some problems with this view of a species, but the semantical point about indexicality does not depend on it. It leaves open the possibility that if "tiger" refers directly to animals like *that*, and if animals like that gradually change in their features over time, and if the meaning of "tiger" is determined by the animals to which we point, then the meaning of "tiger" can slowly change.[3] Meanings change when reference changes. If we take this approach, the parallel point about exemplarism is that what we mean when we say "An admirable person is a person like that" can change over time because the admirable persons to whom we refer can gradually change. The relevant sense of "like that" does not have to be a fixed essence.

What exemplars have in common is their admirability, and that shows us a more important dis-analogy with natural kinds. In the case of water, we notice a similarity of superficial features of taste and appearance, and we suspect that all samples of water have something in common that makes them all water. The superficial properties get our attention only insofar as they fix the reference of "water" so that we have something to investigate, but we are not interested in the superficial properties per se. If it turned out that the stuff we call "water" has no common physical structure that explains its superficial properties, we would lose interest in investigating water. In contrast, we think that admirability is a deep feature of exemplars; in fact, it is what makes them exemplars. Our problem is that we need to investigate them carefully in order to find out what makes them admirable—what the precise features are that explain the overt behavior that elicits our admiration upon reflection. If it turned out that exemplars do not have a single common psychological structure, we would not lose interest in investigating them; it would just make investigation more complicated. But there is a limit to how complicated it can be without making the project of investigating the admirable pointless. If it turned out that exemplars have nothing at all in common psychologically, we would probably conclude that admirability *is* a superficial feature like being colorless and tasteless is for water. But we can deal with more than one kind of exemplar.

The value terms are all terms for forms of good: a virtue (a good trait), a good motive, a good end, a good act, and a good life in two senses of

---

3. Richard Boyd (1988) has pointed out some difficulties with the fact that Kripke takes physical elements like gold and chemical substances like water as his paradigm natural kinds. Gold and water presumably never change, whereas biological kinds do change. This difference can be important for using natural kind terms as models for moral terms. I discuss Boyd's theory briefly in Chapter 8.

good—the admirable and the desirable. I discuss the first four value terms in this chapter, and the terms for a good life in Chapter 6. I discuss the deontic terms in Chapter 7.

Let me begin by going back to the way I introduced these terms in Chapter 1:

(1) A *virtue* is a trait we admire in an exemplar. It is what makes persons like *that* admirable in a certain respect.
(2) A *good motive* is a motive we admire in an exemplar. It is a motive of a person like that.
(3) A *good end* is a state of affairs that exemplars aim to bring about. It is a state of affairs at which persons like that aim.
(4) A *virtuous act* is an admirable act, an act we admire in a person like that.

I believe that the meanings of these four terms are linked together, and in fact are inter-definable. I explain why I think that in the next section. At this stage it is enough to say that each of the above terms refers to something that elicits our admiration and which we continue to admire upon reflection: an act, a motive, an end, a trait, all of which are features of admirable persons that we can discover.

It should be apparent that all of the definitions refer to something outside the mind of the user of a moral term in determining the meaning of the term. To find out what a virtue is, what a right act is, what a good life is, and so on, we need to look carefully at exemplars—at their motives, forms of reasoning, ends, and behavior. I begin doing that with the term "virtue" in the next two sections. We look first at how we find out what a virtue *is*, and then how we find out what the virtues *are*.

3. What Is a Virtue?

Traits of character are discovered by observation of persons. When we observe someone's behavior, we sometimes respond with admiration or contempt, or more often, neither one. We may have other responses like curiosity, which may lead us to look more deeply into the person's acts, ends, and motives. But when we admire someone, I think that in the typical case, we begin by admiring her behavior. The behavior could be an overt act or pattern of acts, but it could also be facial expressions and bodily demeanor, the overt exercise of emotional restraint, the verbal expression of thoughts we admire, or some combination of these features. We saw an example of that in the discussion of Confucius in the last chapter. In each case we think that there is something in the person's psychology that is expressed in the observed behavior, and in fact, most observed behavior has an internal psychological component. What we mean by an *act* is not simply bodily movements, but conscious bodily movements. There is something we take ourselves to be doing when we act, and if the act is intentional, it has other psychological properties. These properties are caused by further psychological features of the person—perceptions, motives, the adoption of ends. I also argued in Chapter 3 that we admire the person *for* the act to the extent that the cause of the act is in psychological features of the person rather than in something external to her agency, and our admiration can change when we discover what those psychological features are. The idea that admirable behavior requires certain psychological causes has deep historical roots, both in the East and in the West.[4]

Next, I propose that we admire the person more when the behavior expresses a psychological disposition that endures over time, and when the disposition is a deep part of her psychology, by which I mean that she consistently expresses the admirable disposition even when tempted not to do so. In Chapter 3 I suggested that a deep and enduring psychological disposition is more admirable than one that is not, and for that reason I postulate that a virtue is deep and enduring. The fact that we admire psychological causes of admirable acts that are deep and enduring in these ways is a testable hypothesis. I think it is likely that Aristotle thought of a virtue as a deep and enduring trait because he thought of a virtue as an admirable trait,[5] and a deep and lasting trait is more admirable than a quality that is fleeting or easily overcome by temptation.[6]

---

4. There is evidence from classical Chinese sources for the idea that behavior is not truly admirable unless it arises from deep features of the person's psychology. Stephen Angle (2009, 53) says that *de*, translated roughly as "virtue," refers to a gift from *tian* (Heaven) in the pre-classical era, and then gradually begins to refer to something that a person attains from within; it comes from inner psychological sources. If the behavior is produced by something external or by an ulterior motive, then even if it looks admirable, it is actually common. Only behavior that springs from one's inner heart counts as *de*. This view has always been the dominant view in the West, but for a differing position, see Julia Driver (2001) who argues that virtues are traits that lead to good consequences, regardless of the mental state from which they arise.

5. Aristotle does not say a virtue is admirable, but he says it is praised, and as I mentioned in Chapter 2, he distinguishes what we praise from what we prize (*NE* 1101b10–25, 31).

6. For a contrary view of virtue, see Thomas Hurka (2001, 2010). Hurka argues that a virtue is located in occurrent feelings, desires, and acts rather than in stable traits. Hurka is not addressing the admirable per se.

In discussing admiration in Chapter 2, I proposed that we admire an acquired trait differently from the way we admire an inborn feature of temperament. The kind of admiration we have for the former is the one relevant to exemplarism. So under these hypotheses, it follows that a good trait of character is *a deep and enduring acquired psychological disposition that is the source of acts and other behaviors that we find admirable.*

When we observe the admired person, we find out what we admire about her. Not every act is part of a pattern of acts, but some acts arise from deep and enduring dispositions, and I suggest that careful and extended observation can reveal to us what the admirable traits are. What we find out may lead us to admire the person more or to admire the person less, or even to withdraw our judgment that the person is admirable for certain behavior. In Chapter 3 I suggested that our admiration is strongly affected by the discovery of a motive of self-interest rather than a motive of care and concern for others. Admiration is much greater when the putative admirable act is motivated by concern for others. A motive of self-interest reduces our admiration and may even eliminate it completely. As I have said, our justification for dividing acts motivated by self-interest from acts motivated by concern for others is our disposition to admiration. We do not need any further justification for separating the dispositions we call virtuous from the non-virtuous other than applying our disposition to admiration suitably tested by reflection. When we use this test, we will no doubt find other motives that arouse our admiration, such as acting from a sense of duty, or from a concern for the truth, or from a desire for peace and harmony among people. I am not attempting to exhaustively list the admirable motives, only to propose a method for identifying them.

Careful and sustained observation of many admirable persons permits us to identify the components of an admirable trait. We know we are looking for something in the person's psychology that explains admirable behavior, but we are usually vague about the place of beliefs, motives, desires, emotions, aims, and intentions in producing such behavior. Historically, all of these psychic elements have been connected with virtue in some way. With the methodology I am proposing, we can identify the components of a virtue by doing careful work in moral psychology that shows us the way these psychic elements are connected, and by dividing the elements that arouse our admiration from those that do not.

In previous work I proposed that a virtue has two major components: a motivational component, and a success component (Zagzebski

1996, 134–137). Both of these components can be subjected to the admiration test, although I did not think of that at the time. First, I believe that each virtue includes a motive disposition that is distinctive of the particular virtue. By a motive disposition I mean a disposition to have a distinctive emotion that initiates and directs action toward an end. My original idea was that virtues are individuated by their motivational component, so there is a distinctive motive for generosity, another for compassion, another for courage, and so on. I thought that both the way the motive feels and the end of the acts it initiates are different for each of the virtues. So not only do compassion and generosity have different intentional ends, but generosity includes a disposition to have an emotion that feels different from the emotion that is a component of compassion. I do not know how we could find out whether it feels different to be motivated by generosity than by compassion, but that is my hypothesis. A general concern for the welfare of others probably underlies a number of distinct virtues, and investigation can tell us whether there is any difference in the emotion that underlies compassion and the emotion that underlies generosity, or benevolence, kindness, and related virtues. In any case, the ends of different virtues differ. I assume that generosity aims to give goods to others, whereas compassion aims at alleviating suffering. These features of the motivational components of virtues can be investigated, and the issue of how one virtue differs from another in its feeling aspect and in its ends can also be investigated. The results of these investigations might change the way we distinguish one virtue from another.

From what we have so far, I postulate that *a virtue is a deep and enduring acquired trait that we admire on reflection and which includes a motive disposition*. A motive disposition that is a component of a virtue is a disposition to have an emotion like that of an exemplar and to aim to bring about the end the exemplar has. All these features are determined by what we admire on reflection. We admire the exemplar, and on investigation, we determine that she has certain emotions that direct her toward certain ends in circumstances of a certain kind. If this investigation reveals a motive or end that we do not admire, then we withdraw our judgment that she is an exemplar.

This approach can be used in conjunction with empirical research on exemplars. For instance, in Chapter 2 I mentioned a study by Frimer et al. (2012) in which participants rated the moral admirability of individuals on a list of *Time* Magazine's most influential persons in recent history. The researchers gave the participants some criteria for moral admirability: (1) a sustained commitment to moral ideals, (2) a disposition to act in accord with those ideals, (3) a willingness to risk their self-interest for these ideals or principles, (4) a tendency to inspire others to act in the same way, and (5) a sense of humility about their own importance. These criteria were taken from the previous study of moral exemplarity by Colby and Damon (1992), who used a panel of twenty-two ethical experts to produce the criteria. The resulting ratings of the most influential people using these criteria should match the ratings of their admirability. If they do not, there is either something wrong with the criteria or there is something wrong with the choice of participants. After the researchers in the Frimer study ranked the most influential people, they examined speech and interview transcripts of both the most admired individuals on the list and the least admired, coding them for implicit self-promoting and other-promoting motives. Both the most admired and least admired persons had motives they call motives of "agency," or acting on the interests of the self, but the admired persons had the ultimate motive of promoting the good of others, or what they call motives of "communion." The motives of the most admired persons were not divided into conflicting self-interested and other-interested sets; rather, their agential motives were instrumental to serving their communal ends.

I do not know whether the speeches of the most admired persons in this study revealed identifiable feelings as well as intentions to act in certain ways, but the results support my claim that part of what is admirable about an exemplar is an admirable motive, and one kind of motive we admire is concern for the welfare of others. I have also postulated that we admire even more a consistent disposition to have such a motive, and that is an element in a virtue, a trait we admire. I surmise that the admired persons in this study were admired more because they exhibited a pattern of admired motives over a period of time. If and when some of them failed to exhibit that pattern, my hypothesis is they would be admired less and rated as less admirable.

This study is an example of how empirical studies can be incorporated into the methodology I am proposing here. First, Colby and Damon asked a set of ethical "experts" to identify common features among their most admired individuals, leading to a set of criteria that could be used in identifying more exemplars. Another group of participants was asked to rate a set of influential persons on these criteria. I am suggesting that the result should correspond to what we as a community admire. If not, the criteria need to be revised. But once we identify some of the criteria for admirability, a study like the one conducted by Frimer and colleagues can fill in some of the substantive features of admirable persons. They have identified one that they interpret as a harmonizing of "agential" motives and motives of "communion" among the most admirable persons. I think this conclusion could use further clarification, but I do not see that as a methodological defect.

So far I have suggested that the virtue of compassion includes a characteristic feeling that motivates the agent to act with the end of alleviating suffering. We do not admire a person who feels compassion but does nothing about it as much as we admire persons who both feel compassion and act on it. For the same reason, we do not feel as contemptuous of a person who has mean or vengeful thoughts but never acts on them as we do for a person who acts on mean thoughts and desires. In general, I think that a virtuous person attempts to reach the end of the virtuous motive. The vicious person aims to reach the end of the vicious motive.

What if a person feels compassion in the appropriate circumstances and tries to alleviate suffering but systematically fails? My hypothesis is that *the second component of virtue is reliable success in reaching the end of the virtuous motive,* and I would make the parallel claim about vice. This component of virtue is contentious, so I want to say something about how we might go about resolving that dispute. To some extent, the success component is already included in the motivational component because normally a virtuous agent learns from her failures. For instance, if a person is properly motivated to help suffering persons and has a reasonable degree of knowledge and understanding of the world, she will find out if her action does not succeed at its end in particular cases, and she will amend her behavior in the future. The same point applies to failures of generosity, temperance, and fairness. But there may still be instances in which the agent is virtuously motivated—characteristically has the appropriate emotion for the circumstances and aims at the end of that motive—but regularly fails to reach that virtuous end through no fault of her own. Is she virtuous? My view is that she is partly virtuous. The full virtue requires regular success. Of course, we would not blame the agent for failure beyond her control, but she fails to have the full virtue, and so she fails to have whatever degree of admirability having a full virtue entails. I think that this is one of the ways in which we can be victims of moral luck. But even though I am still inclined to think that virtue has a component of reliable success in reaching the end of the virtuous motive, I am willing to let this matter be settled by the test of what we admire on reflection.[7]

I do not know of much research about this issue so far, but there is empirical evidence of a success component in judgments of the admirability of particular acts. In a series of studies conducted by Cynthia Pury and colleagues, participants' judgments of courage included success in the following ways:

(1) In a study by Pury, Kowalski, and Spearman (2007), participants overwhelmingly described an act with a successful outcome when asked to describe a courageous act they did personally.
(2) A study by Pury and Hensel (2010) replicated these findings in descriptions of courageous acts of other persons.
(3) In another study by Pury and Hensel (2010), participants rated the degree of courage in a number of scenarios. Successful actions were rated as more courageous than actions that were identical except that they did not have a successful outcome. For instance, if two people rush into a burning building and one succeeds in saving a person's life whereas the other does not, people rated the first individual as more courageous than the second.

As far as I know, the participants in these studies were not asked whether they admire the person who did the successful act more than the one who failed, but their willingness to call a successful act more courageous than an unsuccessful act suggests that that is probably the case. It would be helpful to have other studies on whether success increases admiration for different kinds of virtuous acts besides courageous ones. The generous person aims at giving to those in need; the compassionate person aims at alleviating suffering; the fair person aims at producing a distribution of goods or burdens that have a certain feature—what we call "fair." An

---

7. The Effective Altruism movement is a social movement that purports to use evidence to determine ways of effectively changing the world for the better. I think that it is obviously better to be effective than ineffective, and I am suggesting that a full virtue requires effectiveness. However, I also think that a virtue requires an admirable motive disposition. I have heard of criticisms of the movement on the grounds of excessive concentration on consequences over internal factors of an agent. I am not in a position to know how to evaluate these criticisms, but I think that it is interesting that the movement exists.

act motivated by generosity, compassion, or fairness can fail in its aims. It would be useful to find out whether people admire the person who fails but is well motivated in these ways as much as the one who is both well motivated and succeeds.[8]

In Chapter 2 I gave a list of some persons I admire. It is interesting that every one of them was successful. (I made the list before I read Pury and Hensel.) The only one who was not wholly successful was Leopold Socha. He started by hiding scores of Jews in the sewers of Lvov, but some of them died, and some of them freely left and were shot. Ten survived under his care, quite a remarkable success rate, given the odds. But what if he had not succeeded in saving a single one? Would he have been just as admirable? Perhaps an empirical study would reveal that people would rate him as less admirable, but many readers will find that unfair. Granted, it is doubtful that there would be books and movies about Socha if he had failed, but that might just indicate that success makes a better story, not that we really think that success adds to admirability.

The participants in the studies by Pury et al. seem willing to require success for virtue in a stronger sense than I have claimed. My view is that an enduring trait of character, involving many different acts, does not count as a virtue unless it is generally successful. It does not have to be successful on every occasion. The view that a single act is less admirable when it fails due to circumstances outside the control of the agent is stronger, yet that appears to be what the participants in these studies say about courageous acts. Most heroes get only one chance, but they are usually not even called a "hero" unless they are successful.

For the most part, I do not think that the issue of whether exemplars must be successful affects exemplarism very much as a theory. We all agree that the successful exemplars are exemplars, and we all agree that the unsuccessful exemplars are admirable, even though we may disagree about the degree of the admirability of the exemplars who are unsuccessful on some occasion. But it is important for a community to study unsuccessful exemplars to determine the reason for their failure. Some failures are due to social conditions over which we have some control as a community even though the individual agent lacks control over them. For instance, most social reformers rely on cooperation from many other

---

8. Charles Starkey tells me that he and Cynthia Pury are currently working on a study of people's responses to successful versus unsuccessful acts of kindness.

people, and their success in bringing about the reform depends on external social conditions.[9] We want a society that has the conditions that help virtuously motivated individuals to be effective.

We are ready to lay out the first pieces of our map of the moral. The first piece is the definition of virtue I gave above:

(1) A *virtue* is a trait that makes an exemplar admirable in a certain respect. It makes a person *like that* admirable in a certain respect.

As I have said, proposition (1) tells us what "virtue" means, but it does not tell us what virtue *is*. With the assumptions I have given about what the source of admirable acts is, and evidence of what we admire and do not admire in the sources of acts, I propose the following account of the nature of a virtue:

(1a) A *virtue* is a deep and enduring acquired trait that we admire upon reflection, consisting of a disposition to have a certain emotion that initiates and directs action towards an end, and reliable success in reaching that end.

(1a) can be revised after investigation. It is intended to give us the nature of a virtue, but, of course, it may be mistaken or partially mistaken. Even "Water is H_2O" can be revised, although it is not very likely that revision will be necessary, given current science. As I said at the beginning of this chapter, investigating admirable persons has more in common with investigating a biological species than with investigating a simple substance because of the complexity of its elements and the permitted variations within the kind.

Given (1a), we can say more about (2) and (3): (2) says that a good motive is a motive of an exemplar, and (3) says that a good end is an end of an exemplar. If a virtue has as a component a disposition to have a

9. Julia Annas (2011) observes that ancient Roman slavery was embedded in every aspect of society, and it was not as open to a slave-owner to free his slaves as it was open to a slave-owner in the American South. There was no way for a Roman to opt out of the system, no place to go. Annas remarks, "A would-be reformer would have been silenced, either by ridicule or literally. (So if there were any would-be abolishers of ancient slavery, we will never know about them)" [parentheses in original, 60]. It would be interesting to think about whether we admire the "would-be" reformers as much as actual, successful reformers in later ages.

characteristic motive that initiates action toward an end, then we can refine (2) and (3) as follows:

(2a) Good motives are the motives that are the components of virtues.
(3a) Good ends are the ends of virtuous motives.

According to (4), a virtuous act is an admirable act. If we have identified virtue correctly as a disposition out of which admirable acts arise, then it follows that

(4a) Virtuous acts are the acts that express virtues.

I have proposed that we begin the construction of our map of the value concepts by admiring certain behaviors, in particular, acts. We move backward to identify virtues as the psychological sources of those acts, and then we move forward again to identify more acts that arise from those sources. Roughly, those are the virtuous acts. If I am right in (1a), then virtuous acts arise out of distinctive motives with distinctive aims. We have already discussed ambivalence about whether a virtuous act must be successful in its aim. I have not claimed that every virtuous act must succeed, although (1a) says that a virtue requires reliable success. These features are disputable, and (4a) can be interpreted in a way that is compatible with either position.

Since admiration drives the theory, we are justified in revising our identification of exemplars if we find that they have motives or ends that we find dis-admirable. As I have said, we have pre-theoretical judgments that moral theory attempts to explain and justify. Among those judgments, there are judgments that certain ends are mistaken. It will not simplify and justify our pre-theoretical moral judgments if we take someone whose end we believe is mistaken to be an exemplar. But we disagree about ends, and that disagreement is important because our awareness that the person has a certain end affects our judgment of her admirability as an exemplar. For instance, it seems to me that people rarely recognize as an exemplar someone who dies for a cause that they do not believe in, or someone who rescues someone they do not believe needs rescuing, or someone whose behavior they believe is unselfish but harms more than helps. Thousands of pacifists were jailed during World War I, some of them subject to harsh treatment, occasionally leading to death, but few non-pacifists would mention these persons as exemplary, although they would not hesitate to mention them if the same persons had been imprisoned for a cause the non-pacifists believe in.[10] Books are written about Holocaust rescuers and slave rescuers, but usually only abortion opponents treat abortion rescuers as heroes. Nobody can deny the unselfishness of persons who give to the poor, but differences in opinion about the benefit to the recipients affects observers' judgments of the degree of admirability of people who give to anyone who appears needy, such as panhandlers.

There are empirical studies relevant to the issue of whether a virtuous person must have an end that is judged to be right independent of the agent's point of view. Pury and Starkey (2010) argue that there are two distinct streams of courage research. One focuses on what they call process courage, or the psychological process of acting in the face of fear for the sake of what the agent considers to be a noble goal, and the other focuses on accolade courage, which entails commendation and endorsement on the part of the person making the judgment. Pury and Starkey propose that the term "courage" is used in these two different ways and that part of the reason for conflicting views on whether the 9/11 terrorists were courageous is that some people think that calling them courageous includes endorsing the attack and its ends, whereas others think that it is the terrorists' perception that is relevant. Sometimes it implies endorsement of the courageous person's ends, and sometimes it does not. In their study, participants were not asked whether they admire the person performing the putatively courageous act, but as with the other Pury studies I mentioned earlier, I would not be surprised if the difference Pury and Starkey detect in the use of the term "courageous" is reflected in a difference in the emotion of admiration and in judgments of admirability.

If Pury and Starkey are right about an ambiguity in the use of the term "courage," that could arise from ambivalence in the emotion of admiration, but I think it is more likely that it reveals different components of virtue. If we admire a terrorist act in one way but find it contemptible in another, that probably means that there are admirable psychological characteristics that are separable from the ends at which they are directed. Our response to the terrorists is a good way to bring to our attention the

---

10. Maximilian of Tebessa was a third-century martyr from what is now Algeria, who was executed for refusing to serve in the Roman army because he was Christian (see Brock 1994). Some interpreters think his reason was that pacifism was the Christian position, and so he was executed for pacifism, but others think his refusal was based on the fact that in the army he would be required to pay homage to false gods. I find it interesting that Maximilian is rarely mentioned as a hero outside the pacifist literature.

distinctness in the components of virtue and vice. We could decide to use the term "courageous act" to refer to acts expressing fearlessness in the defense of a perceived value, but then we would need another word to refer to acts expressing fearlessness in the defense of an end we admire on reflection. I think it is most reasonable to use "courage" in the latter sense, but there is nothing in exemplarism that requires that.

The issue of how we respond to the discovery of the motives and ends of putative exemplars shows how important it is to place virtue in the wider context of a person's life. As we saw in the interviews with Holocaust rescuers and L'Arche caregivers, a person's acts arise out of a structure of motives, beliefs, and ends that are adopted as part of a life story that appears different when told in the first person than when it is told in the third person. The pacifist, the abortion rescuer, the L'Arche caregiver, and the person who shares all her wealth with the poor have ends that cannot be understood outside a narrative of the world as they see it, and the place they believe they have in that world. We often can learn something from a person's own perspective on her life that is hidden when we view it from the outside. Our conception of what counts as an admirable end is mostly determined by our perspective on our own lives and an outside perspective on other people's lives, but it is difficult to critique our perception of the admirability of particular ends without an appreciation of the perspective of people who actually adopt those ends.

In this section I have proposed a series of simple definitions of the value terms "virtue," "good motive," "good end," and "virtuous act," each of which can be defined by direct reference to exemplars. Given my hypothesis about the psychology of admirable persons, the definitions can be filled out in the way I have suggested, making these concepts interdefinable. So a good motive and a good end are constituents of a virtue, and a virtuous act expresses a virtue. But if what we call a virtue is a trait that leads to admirable acts, then a good motive is the motive of an admirable act, and a good end is the end of an admirable act, so the series of definitions does not have to begin with the definition of a virtue, as I have done in this section. Furthermore, since I am using "good" in the sense of the admirable, and since the admirable is judged by reflective admiration, a virtue is a trait we admire on reflection, a good motive is a motive we admire on reflection, a good end is an end we admire on reflection, and a virtuous act is an act we admire on reflection. The hypotheses I have formulated in this section are attempts to make these definitions conform to observations of admirable persons and their behavior, and it

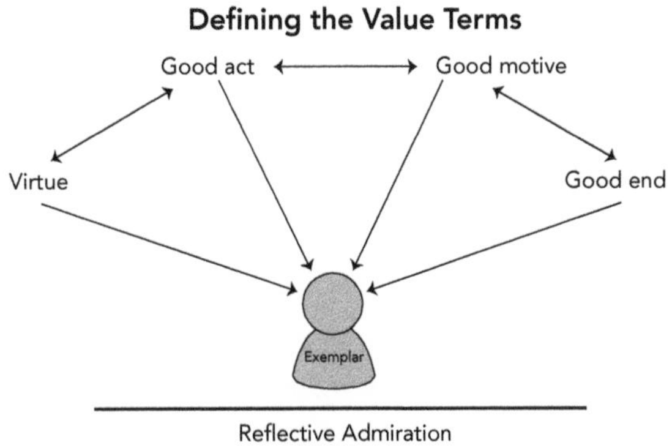

Defining the Value Terms

FIGURE 4.1 Defining the value terms

is also intended to permit the mapping of the territory of value terms in a way that not only simplifies the territory but also gives us ways to check our identification of exemplars and our identification of admirable traits, ends, and acts. Each of these terms is justified by its place within a network of terms. Admiration is both my principle of simplification and my principle of justification of the network.

4. Discovering the Virtues in Exemplars

4.1 The Scope of Particular Virtues

There are a number of advantages of mapping the individual virtues by direct examination of exemplars. I have argued in this book that we can identify what we admire on reflection in advance of knowing what is admirable about it. We do not need a theory of virtue to tell us what we admire, and in any case we are often more certain that certain individuals are admirable than we are of any theory. In Chapter 3 I described three exemplars as exhibits for the method of exemplarism and showed how we can identify particular admirable traits in those exemplars. Leopold Socha displayed courage, ingenuity, and virtually boundless love for the people he cared for. Confucius displayed reverence, civility, and the distinctively Confucian virtue of *ren*. Jean Vanier displays love, deep understanding and acceptance of human beings in all their frailty, and something else that is harder to name, but which I describe in more detail here. In each case, we can say that what we mean by courage, love, civility, and so on are *what they display*. I am using only a few cases of exemplars to illustrate the model, but we will not be adequately connected to the network of users of a word like "courage" and properly identify its extension unless we observe a number of other exemplars who have these virtues. We do something similar in the observation of a species of animal. In a sense it only takes one paradigm tiger to tell us what a tiger is, but we will not be properly connected to a network of users of "tiger" without a grasp of the differences between one tiger variety and another. We are much better at identifying the extension of "tiger" if we can do that, and similarly for virtue terms.

Another advantage of letting the virtue terms be defined by direct observation of exemplars is that the most exemplary persons show us acts in the extension of "virtuous act" that surprise us and make us grow morally. They can show us that the scope of a virtue term is wider than we thought. For instance, most of us can recognize hope. We see persons who hope when others have given up, and so we say that hope is like that. We know what hope feels like in ourselves, and we hope for many ordinary things. But exemplary hope not only shows us hope that is more intense, but more important, it shows us *what* we can hope for.

Jean Vanier does that for us in his story of Claudia (1998, 20–22), whom I briefly mentioned in Chapter 3. In 1975 they welcomed Claudia into their L'Arche community in a slum area of Honduras when she was a blind and autistic seven-year-old. She had spent almost her entire life in an overcrowded asylum that left her fearful of relationships and filled with inner pain and anguish. When she arrived at the community, her anguish seemed to increase terribly, and Vanier says that that was probably because she had lost the few reference points for reality she had left. "Everything and everyone frightened her; she screamed day and night and smeared excrement on the walls. She seemed totally mad; overwhelmed by insecurity, her personality seemed to be disintegrating" (21).

Vanier goes on to say that in L'Arche they have learned from their own experience and with the help of psychiatrists that what we call madness has meaning. It comes from somewhere and is comprehensible. It is an immense cry of pain in a world where the pain has become too great. "But there is an order in the disorder that can permit healing, if only it can be found," he writes. What is most remarkable to me about this story is that they were able to find the key to healing Claudia. Twenty years later when Vanier visited the community again, he found her quite well and thriving. She was still blind and autistic, but she was at peace and able to participate in the community activities. One day he asked her, "Claudia, why are you so happy?" Her answer was simply "Dios." He asked Nadine, the community leader, what Claudia meant. Nadine said, "That is Claudia's secret."

Claudia's story is one of many stories I have read in accounts of L'Arche communities that show the tremendous power of hope in the capacities of each individual person, no matter how far she is from normality. The assistants who care for people like Claudia see a person's inner humanity when others do not, and by believing in it and showing her that they believe in her, her humanity can blossom. Hope sees the good that is possible when most of us do not grasp the reach of those possibilities. People with exemplary hope have exemplary vision. Narratives of their hope show us what hope is in a way that is profoundly more penetrating than a conceptual definition ever could be. It is also more motivating, of course, but that is the topic for Chapter 5.

4.2 The Connection of One Virtue to Another

Exemplarism can show us dividing lines between the virtues. If we find exemplars of one virtue who do not have another, that suggests that they are two distinct virtues. With this approach, we have no guarantee that the virtues will be individuated in the traditional Aristotelian way, although I think that the fact that something close to the Aristotelian list has withstood the test of time indicates that many of the virtues on Aristotle's list will also survive the approach of direct observation of exemplars.

However, our experience of exemplars might also give us reason to think that there is a master virtue that covers the whole range of human life, such as the Confucian virtue of *ren* or the Aristotelian virtue of *phronesis*. If there is a virtue like that, we would expect it to be possessed by persons who are exemplars all things considered. It would be a shame to ignore *ren* or *phronesis* in the development of a theory of virtue, and an exemplarist approach has the best chance of showing us what a virtue like that is. As already noted in Chapter 3, Olberding argues that the *Analects* defines *ren* by direct reference to the person of Confucius. We cannot say anything very illuminating about the content of *ren* without pointing to exemplars who embody the virtue and telling extensive stories about them.

Phronesis, or practical wisdom, is another big virtue. As I have mentioned, Aristotle maintained that *phronesis* is an intellectual virtue that is both necessary and sufficient for the possession of the moral virtues (*NE* 1144b30–31). It includes appropriate perceptions of the details of situations as well as appropriate emotion dispositions and the ability to adjudicate the demands of the various virtues as they apply in a given situation. This virtue might be easier to describe than *ren*, but it also is inadequately captured by any description, and it is best identified directly. These master virtues suggest that even if there is a multitude of virtues, there may be a unified structure among the virtues. To understand that structure, we need close investigation of exemplars. So one thing we learn from observation of exemplars is whether there is a master virtue that unifies the psyche of a good person and gives her the ability to determine a single course of action in response to the multiple moral demands of the circumstances of life.

Observation of exemplars can also give us a way to test the ancient "unity of the virtues" thesis. There is more than one version of this thesis, but the version endorsed by Aristotle is that there are lots of virtues, but anyone who has one virtue fully has all the rest. In contemporary philosophy John McDowell (1979) has argued for a version of this thesis.[11]

Narratives of exemplars and near-exemplars can show us whether a single vice can prevent someone who is mostly virtuous from acting virtuously in some set of circumstances. One interesting example involves the connection between justice and the improper handling of money. Thomas Jefferson's attitude toward freeing his slaves was apparently complex, but there is evidence that he was motivated to free them. However, he was always in debt due to his profligate lifestyle, and he would have run into difficulties with his creditors if he gave away his assets.[12] This seems to show how the vice of overspending can prevent one from having the full virtue of justice. It is an interesting example because injustice and the inability to manage one's finances may seem to have nothing to do with each other.[13] Jefferson seems to have been a just person, far better than most, but it could be argued that he was not able to be fully just given his problems with money.

---

11. McDowell says that virtue is a type of sensitivity that consists of a number of sensitivities working in harmony. There is a sensitivity operating in kindness, a sensitivity in justice, one in courage, one in generosity, and so on, but these sensitivities are not independent. It seems to me that McDowell's position is virtually impossible to confirm empirically without examining exemplars.

12. But Paul Finkelman remarks that Jefferson could have hired out his slaves to pay what he owed, with the understanding that they would be freed once his debts were paid off. Apparently that was done by Herbert Elder (1994, 220, note 91).

13. It is not surprising that injustice and the inability to handle money are connected in entities like governments, as Christian Miller has pointed out to me.

I am not supporting a unity thesis, but it seems to me that the connection among the various virtues deserves more empirical study and that exemplars are important because they are candidates for having all the virtues. Furthermore, since the exemplars we find for study are not perfect, their defects can be as illuminating as their virtues. There are ways to tell whether their defects are psychologically isolated from their admirable traits, or whether, like Jefferson, those defects prevent them from being fully admirable even in their most admirable qualities.

Regardless of whether the unity of virtue thesis is right, there are clearly causal connections of various kinds between and among the individual virtues. Narratives of people who grow morally into exemplars can be especially useful in revealing those connections. I find the story of Leopold Socha helpful for that purpose. Once he decided he was going to save the Jews, he had to develop character strengths that he had not fully developed into virtues. He had to exercise ingenuity, self-control, and perseverance, in addition to courage. He had to become a peacemaker for the people in his care who were sometimes at odds with one another. He had to convey his trustworthiness to them. He had to restrain his drinking. He had to become a consummate actor, playing the part of a friend of the Nazis while secretly going about his daily business of finding provisions for the people hidden in the sewers. His former life as a thief probably helped him develop clever strategies for smuggling goods underground. His religious faith intensified during the long ordeal and gave him a sense that his mission was a calling from God. It is hard to say exactly how these qualities were related. Would he have been as persevering without his religious faith? How much of his ingenuity was a natural talent and how much an acquired trait? Whatever we think of the answers to these questions, the story of Socha shows connections among his traits both in their motivational components and in their successful exercise. He passionately wanted to be successful and that demanded all of his resources, as well as a lot of luck.

Exemplars can also be useful to test my thesis that the intellectual virtues are among the traits admirable in the same way as the moral virtues. We can see whether the most admirable persons have such virtues as open-mindedness, intellectual courage, and intellectual carefulness as well as the standard moral virtues. If there are connections between the possession of one moral virtue and another, there may also be connections between an intellectual virtue and a moral virtue. I suspect that the connections between certain intellectual virtues and certain moral virtues are at least as strong as the connections between one moral virtue and others. It would be important to find out if exemplars of courage are also intellectually courageous, if especially tolerant and sympathetic people are also open-minded, if people who are paradigmatically humble in their treatment of others are also intellectually humble, and so on. The people who possess a virtue to a superlative degree are ideal subjects to help us answer questions of this kind.

It seems to me possible to identify a virtue by close observation of a single exemplar, but a difficulty in attempting that is that a virtue needs to be emulable, which means it must be a shareable trait. To identify such a trait in an empirical study, we would have to follow an exemplar around for a month or more to find out what motivates him and how he makes decisions. A fine-grained approach to studying him would make it easier for others to imitate him.

An interesting new method that could be applied to the observation of exemplars is the use of the EAR (Electronically Activated Recorder) in tracking people's verbal behavior and interactions with others over a period of time. This is a micro recording device developed by M. R. Mehl and associates, (2001 and 2012, Chapter 10), programmed to periodically record brief snippets of ambient sounds. Participants wear the EAR while going about their normal lives. In its typical use, the EAR yields about seventy samples of a person's acoustic social environment per day, or about thirty-five minutes of ambient sounds. The EAR provides a random acoustic log of a person's day from the point of view of a hidden bystander. This permits the observer to get quite a large amount of observational data about the subject, including the kind of subtle interactions with other persons that cannot be obtained by ordinary empirical methods.

Mehl and his colleagues (2013) have used the EAR to study virtue in order to examine the convergence among behavioral, self-report, and informant-report measures of moral character, and to study the stability and variability of virtuous behavior relative to neutral and negative behavior. As far as I know this method has not yet been used to study exemplars, but it is fascinating to imagine what it would have been like if Confucius had walked around with an EAR. We might find out some surprising things about an exemplar walking around with an EAR (like Mother Teresa's bouts with doubt and discouragement), and we also might find out some interesting ways in which different virtuous motives are connected. If McDowell is right that there is a connection among the sensitivities involved in kindness, generosity, and other virtues, we would be more likely to discover that with an EAR worn by the people in whom those sensitivities are most developed than with traditional approaches.[14]

Real admirable persons also show us the scope of the individual virtues. Empirical work can reveal the way they generalize their behavior from one situational context to another. If they do not generalize in a way we expect, we can also see how they judge their own behavior or motives later. There are no doubt natural ways in which people generalize their emotions and behavior, and ways in which they do not. But when they do not, they might judge that they should have. If an exemplar is not perfect, we might trust her judgment more than her actual behavior. That would be a reason to demarcate the scope of a virtue by the exemplar's reflective judgment rather than by her behavior.

A study of exemplars gives us a different way to interpret data that allegedly show that most people are not consistently fair or courageous or compassionate.[15] What happens if we combine that data with the evidence of the existence of exemplars who are extraordinary in their possession of some virtue? Suppose we find out that many of the people who are not consistently compassionate (fair, courageous, generous, etc.) admire exemplars of the virtues they themselves inconsistently exhibit and are motivated to emulate the exemplars? We would not want to classify such people with those who fail both in virtuous behavior and in the motive to act virtuously.

The same point applies to data that indicate that there are highly admirable people who are inconsistently virtuous all things considered. Oskar Schindler was courageous and compassionate in his work of saving Jews from the Nazis and could be considered an exemplar of those virtues, yet he was greedy for money and was habitually unfaithful to his wives. A natural interpretation is that courage and compassion are distinct from faithfulness and liberality, but there is another possibility. How did Schindler react to the awareness of persons who were highly virtuous in the ways in

---

14. The EAR has some limitations that could be serious. The context is often hidden because the events immediately prior to the activation of the recorder are not recorded, and negative words and behavior might be justified by unrecorded events. The recorded words and exchanges have to be interpreted and coded by the experimenter, and there are problems in identifying certain classes of acts. For instance, how does the experimenter know when the subject is lying? But if the subject is an exemplar who has already been identified as extraordinarily admirable, the EAR might be very helpful in shedding light on how she behaves in many specific circumstances and what her weaknesses are.

15. See Chapter 3, note 3 for references.

which he was weak? I do not know the answer to that question, but I think that our understanding of a virtue requires a distinction within the class of inconsistently virtuous persons between those who aspire to be consistent and those who do not.

In this subsection I have summarized some of the advantages of studying individual virtues by direct observation of exemplars. (1) It can show us whether there is a master virtue like *ren* or *phronesis* that governs most situations of moral choice. (2) It can be used to test the unity of virtues thesis. (3) It shows us a natural way to individuate the virtues that may or may not correspond to standard lists of virtues. (4) It can be used to test the connection between intellectual and moral virtues. (5) It shows us the scope of the individual virtues. (6) It permits us to make an important distinction within the class of imperfectly virtuous persons.

4.3 Virtues without a Name

A different advantage of the observation of exemplars is that it can reveal virtues that are not on standard lists. I have already mentioned Confucian civility, but there are others. Alasdair MacIntyre (1999) mentions a virtue of the Lakota tribe that they call "wancantognaka," a virtue that cuts across justice and generosity and is demarcated by social and familial connections. This is how MacIntyre describes it:

> That Lakota word names the virtue of individuals who recognize responsibilities to immediate family, extended family, and tribe, and who express that recognition by their participation in ceremonial acts of uncalculated giving, ceremonies of thanksgiving, of remembrance, and of the conferring of honor. "Wancantognaka" names a generosity that I owe to all those others who owe it to me.... Because I owe it, to fail to exhibit it is to fail in respect of justice; because what I owe is uncalculated giving, to fail to exhibit it is also to fail in respect of generosity. (120–121)[16,17]

---

16. MacIntyre refers to Soldier (1995).

17. It seems to me that there is something like wancantognaka in the practice of giving gifts for special occasions such as Christmas, birthdays, and weddings. To fail to give a gift is ungenerous, but it is not ungenerous in the sense in which it would be ungenerous to fail to give to charity. It is a violation of the duties of a relationship and hence is a failure of justice in one of its forms.

This virtue is in a category MacIntyre calls virtues of acknowledged dependence, virtues that are necessary for goods of networks of giving and receiving. These virtues are neither altruistic nor self-interested, and he believes that they reveal the artificiality in the alleged dichotomy between altruism and self-interest. The Confucian virtues of the *Analects* also blur the distinction between self-interest and other-interest. These virtues extend outwardly from responsibility to family to responsibility to extended family and community. For instance, *yi* (honesty) and *xin* (living up to one's word) are virtues that express both what we can expect from others and what others can expect from us as members of a family or community. We have seen another example of the kind of network MacIntyre has in mind in L'Arche communities. Jean Vanier created a new kind of community in which mentally disabled persons can flourish, but as the caregivers stress repeatedly, these are not communities where the caregivers give and the core members receive. The giving and receiving go both ways. The virtues exhibited in L'Arche communities seem to be an example of what MacIntyre has in mind, and I do not think these virtues have a common English name.

I think that the exemplarist approach can also allow us to identify completely new virtues, virtues that have no name. My student, Ben Polansky (unpublished) has identified a virtue of restraining one's powers. Here is a story he tells that shows why we need a word for this virtue:

> A Japanese Go master of the last century used to ride the public trains incognito from match to match, playing games with amateurs to pass the time. It did not matter to him whom he was playing, whether they were strong or weak, beginners or experts, he always won—that is, every single game—by exactly one-half point, the slimmest margin by which it is possible to win in a game in which the discrepancy in points can be 350 points.[18]

Polansky says there is something god-like about this man's mastery, superiority, dominance, and control, so quietly, so obscurely expressed. The Go master had to know his opponent better than the opponent knew

---

18. Polansky got this example from a series of eyewitness newspaper articles written by the Nobel Prize winning novelist, Yasunari Kawabata, covering the famous 1938 match between Honinbo Shusai, an old-world Go master, and a rising star who represented a modern generation of Go players coming up in Japan. The match, now one of the most famous in history, was recreated by Kawabata in his chronicle-novel, *The Master of Go* (1996).

himself. Having never before played against the opponent, the master needed to be able to anticipate which of all the points available to his opponent on the board he would take himself. He would need to be able to give the opponent points without the opponent's knowledge. The Go master did this even though what he was accustomed to doing with peers was making the strongest move available to him at every turn. His play was so skillful, it is said, that no one ever noticed who he was, even though Go masters were celebrities in Japan at the time.

I agree with Polansky that the Japanese Go Master displayed a virtue, and I do not know the name of it. Polansky believes that the virtue should be called "moderation," in a sense that coincides with what Plato calls "*sophrosyne*," but not the virtue Aristotle calls by that name, and he thinks it can be found in the writings of Charles Sanders Peirce, Ralph Waldo Emerson, and Henry David Thoreau. It involves a restraining of one's powers to make a difference to the world. It is not focused on restraining one's indulgence in pleasure, so it is not what people ordinarily mean by temperance, and it is not simply self-control because the self is not the target. One can exercise it in restraining the exercise of one's powers to make them appear less in comparison to others—intelligent, skilled, strong, and so on. The self and its powers remain the same before and after the virtue is expressed; what differs is the use or non-use of those powers in relation to other people and the surrounding world. This virtue is particularly interesting to me because it is not just a modification of some other virtue or vice—like the virtue of proper ambition or the vice of excessive generosity. We would not think of it by studying a list of ordinary words for virtue, and I do not think we would think of it by studying any standard account of virtue. We think of it because we see it displayed in an exemplary way.

There are also virtues that have a name but have become so rare that people have a hard time explaining what each one is. For example, if you ask people what magnanimity is, they give an answer that is meager and vague by their own admission. That problem can be remedied by vivid narratives of exemplars of the virtue like Abraham Lincoln, whose magnanimity was described by Secretary of State William Seward as "almost superhuman" (Goodwin, 364). He did not hold grudges, tolerated rudeness and insolence, gave credit to others when it was due, and admitted his own mistakes. Perhaps his most amazing act of magnanimity was to appoint as secretary of war Edwin Stanton, a man who had openly disdained him, because, as Lincoln explained, Stanton was the best man for the job. In his moral biography of Lincoln, Thomas Carson (2015) argued that the magnanimity of

Abraham Lincoln was central to his greatness as a leader. Carson observed, "Had he acted on the promptings of a normal human ego, Lincoln would not have enjoyed the services of the people working for him, he would have been greatly distracted by the numerous slights and slanders that assailed him, and he would not have succeeded in the tremendously difficult tasks of his presidency. Lincoln's magnanimity was essential for his success as president" (239). This is an example of how well-told stories can not only show us what a virtue like magnanimity is, but they can reveal the way virtue can contribute to success in domains that might otherwise seem to make virtue a liability, such as the military and political domains.

In Chapter 3 I mentioned that one of the issues the HABITVS research group has explored is the connection between laboratory giving behavior and laboratory rescuing behavior. These studies do not go very far in exhibiting connections between one kind of virtuous behavior and another, and the studies of Holocaust rescuers discussed in that chapter do not focus on a single individual in enough detail to permit us to see the relationship between rescuing and their other behavior, nor do they tell us anything about motives. In contrast, an important historical figure like Abraham Lincoln is a person who was both morally extraordinary, and whose life has been studied in great detail, amounting to roughly 16,000 books about him from every point of view, and we have a large number of his own writings and letters, as well as hundreds of eyewitness accounts.[19] Lincoln was a rescuer as well as a magnanimous, compassionate, just, and intellectually fair person. During the Blackhawk War, Captain Lincoln risked his life to save an old Indian man who wandered into his camp. Lincoln's men, who were armed, wanted to kill the old man, but Lincoln interposed himself between his men and the old man and said that they would have to fight him if they tried to kill the man. His men backed down and the old man was spared. Arguably, Lincoln's actions were even more virtuous, given that his family despised American Indians (Carson 2015, 247 and 398–399). In Lincoln we also see vividly the connection between rescuing behavior and his many acts of kindness and compassion. There is story after story of his tenderheartedness toward all people and animals. He could not bear to see others suffer and was willing to take personal risks to help them, sometimes even at the risk of his life. We are able to see patterns in Lincoln's behavior because of the enormous quantity of material on the man.

---

19. I thank Tom Carson for impressing this point on me in correspondence.

It is highly unusual to have as much material on historical exemplars as we have for Lincoln, but it is not unusual in people's personal lives to know an admirable person intimately and for a long period of time. Most of us do not know someone whose life is saintly enough or sagely enough to make a good narrative for large numbers of other people, but we may know someone whose admirability is an inspiration in our own lives. We can see the way their traits connect and disconnect, and how their responses to their own mistakes can be as revealing as our own responses to their admirable acts and feelings.

In this chapter I have argued that exemplarism has a number of advantages in the study of virtue. It helps us identify the psychological structure of a virtue. It can show us whether there is one big virtue like *ren* or *phronesis*. It helps us to individuate virtues and the scope of a single virtue. It shows us how the virtues are connected in a life. If the virtues are unified, studying exemplars will show us that also. It reveals non-standard virtues for which we were not searching. It can show the artificiality of separating intellectual from moral virtues. And it shows us through narratives how virtues are applied. But the biggest advantage is the advantage of semantic externalism. It allows us to map value terms without relying upon a conceptual foundation.

5

Emulation

1. Introduction: Imitation and Emulation

In an essay on the place of classics in education, Alfred North Whitehead made a statement that has been repeated many times: "Moral education is impossible without the habitual vision of greatness" (1929, 69). To sympathize with Whitehead's remark one need not deny that there is an innate moral sense,[1] but we ought to recognize that our innate moral sense does not get us very far in developing our moral capacities. In the first four chapters I have tried to pique the reader's interest in the idea of using exemplars of admirability to structure a moral theory. So far I have focused on the theoretical purpose of mapping the moral domain, but now I want to turn to the practical purpose of moral education. I believe that exemplars not only show us what morality is, but they make us want to be moral and they show us how to do it. This chapter is devoted to the way exemplars can serve as a guide for moral training. Some of that training is directed from the outside, in the moral education of children by their parents and teachers. Some of it is directed from the inside, as we attempt to improve ourselves morally. My focus is on the learning of virtue by imitation. Since virtue has a number of components, we need to consider whether all the components of virtue can be learned by imitation, including both virtuous motives and virtuous behavior. If the virtuous person acts from reasons, we will want to know whether we can acquire the reasons by emulating a virtuous person. I then consider an objection to emulation on the grounds that it is incompatible with autonomy.

---

1. See Paul Bloom (2013) for research indicating that babies have a moral sense before they can walk and talk. See also Hamlin, Wynn, and Bloom (2007) and Hamlin, Wynn, Bloom, and Mahajan (2011). For references supporting "primate proto-morality," see Haidt (2001, 826).

There is a multitude of evidence of the way we acquire both behavior patterns and desires and emotions from other people. Here is a particularly vivid example, written around AD170 by the Stoic philosopher and Roman emperor, Marcus Aurelius:

> From my grandfather Verus I learned good morals and the government of my temper.
>
> From the reputation and remembrance of my father, modesty and a manly character.
>
> From my mother, piety and beneficence, and abstinence, not only from evil deeds, but even from evil thoughts; and further, simplicity in my way of living, far removed from the habits of the rich.
>
> From my great-grandfather, not to have frequented public schools, and to have had good teachers at home, and to know that on such things a man should spend liberally.
>
> From my governor, to be neither of the green nor of the blue party at the games in the Circus, nor a partisan either of the Parmularius or the Scutarius at the gladiators' fights; from him too I learned endurance of labour, and to want little, and to work with my own hands, and not to meddle with other people's affairs, and not to be ready to listen to slander. (1997, beginning of Bk I).

Marcus Aurelius wrote these words in middle age, while on military campaign. Like the other Stoics, he thought of imitation as an extension of natural human development, of acquiring the right attitude toward the value of things.[2] But the imitation mechanism applies much more widely than the learning of morality. We share it with other animals and continue to use it throughout life. It is the best way to learn practical skills such as cooking and dance movements, and how to play games and sports. In babies, imitation is automatic. It is fun to mimic sounds and gestures, and babies laugh at an echo. When our twin sons were infants, they would trade sounds in an increasingly high pitch until they fell over in their cribs, laughing. We still find mimicry amusing in adulthood, but as we mature, imitation becomes more discriminatory, more targeted. We find some things deserving of imitation and others not. We become conscious

---

2. See Brennan (2005) for an engaging recent discussion of Stoicism and an interesting account of the "befitting." I thank Danny Munoz-Hutchinson for bringing this book to my attention, and conversation about the links between my theory and Stoicism.

of our own imitation mechanism, and gradually become aware of the purposes it serves.

Emulation is a form of imitation in which the emulated person is perceived as a model in some respect—a model of cooking, dancing, playing basketball, doing philosophy. The emulated person might be like James Dean in *Rebel without a Cause* (1955), a model of the daring teenager. Unfortunately, some teens imitated the game of racing their cars toward the edge of steep cliffs, and some were killed. They were not merely imitating for the fun of imitating, like the baby imitating a sound; they were emulating a model of something they wanted to be.[3]

There are ways in which we can control what we emulate and how we do it, and there are ways in which adults can influence the process by which children emulate others.[4] It is important to know how children are affected by narratives because it can be surprising to find out that classic stories like "Pinocchio" and "The Boy Who Cried Wolf" fail to reduce lying in young children, whereas the story of "George Washington and the Cherry Tree" significantly increases truth-telling.[5] This seems to be evidence that children emulate an exemplar but are not likely to learn from a negative example.[6]

Studies of adults have also indicated that witnessing morally good acts can lead to imitation. For instance, Rushton and Campbell (1977) found that people will imitate the actions of an exemplar who signs up

3. Classic work on imitation by Bandura, Ross, and Ross (1963) and Albert Bandura (1977, 1986) was partly a reaction to the sometimes fatal imitations of James Dean.

4. For early studies on imitation of altruistic behavior in children, see Bryan and Walbek (1970), Bryan et al. (1971), Rice and Grusec (1975), and Rushton (1975). These studies found that children were much less influenced by being told to engage in altruistic acts than by observing such an act.

5. See Kang Lee et al. (2014). The children in the study were three to seven years old. They were put in a situation in which they had to decide whether to lie. Children who had been told the story of George Washington were much less likely to lie than children who were not told a story. The story of Pinocchio did not affect their behavior. The study showed further that if the story of George Washington was modified to one with a negative outcome like the story of Pinocchio, it had no effect on the children's behavior. Only the story with the positive role model and positive outcome had an effect. See also Wang (2014) for a *Wall Street Journal* story on the study.

6. However, in a set of experiments by Peter Blake and associates, children watched as their parents chose to give resources to another adult. Some parents acted generously, others selfishly. Later when deciding whether to give their own resources to another child, the children in the study showed greater imitation of the parent when the parent acted selfishly. One interpretation was that the children wanted an excuse for bad behavior, and the parent provided it.

for blood donation, and Spivey and Prentice-Dunn (1990) have found the same type of imitating behavior in the donation of money. More recently, Simone Schnall, Jean Roper, and Daniel M. T. Fessler (2010) have done studies on the connection between the feeling of admiration (which, following Haidt, they call "elevation"), and the desire to help others. They began by measuring elevation among participants in an elevation-inducing condition to determine whether witnessing altruistic behavior elicited elevation. In the first experiment, participants experiencing elevation were more likely to volunteer for a subsequent unpaid study than were participants in a neutral state. In the second experiment, participants experiencing elevation spent approximately twice as long helping the experimenter with a tedious task than participants experiencing happiness or a neutral emotional state. Further, they say that among the participants in their studies, feelings of elevation predicted the amount of helping, but not feelings of happiness. They conclude that witnessing another person's altruistic behavior elicits the emotion they call elevation, and that in turn leads to measurable increases in helping behavior. They suggest that even brief exposure to another person's "prosocial" behavior motivates such behavior in individuals, an important outcome in "large societies characterized by anonymity and cultural heterogeneity," where it is often difficult to create an empathic connection (Schnall, Roper, and Fessler 2010, 319).

What about the imitation of a whole person rather than a single act? The experience of centuries of religious literature testifies to the power of uplifting emotions to lead to the imitation of Christ in the lives of devout Christians, and there are many personal stories of the influence of saintly persons in the lives of people who know them or read narratives about them.[7] But only recently have there been empirical studies of individuals emulating a person rather than an act. A new series of studies by Laura E. R. Blackie et al. (forthcoming) tests a theory of moral paragons, where what they mean by a paragon is a person who is admired and esteemed as a whole person, unlike a role model, who is domain-specific. They propose that people obtain their moral grounding and life guidance

---

7. Palmer et al. (2013) discuss the power of saints and argue that morally elevating acts, stories, and images have a "cascading effect" (109), encouraging such acts generation after generation, and they hypothesize that these acts may have played a role in the evolution of our species.

from paragons who exemplify how to be a good person. In their first study they identified cultural paragons in American society, which included inventors, actors, entrepreneurs, social activists, and fictional characters. In the second study they found that individuals felt virtuous and authentic when they acted like their personally chosen paragons. A third study supported their hypothesis that there was a causal relationship between paragon emulation and moral self-regard.

The paragons chosen by the individuals in the study included Mother Teresa, the Dalai Lama, and Gandhi, but also Tom Hanks, Robin Hood, Joan of Arc, Lebron James, and Margaret Thatcher, among others. Emulation was stronger for personally chosen paragons than for "universal paragons," those persons who obtained the highest scores for admiration among all the people in the study. During the study, people were asked five times a day to rate how much their behavior resembled their personal paragon. For instance, people whose personal paragon was Tom Hanks were asked each time to rate how much their behavior resembled Tom Hanks's behavior at the moment, and they were also asked how good they felt about themselves as persons. As predicted, when they felt their behavior resembled Tom Hanks's behavior, they felt more moral and better as persons than when their behavior did not resemble his behavior (24).

What are these people doing? Are they imitating behavior only, or are they imitating attitudes and emotions? Are they taking on some of Tom Hanks's beliefs? What about his reasons for his acts? If asked, would they attempt to identify his reasons, or would they have their own reasons? A more basic question is whether they refer to reasons at all. If asked to justify their acts, do they point to justifying reasons, or do they simply say that they are acting like their personal exemplar? The connection between reasons and morally virtuous acts is one of the issues I look at in this chapter because emulation functions differently for different parts of a person's psychological structure.

2. How Can Emulation Produce Virtue?

Aristotle argued that human beings acquire virtue by habituation. As Myles Burnyeat (1980) describes the process in a classic paper, children are told what is fine or noble (*kalon*) by their parents, but they do not yet see for themselves that acting virtuously is noble. Parents use reward and punishment to make their children act as virtue requires, and through the repetition of good acts, the child acquires a habit that she associates with pleasure. Eventually, as she gets older, she comes to take pleasure in acting virtuously for its own sake. Only then does she have the virtue.

This well-known picture of moral learning raises some questions about the learner's motivation. For Aristotle, the virtuous person takes pleasure in the virtuous act (*NE* 1104b5), but a virtuous person performs the act for its own sake (*NE* 1105a32), not for the sake of pleasure. However, as Hallvard Fossheim (2006) points out, "It is hard to see how motivations based only on pleasures and pains can magically transmute into anything essentially different from themselves. . . . [M]ere association cannot bridge the gap between pleasure and the noble, and a 'hooking up' of the good and the noble by associative training cannot be enough to give the learner access to the noble as a motivation in its own right" (107–108). Fossheim's answer comes from Aristotle's *Poetics*. *Mimesis*, or imitation, precipitates virtuous behavior, and the basic human pleasure in *mimesis* provides the initial motivation to act as virtue requires. But *mimesis* leads to the performance of a virtuous act for its own sake because what is aimed at in the *mimesis* of an activity is just the activity. "Mimetic desire ensures that, whatever the learner fastens on, relating mimetically to it will at the same time mean relating to it as something to be savoured for its own sake. Thus an action which might otherwise be done in order to receive a reward or to avoid a punishment will, if it is instead performed mimetically, be done without any ulterior motives" (Fossheim 2006, 113).

It is not yet clear how this model gets beyond pleasure as the motive for an act. Fossheim says that *mimesis* is motivated by the natural pleasure in imitation, and eventually, through repetition of the appropriate acts, pleasure in imitating is replaced by pleasure in doing the act itself. Acting in that way does not have an ulterior motive. But lacking an ulterior motive is not sufficient for acting out of virtue. The virtuous agent not only gets pleasure in the doing of the act, but the act must have the right motive for the kind of act that it is—for example, respect for others, in the case of honesty; caring for others' welfare, in the case of generosity. To bridge the gap between pleasure and the noble, it is not sufficient that the agent gets pleasure in telling the truth as opposed to telling the truth for the sake of avoiding punishment. Telling the truth must be motivated by the motive characteristic of the honest person, which is presumably something like respecting the need of others to know the truth.

Second it is not clear how *mimesis* leads to doing acts with moral value. Since children get pleasure in imitation per se, it does not matter for the pleasure of imitation whether they are imitating something good or something bad. When the learner imitates a good act, if she would just as easily have imitated a bad act, it is hard to see how imitating a good act produces an act that is morally good, even if done repeatedly, and eventually with pleasure in doing the act. Fossheim recognizes this problem, and says that that is why it is so important for children to have good models (115–116). I agree with him about the importance of good models, but if children cannot distinguish good from bad models, the process of *mimesis* makes it look as though the child's motive is good because of the accidental fact that the child was imitating a good rather than a bad model, and that is not plausible.

Both of these problems can be solved if the moral learner admires the person she emulates. Admiration explains why she would want to be like the person she emulates, not just for the pleasure of imitation, but because she sees the person she emulates as good. She emulates the admired person qua good, not just qua something it would be fun to imitate. Admiration also explains why she is motivated to emulate the admired person's motive for the act as well as the behavioral component of the act, assuming that part of what she admires in the person is the motive. Emulation arising from admiration can explain how virtuous motives develop. Pleasure alone cannot do so.[8]

If the moral learner is already partially motivated to act from the exemplar's motive, it is not hard to see how emulation can produce the right act from the right motive. For instance, in Chapter 3 I mentioned a study by Michael Gill et al. (2013), which shows how consistent contributors function to "energize" the moral values of those who profess to value altruistic giving. These researchers found that in a social dilemma situation that contains no consistent contributors, self-professed altruistic values do not predict a participant's level of giving to the collective. In contrast, if a consistent contributor is present, the giving of those with self-professed altruistic

---

8. I think that Fossheim would be happy with the addition of admiration to the model. In one place he refers to the "object of admiration" when explaining the process of mimesis (111). In subsequent private correspondence, he agrees. He has suggested to me that the good and the bad are not equally forceful mimetic objects. I do not pursue that idea in this book, but it is a fascinating one, and it is related to the view that humans have an innate moral sense.

values increases markedly. These studies support the idea that there are people who are exemplary in generosity in the conditions created for the study, and that their exemplarity leads other people to emulate them when those people share their altruistic values, but need a nudge to act on it.

But how does emulation lead the learner to acquire a good motive if she does not already have it? We know that *mimesis* or emulation is not mere copying, and in any case, the learner cannot copy a good motive the way she can copy sounds her mother makes when she is learning to talk. She can emulate an overt act, such as sharing her toys with a visitor, but emulating the motive of generosity is much trickier. Fossheim mentions seeing one's ideal self in the admired person (117), and I think that this is the key to emulating motives.

David Velleman (2002) has described a process by which admiration leads to the emulation of an admired person's motives through wishful picturing of oneself in the image of the admired person. One imagines oneself as a generous (honest, kind) person, and then goes about enacting this self-image. Emulation flows directly out of admiration because "wishfully picturing oneself in the image of an ideal is not a distraction from the business of admiring him: it *is* the business of admiring him" (101). Confucius speaks of doing this himself when he frequently dreamed of his exemplar, the Duke of Zhou, and expressed sadness when he stopped doing it (*Analects* 7.5). He associated his admiration and emulation of the duke with dreaming of the duke as an ideal. I think that what Confucius was doing is what Velleman proposes. In projecting oneself into the image one then enacts, one gradually becomes the person one wants to be.

This model does not apply to young children, but is applicable to adults and to older children who have reached the point in their moral learning at which they can acquire the virtues. I think the model can work because even though imagining ourselves with a motivating feeling is not the same thing as having the feeling, imagining is very close to having, and an imagined feeling can cause an actual feeling, especially when we want to become a person with such a feeling. There are many examples of this phenomenon. Women can sometimes fall in love with a man by spending a long time imagining themselves in love with him. People often become angry with someone or intensify their anger by imaginatively dwelling on the anger and the situation in which they became angry. Sometimes agitated persons can make themselves contented by imagining themselves as content. The same thing can happen when the emotion is clearly unwanted, as when a vividly imagined fear turns into a real fear.

Many actors attempt to acquire the emotions of the character they are portraying. They take on the perspective of the character in imagination and that leads them to temporarily acquire the character's feelings.[9] Some actors reportedly immerse themselves so thoroughly in the character they are playing that they remain in character off-stage for the duration of the project.[10] Presumably, they do not permanently acquire the traits of the imaginary character, and it is questionable whether they even have the traits temporarily,[11] but the fact that some people can create the appropriate motivating emotions through a process that occurs purely in their imagination suggests that ordinary people might be able to do something similar in the process of making those traits a part of their actual character.

In Velleman's model we acquire virtue by playing a role that becomes part of us. This raises lots of questions about how a character I am pretending to be can become myself, but Velleman seems to be suggesting that wanting to be like an exemplar, when conjoined with imagining that I am like that exemplar, can make me like that exemplar. The model seems plausible, but it would be helpful to see more empirical work on creating the self through imagination.

It seems to me that we cannot imagine ourselves as a certain kind of person, as Velleman describes, unless we know what it is we are imagining. We have to be able to grasp what that person is like. But we cannot grasp that by superficial observation, certainly not by observing overt behavior. We need to be mind readers. Simulation theory is one model of how we do that. Karen Shanton and Alvin Goldman (2010), and Goldman

---

9. The great Russian actor and theoretician, Konstantin Stanislavsky, developed a system of acting that became known as "the Method," adapted by Lee Strasberg in the United States. Some followers of method acting use techniques to make them feel and think as if they are the imaginary character in the play. Robert C. Roberts (2013, 208–209) gives a brief discussion of Stanislavskian role-playing as a model for learning virtue in his recent book on emotions in the moral life.

10. Daniel Day-Lewis is a good example. See Segal (2005).

11. Does the actor take on a temporary character trait? This question is particularly intriguing when the actor is playing an evil character. Daniel Day Lewis is good at that also. Philip Zimbardo's famous Stanford Prison experiment suggests that intense role-playing can make a person take on the motives and feelings of the character even when it is evil. The students playing the role of prison guards became so brutal that the experiment had to be stopped.

(2008) have drawn on work in cognitive neuroscience in developing an account of how a "mentalizer" simulates another person's mind by creating pretend states that correspond to those of the target, which she then inputs into a suitable cognitive mechanism to generate a new output—for example, a decision. We engage in the same sort of process when we simulate our future selves, a process they call prospection. Simulation requires a certain degree of similarity between exemplar and moral learner if the simulation is to be accurate. For instance, we could not simulate the exemplar's feeling of compassion and the way that compassion motivates acts unless we had a suitably similar system of emotion dispositions and mental structure linking emotions of the relevant kind with acts of the relevant kind. I think that this is what we would expect in the process of emulation on Velleman's model. We would not be able to see the exemplar as an ideal self without a basic similarity in psychic structure between ourselves and the exemplar. An exemplar with a radically different psychic structure would be unrecognizable.

My hypothesis, then, is that the primary components of virtue—a virtuous behavior disposition and a virtuous motive disposition, can be acquired through emulation. The model I am proposing starts with admiration of an exemplar, which leads to an imaginative ideal of oneself, which in turn produces emulation of the exemplar's motives and acts. The moral learner does the virtuous act from a virtuous motive because the learner is emulating someone who does that act from that motive. With practice, the agent becomes disposed to doing acts of that kind from motives of that kind. I am not suggesting that this is the only model of moral learning, but I think it is a common one, one that can be easily combined with varieties of Aristotelian psychology, such as the one described by Fossheim, and it has the advantage of explaining how emulation can lead both to virtuous behavior and to motives that move beyond pleasure to the noble.[12]

There is one more psychological puzzle about emulation that I want to address in this section. Velleman (2002) raises the worry that if one is motivated to be generous by the desire to emulate a generous person, one's act is not motivated by generosity after all (100). The motive to imitate is not the motive the virtuous person has. That is why Velleman proposes that the desire to be generous will meet with better success if one first

---

12. Julia Annas (2011) defends a skill model of virtue that is Aristotelian in spirit, and also fits well with the model of moral learning I am proposing here. Annas argues that like skills, virtues are importantly connected to both "the need to learn" and "the drive to aspire" (16). The way in which virtue is acquired is part of what makes it a virtue.

imagines oneself in the image of the generous person and then attempts to enact the image. Velleman is surely right that the desire to emulate cannot be the motive for the act if the act is virtuous. The act must be motivated as it is in the virtuous person. So the desire to be like that person must be a higher order motive: the motive to (a) acquire the motive of the exemplar, and (b) to act like her. The motive for the moral learner's act is the same as the motive of the admired person. The motive to acquire the motive of the admired person is the desire to be like her. The motive to be like her is not the motive of the act.[13]

I think this shows that a common puzzle about emulation has a solution. The puzzle arises for emulating anyone who did not himself acquire his admirable traits by emulating someone else. For instance, philosophers emulate Socrates, but, the argument goes, such a project is doomed because Socrates wasn't emulating anybody. I remember saying to a student one time, "If you want to be like Aristotle, don't imitate Aristotle." I was wrong to say that because the puzzle disappears once we see that we can distinguish between the process of emulation and the object of emulation. Emulation is a way of becoming like someone else in a certain respect. That respect need not, and in general does not, include the process of emulation. There *would* be a problem if the exemplar would not emulate anyone, if there is something dis-admirable about emulation, and some people have argued that that is the case. In section 4 I will discuss the issue of whether the moral ideal is a kind of autonomy that is incompatible with emulating another person. However, I do not see that there is any problem in emulating a person's admirable properties on the grounds that the person emulated did not acquire those properties by emulation.

3. Moral Reasons

3.1 Are Moral Judgments Based on Reasons?

Accounts of virtue sometimes maintain that we do not act virtuously unless we act for the right *reasons*. For instance, Alison Hills (2009) says

---

13. According to Simulation Theory, an integral part of mind reading consists in a suspension and quarantine of one's present psychological state, which makes room for inhabiting imaginatively the psychological state that one attributes to another or to one's future self. I interpret this to mean that one's admiration for an exemplar can be suspended while one inhabits the psychological state of the exemplar and feels whatever the exemplar feels. One's motive for acting in this way can then be the same as the motive of the exemplar, not admiration.

that a virtuous action must be performed from the right reasons, where having the right reasons is not just a matter of having the correct moral beliefs but of understanding how those beliefs justify the act. Many other philosophers have connected virtue with the function of reason, although it is not obvious that what we mean by *a* reason is always a deliverance of the faculty of reason. How are we to understand the claim that virtuous action requires acting from right reasons? If the claim is true, can exemplars help us in our acquisition of the reasons we need for virtuous action? If we cannot emulate the possession of reasons, does it follow that we cannot acquire virtue by emulation?

I define a reason as something on the basis of which a rational person can act or believe, and on this definition, there are both epistemic and practical reasons. An epistemic reason is something on the basis of which a rational person can settle for herself whether a proposition p is true. A practical reason is something on the basis of which a rational person can settle for herself whether X should be done, that it would be right to do X. A reason need not be sufficient to settle the matter of whether a certain proposition is true or a certain act ought to be done, but it is the sort of thing that can do so, normally in conjunction with other reasons. Notice that my interpretation of a reason does not require that a reason be a belief or a proposition. It must be something a rational person would use in supporting either the truth of a belief (an epistemic reason) or the rightness of an act (a practical reason).

There are epistemic reasons in the moral domain as long as there are true propositions with moral content. The idea that there are moral epistemic reasons need not assume that moral propositions are true in the same sense as non-moral propositions. It assumes only that we have moral beliefs that can be right or wrong in whatever sense of right and wrong is appropriate for moral beliefs. As I have said in discussing emotions, we have psychic states that aim to fit their objects. Emotional states aim to fit their intentional objects. Beliefs aim to fit the part of the world the belief is about. The belief could be about some part of the natural world, some part of the supernatural world, some part of the social world, or part of the self. So a moral epistemic reason is something on the basis of which a rational person can determine that a given moral belief fits the part of the world the belief is about, whatever that may be. A moral practical reason is something on the basis of which a rational person can determine that it would be morally right (or appropriate or fitting) to do some act X. Acts are based on beliefs. If an act is not justified unless the beliefs on which it is based are justified, and if a belief is not justified unless it has epistemic reasons, then a rational person cannot determine the right thing to do without having epistemic reasons.[14]

It is common to think of an epistemic reason as something that can be consciously grasped and laid out for others to evaluate, a task in which moral philosophers are more than willing to engage. It is also common to think that epistemic reasons must themselves be justified by other epistemic reasons, and some philosophers would be willing to say that a moral epistemic reason needs to be based on some fundamental moral principle from which the immediate reason for the act can be derived.

But now we seem to encounter a problem because cognitive psychologists say that only a small percentage of human behavior is consciously calculated (e.g., Kahneman 2011), a position that has been applied to moral behavior and to moral judgment. So Jonathan Haidt et al. (1993) and Schnall et al. (2008) have argued that people will make a moral judgment out of an emotion such as disgust without any further reasons to which they can point to justify the judgment. For instance, when asked why they morally disapprove of incest, or eating one's dog, or using an American flag to clean the toilet, they will often look for reasons to justify their judgment after they make it (e.g., incest leads to birth defects), but such reasons do not cause the judgment, and in many cases, people can find no reason for their moral disapproval other than the emotion itself. The real reason for the judgment is the disgust. Haidt has used these studies as evidence for his view that in human beings "the emotional dog wags the rational tail" (2001). Haidt maintains that people make moral judgments out of emotion, and then offer post hoc reasons to justify the judgment to other people. Haidt thinks this shows that philosophers and others who believe we need reasons for a moral judgment are mistaken. We merely use reason to bolster the deliverance of emotion, and in a social context in which we are asked to justify our acts to other people.

Haidt (2007) argues further that social psychologists have increasingly adopted a version of the "affective primacy" principle "in light of evidence that the human mind is composed of an ancient, automatic, and very fast affective system, and a phylogenetically newer, slower, and motivationally weaker cognitive system (998)." Affective reactions come first. Higher level thinking comes afterward, and generally it is used to bolster the affective response.

---

14. I am leaving open whether a practical reason is sufficient to motivate the behavior it justifies.

What are we to make of this claim? It seems to me that the empirical studies cited by Haidt and others can falsify the view of those philosophers who say that moral judgment and moral behavior must have justifying reasons only if we make certain assumptions:

(a) What subjects do in an experimental setting is closely connected to what they are justified in doing/judging.
(b) Emotions are not reasons in the relevant sense.
(c) Any reasons to which subjects can point after they make a moral judgment do not justify the judgment.
(d) Justifying reasons must be conscious.

I think that all four of these assumptions are false.

Let me begin with the preliminary point that it is not necessary for the purposes of exemplarism to adjudicate the putative conflict between philosophers and psychologists about moral reasons. Exemplarism has the advantage of neutrality on the relative place of reasoning and emotion in moral behavior. If exemplars have reasons for acting in the sense of justifying propositions that can be laid out for others to evaluate, we ought to be able to find out what those reasons are.[15] If instead, they have no such reasons, or are not conscious of them, that also is something we can discover. Likewise, we should be able to discover the role that emotion plays in their moral decisions and whether they treat their emotions as justifying their behavior. If the reasons exemplars have for acting differ from the reasons ordinary people have, that is another thing we ought to be able to discover through investigation.

Let me comment first on assumption (d). Even though the evidence suggests that most behavior is without reflection, that is compatible with what philosophers typically mean when they say that we need moral reasons. Moral reasons are justifications for acting in one way rather than another. These reasons need be conscious only when the choice is difficult, or is challenged by someone else, or when one's professor surprisingly insists that there needs to be a defense of a judgment about which almost everyone agrees—like the judgment that incest is wrong. But most of the

---

15. This might actually be rather difficult to do because some exemplars would not cooperate, as Ben Polansky has reminded me. If you ask Jesus for his reason, he gives you a parable. Think also of the reasoning Socrates gives his friend Crito in the jailhouse. Crito asks for and Socrates gives him a *logos*, but it is unlikely that that was Socrates' own *logos* for staying and drinking the hemlock.

time our behavior is like our previous behavior. The choice to do whatever we are doing is not difficult and nobody is challenging it. The same point applies to our moral judgments. Most of the time our judgments do not raise any difficulties from either the outside or the inside. That does not mean that we act or judge without reasons, but it does mean that we do not often attend to our reasons. Perhaps we do not reflect as often as we should, but that is hardly news, and it does not raise any special problems for the view of philosophers who say that moral judgment requires justifying reasons.

This point also has implications for assumption (c). If a reason is not conscious and is only brought to consciousness when questioned, it would not be surprising if the reasons justifying a judgment were not revealed until after the judgment is made. But in some cases, even after questioning, it appears that a person has no reason other than the emotion. Haidt emphasizes this point in discussing the studies on disgust. A person who judges that incest is wrong, and when pressed for a reason, says that it increases the chances of birth defects is presumably confabulating. If it turned out that incest did not increase birth defects, they would continue to judge it wrong based on the fact that they find it disgusting, and in any case, they no doubt judge its degree of wrongness as exceeding the wrongness of other acts that increase the likelihood of birth defects, such as having sex with someone who is known to carry the gene for a serious disability.

In Chapter 7 I argue that the justification for moral judgments is possessed by the community as a collective body, and that certain persons in the community, such as philosophers and religious leaders, have the social role of providing those reasons. But for the purposes of this chapter, I want to look more closely at the prior question, assumption (b): Emotions are not justifying reasons.

I have argued in Zagzebski (2012) that emotions can *be* reasons, and that admiration is a good example of an emotion that operates as a reason.[16] To see how an emotion can be a reason, let me return to what I said in Chapter 2. There I proposed that an emotion includes a cognitive

---

16. In Zagzebski (2012) I distinguish between third person and first person reasons. I think of a third person reason as a proposition that can be laid out on the table for all to consider. Typically, what we mean by evidence is in this category. What I mean by a first person reason is a psychic state that directly justifies a belief for the person who has it, and only for the person who has it. I argue that emotions can be first person reasons, as can one's beliefs, perceptual states, memories, and intuitions.

state even if it does not include a belief or judgment as a component. In an emotional state, the intentional object of the emotion appears in a distinctive way to the subject. In a state of fear, the object appears fearsome; in a state of pity, the object appears pitiable; in a state of admiration the object appears admirable, and so on. When the subject sees something *as* pitiable or *as* fearful or *as* disgusting, she is in a cognitive state. If she trusts the way the object appears to her, she can express that in a judgment: "That is disgusting," "That is fearsome," "That is pitiful," "That is admirable," and so on (Zagzebski 2003, 2012). Assuming that a reason is something on the basis of which a rational person can determine whether p, then judgments of this kind are *reasons* for other judgments, such as the judgment, "That act is wrong." So the expression of an emotion in a judgment like "That act is disgusting" can be a reason for the judgment, "That act is wrong." A judgment based on disgust is based on a reason. Of course, the reason could be mistaken. It would be mistaken if the object is not disgusting. Maybe nothing is disgusting. But if so, it is not because disgust is an emotion.

I suggest, then, that a simple pattern whereby an emotion becomes a reason that justifies a propositional moral judgment is as follows:

1. A person S is in an emotional state—say, one of disgust at an act X.
2. S's state of disgust is rational if it survives conscientious reflection. That is, after reflecting on her disgust, comparing it with the emotions of others she trusts, and reflecting on its coherence with her other beliefs, emotions, and experiences, S might find her disgust trustworthy. S can express her trust in her emotion by asserting, "X is disgusting." The expression of the reflectively endorsed emotion is the judgment "X is disgusting," and in these circumstances the judgment is rational.[17]
3. The judgment "X is disgusting" gives S a reason to judge "X is wrong."

I proposed above that an epistemic reason is something on the basis of which a rational person can determine whether a proposition p is true. If so, then since the judgment "X is disgusting" is an expression of the reflectively endorsed emotion of disgust, it follows that an emotion can be an epistemic reason. Further, if a practical reason is something a rational person can use as the basis for determining whether or not to do X, then

---

17. I assume, of course, that most rational judgments are defeasible. That is, a rational person is prepared to give it up if future reflection warrants it.

since the judgment "X is wrong" is a reason not to do X, it also follows that the emotion of disgust can be a practical reason not to do X.

Let us look now at how admiration can be a reason. If I admire E and reflectively endorse my state of admiring E, I have a reason to judge "E is admirable." The judgment "E is admirable" can be a reason to emulate E in the respect in which I admire E. Admiration is a reason for doing what E does. Given what I said earlier in this chapter, it is a reason to acquire the motives E has in doing what she does. It is reasonable for me to act in the way E does with the motives E has because it is reasonable for me to do what I reflectively endorse. Admiration is a reason to do what E does from E's motives. If E's motives are emotions, and these emotions are reasons for E to act in a certain way, then my emotion of admiration is a reason to acquire E's emotions, and these emotions are reasons for me to do an act like the one E performs. If the exemplar is like Haidt's emotional dog, I can acquire the virtues of the exemplar and act virtuously by emulation. When I do so, my acts have reasons, and the exemplar's acts have reasons. If this is what is happening, there is no inconsistency between the philosopher's insistence that virtuous acts must have reasons, and the psychological literature that allegedly shows that human beings primarily act on emotion.

In this subsection I have looked at the alleged conflict between some cognitive psychologists and philosophers on the issue of whether a moral judgment must be justified by moral reasons. Jonathan Haidt interprets recent empirical studies as indicating that people typically make moral judgments on emotions such as disgust, and then look for justifying reasons after the fact. I have argued that the results of his studies conflict with the position of philosophers and others who think that moral judgment requires justifying reasons only if (a) what subjects do in an experimental setting is closely connected to what they are justified in doing/judging, (b) emotions are not reasons in the relevant sense, (c) any reasons to which subjects can point after they make a moral judgment do not justify the judgment, and (d) justifying reasons must be conscious. I think, however, that a justifying reason need not be conscious, and in fact, need not even be accessible to the individual at the time of the judgment. Further, I have argued that an emotion can *be* a justifying reason for the person who has it, apart from the reasons to which she can point for general discussion and debate in a community. I have not yet commented on the fact that what subjects do in an experimental setting might not be what they ought to do. I think that what they ought to do is what the exemplars do, the topic for the next subsection.

In arguing that the alleged conflict between the Haidt studies and the position that moral judgment requires moral reasons is more apparent than real, I have made claims that would be controversial on both sides, and I think that the emotion versus reasons debate is much more complex than I have discussed here. It is certainly more complex than it appears in the literature in cognitive psychology.[18] Exemplarism is neutral on the outcome of this issue, but I want to turn next to the question of how exemplars make moral decisions and moral judgments because I think that their behavior can illuminate the problem.

3.2. Do Exemplars Act on Reasons?

The moral psychology of exemplarism is partly determined by the outcome of empirical work. It is an open question how exemplars make their moral choices. Maybe they are like the people in the studies cited above, but maybe they are not. It could turn out that exemplars base their moral judgments on propositional reasons rather than emotions, and it is also possible that those reasons are the result of a process of reasoning. If so, there is a problem with assumption (a) above. If exemplars differ from ordinary people in the place of reasoning in their moral judgments, then what participants in these studies do is not the same as what they ought to do. What they ought to do is to imitate exemplars in their process of moral judgment.

Since I think it is an open question whether exemplars are like the participants in the studies cited by Haidt, let us consider both possibilities. Suppose first that exemplars base their moral judgments on moral beliefs that they arrive at through a process of reasoning. If so, we cannot do what they do by imitation. We can acquire an exemplar's emotion by emulation, and we can imitate the exemplar's behavior, but we cannot acquire a belief by imitation. I cannot make myself believe something simply because I admire someone who has that belief. I can admire a vegan who believes it is wrong to eat or use animal products, but admiring her, and even admiring her *for* her belief, is not sufficient to get me to believe it because I cannot believe something unless I think it is true. The

---

18. Peter Railton (2014) has argued in a lengthy paper that our spontaneous, non-deliberative intuitions have been shaped by a history of affective attunement to the social environment that makes our affective reactions much more than a primitive, automatic emotional response. He says that his paper is in part a response to Haidt and others, but it is also an occasion for him to present in detail his position on moral intuition.

model Velleman describes of wishfully picturing myself in the image of the admired person is not going to work if what I am wishfully picturing is a person with certain beliefs. I can acquire the exemplar's motives of generosity or courage by wishfully picturing myself as generous or courageous, but I cannot acquire the exemplar's beliefs by wishfully picturing myself with her beliefs.

In *Epistemic Authority* (2012) I argued that if I admire a person epistemically, then in many circumstances I have a second order reason to believe that her beliefs are true.[19] If my admiration for the exemplar includes admiration for the way she forms her moral beliefs, and I think she has the relevant background knowledge, I see her as more likely to get the truth about the relevant issue than I would be on my own. If so, the fact that she believes p is evidence for me that p is true. It is reasonable for me to believe that p on the basis of my judgment that (a) the exemplar is more likely to get the truth whether p than I am, and (b) the exemplar believes p. In this way it is no harder for me to believe p on the basis of the fact that I admire the exemplar in a certain way than it is for me to believe p on the basis of ordinary inductive evidence. It is no harder and it is just as rational. If virtue requires having certain beliefs, I can acquire those beliefs from an exemplar in this way.

So if the exemplar arrives at her moral beliefs by a process of reasoning, I can adopt the reasoning from her also, but only if the reasoning appeals to my own faculty of reason. I can acquire neither her beliefs nor her justifying reasoning by emulation, but I *can* acquire them from her. I think it is important, then, to find out the place of propositional reasons and reasoning in the process exemplars use to make their moral judgments. If their virtues include the disposition to engage in a reasoning process of a certain kind, we need to find that out because we acquire beliefs and supporting reasons by a different process than by emulation.

Suppose instead that exemplars are like ordinary people in their moral acts and judgments as described by cognitive psychologists. That is, they act on emotion and not on reasons in the sense of justifying propositional beliefs. It would not be surprising that that is the case if Haidt (2007) is right that the human affective system is faster and more basic than the cognitive system. That would give us reason to think that affective primacy is deep in human nature. Whether exemplars are like ordinary

---

19. I also argue that this is one way in which it is reasonable to acquire beliefs on authority (2012, Chapter 7).

people in this respect is also something that we should be able to discover empirically.

The mental behavior of exemplars is a huge question and we do not have enough evidence, but the evidence we have does not support the position that moral reasoning is an important part of the moral judgments of exemplars.[20] In Chapter 3 I mentioned Colby and Damon's studies of twenty-three exemplars with widely differing backgrounds. Colby and Damon observed a number of common features such as a moral awakening, sometimes in childhood and often inspired by faith, and they postulated that what distinguishes these exemplary individuals from ordinary people is not in their professed values, but in the way these values are integrated into a sense of self. I do not think any of them described a deliberative process of reasoning leading to the acts that led Colby and Damon to study them. I acknowledge that the lack of evidence of a reasoning process is not the same as evidence for the lack of a reasoning process, so I think that these studies should be treated as indeterminate on this issue.

Kristen Renwick Monroe's in-depth interviews of five Holocaust rescuers, also discussed in Chapter 3, shows us something stronger. The people interviewed in that study clearly saw their rescuing activities as justified from the point of view of their personal life narrative. A rescuer named "Irene" is quoted as saying, "I did not ask myself, should I do this? But how will I do this? Every step of my childhood had brought me to this crossroads. I must take the right path, or I would no longer be myself." How did she know it was the right path? The rescuers in the studies I have seen apparently thought it was obvious. If they had any propositional belief such as "These people deserve to be rescued," it was not something they based on a reasoning process. At least, it was not a reasoning process that included more than one step. We see the same thing in the biographies of Leopold Socha, who told Paulina Chiger that when he first saw her huddled in her cellar with her two little ones, he knew immediately he would save her.

Jean Vanier is an articulate and eloquent writer and speaker, and he gives us much insight into his motives for founding L'Arche and devoting

---

20. Jonathan Haidt (2001, 824) says that exemplars do not differ from ordinary people in their moral reasoning, referring to Hart and Fegley (1995) and Colby and Damon (1992). He says "both [research groups] compared highly prosocial moral exemplars with nonexemplars and found that the groups did not differ in their moral reasoning ability assessed by Kohlbergian techniques." But it needs to be noted that Kohlbergian techniques do not exhaust the resources of human moral reasoning.

his life to it. He also gives a justification for these communities in his many writings. As I interpret his works, he is motivated by a vision of a community in which "the poor" and "the rich" live together in a way that allows the flourishing of all. It is revolutionary, so it is unlikely that the vision is justified by common moral principles. Vanier clearly engages in reasoning, but it is not the type of reasoning that would be used in a philosophy class or a professional journal. It seems to me that he is an example of someone who blurs the distinction Haidt makes between emotion and reasons. But whatever Vanier does, it can be emulated because many people have already emulated it.

What about Confucius? One gets the sense that for Confucius, moral reasoning is given in response to questions from someone who asks him why he did what he did. His explanations are usually general statements about what virtue entails or what a virtuous person would do. He is telling a learner what to think about. But it is questionable whether that is the same thing that Confucius was thinking about when he acted. We see something even more striking in Mengzi, who explains his moral accomplishment as having developed "floodlike *qi*," suggesting that the moral-emotional orientation of the sage simply flows like waters with a force that makes his reactions more like automatic instinct than the result of a process of reasoning.

The use of reasoning in the *Analects* hints at two different functions of moral reasoning. One is support for a moral decision or judgment one is making oneself. I am skeptical that reasoning figures significantly in the judgments of moral exemplars in this way, although as I have said, I think that that is an issue that should be settled by further investigation of exemplars. But there is another function of reasoning that I think is much more important. Reasoning justifying the moral judgments of exemplars and ordinary people serves a significant social purpose. It can lead to new moral practices, and it can lead to a change of direction in the lives of the persons in a community. In Chapter 7 I give my proposal that moral reasoning is a role assigned to certain individuals in a society—typically, philosophers and theologians. The link between that reasoning and what exemplars do is an application in the moral domain of Putnam's Division of Linguistic Labor. Some people are "experts" at moral judgment because of their moral wisdom and insight; others are "experts" at providing the reasoning supporting the judgments of the wise. Ordinary people are expected to grasp a small part of that reasoning, but they are not expected to have the ability to give extended arguments any more than they are expected to give an explanation of the chemical structure of gold. A virtuous person need not be adept at moral reasoning, but her judgments should track moral truth and be justifiable by the community as a whole.

4. Emulation and Autonomy

In section 2 I asked whether there might be something dis-admirable about emulation. One ground for criticism is the suspicion that emulation is incompatible with autonomy.[21] To become like another person is not only to be different from what one previously was, but to let the consciousness of another person replace one's own consciousness in the relevant respect. I assume that there is no objection to wanting to be as good as one can be, but we still want to be ourselves. Being oneself is often interpreted as making up one's own mind about what to do, not letting someone else's feelings dictate one's own, nor letting someone else direct one's life. That is what an autonomous person allegedly is. To act autonomously in the Kantian sense, one must submit to reason, but it is reason in oneself that is the authority. According to Kant, even when confronted with Christ, a man consults his own reason, as Iris Murdoch (1970, 80) reminds us.

I have argued previously that this ideal cannot be identified with Kantian autonomy (2012). The autonomous person is self-governing, but the process of conscientiously governing oneself in accordance with reason does not result in self-reliance. In fact, I have argued that it results in dependence on others whom one is required by reason to trust, and it includes the acceptance of epistemic and practical authority. My position is that autonomy is conscientious self-governance, and the test of whether one is governing oneself well is that one's beliefs, emotions, acts, and other aspects of the self, such as putative memories, survive conscientious self-reflection when we are doing the best we can to make the states of the self that have external objects fit those objects—to make our beliefs true, our memories veridical, our emotions appropriate for their objects, our acts right or good, our goals realistic. If we rely solely upon our own individual reason in governing ourselves, we are less likely to become a conscientiously governed self than if we take some of our beliefs, attitudes, intentions and goals from others. That is because there are other people

---

21. A related objection is that imitation is a betrayal of one's true self. See Warnick (2008, 18–26) for a discussion of the Enlightenment criticism of imitation of exemplars and an emerging alternative view of the educational role of exemplars.

whose conscious states are more likely to survive our own conscientious reflection than the states we acquire independently. And we can discover that by the conscientious use of our own reason and other states of mind that we trust, such as our emotion of admiration. The self-reliant romantic hero does not express the ideal of autonomy.[22]

If I admire a person and reflectively endorse my admiration, I will rationally judge the person to be admirable in the relevant respect, and if I am right that emotions can be both epistemic and practical reasons, then my judgment that the person is admirable is a *reason* to emulate the admirable person, arising from my own critical self-reflection. Emulation in such a case is a dictate of self-direction. I am autonomous because I am acting on my own reasons for my own ends.

There still remains an issue about self-governance in the learning of virtue. The so-called paradox of virtue education is that virtue education in the Aristotelian pattern of repetition and the acquisition of habit under outside guidance is somehow supposed to turn into reflective virtue and critical self-governance, and Kristjan Kristjánsson faults positive psychologists for ignoring this problem (Kristjánsson 2013, 202–205). He identifies two paradoxes—one a psychological puzzle and the other a moral puzzle. The psychological puzzle is the paradox that the goal of educating people to conduct themselves by the governance of their own intellect is supposed to be served by making them develop habits by repetition of behaviors motivated by reward and punishment. If this puzzle can be solved, there remains the moral puzzle of how it can be justified.

I think we have already seen a way to solve both paradoxes. My view on the justification of authority applies to the justification of emulation. In both cases the subject takes direction from an exemplar or an admirable person because of something in herself that she reflectively endorses. If she admires a person and reflectively endorses her admiration, she judges the person to be admirable, and her judgment that the person is admirable is a reason to emulate the admirable person arising from her own reflections. Emulating the admired person is something she does in virtue of her trust in herself. It is a dictate of self-direction. Similarly, if the subject judges that another person is more likely to have true beliefs in the relevant domain than she is herself, and she has the desire for truth, she

---

22. *Epistemic Authority* (Zagzebski 2012) is an extended argument against epistemic self-reliance. I defend the compatibility of autonomy with epistemic authority, focusing on the nature of autonomy in the first and last chapters.

has a reason to believe what the other person believes. Her reflection on her own ends leads her to adopt the strategy of taking certain beliefs from the other person. Reason leads her both to emulate the admired person and to adopt the admired person's beliefs relevant to moral action. She is autonomous when she does so because she is acting on her own reasons for her own ends.

Autonomy is preserved when virtue is acquired by self-direction, but can we foster virtue in the young while respecting their autonomy? Here I think it is relevant to distinguish two senses in which "autonomy" is used in moral and political discourse. An individual or nation suffers an attack on its autonomy in one sense when another individual or nation exerts undue influence over its decisions or range of activity, preventing it from exercising the power of self-direction. This sense of autonomy corresponds to one of the two ways in which Kant says a will can be heteronomous. A will that is controlled by a will outside of it is heteronomous in this sense. Its autonomy is being violated. A will is heteronomous in the second sense when it is controlled by forces in the self other than reason—by inclination or what Kant calls "empirical" forces. In this sense of autonomy, it is something that admits of degree. A will can be more or less autonomous, and moral education aims to make the will more autonomous by training its bearer to direct itself by reason rather than by desire and outside influences. The duality in the ways a will can be heteronomous produces a paradox of education for autonomy that has nothing to do with education for virtue. The paradox here is that the will of the child starts out heteronomous because the child is dominated by desire and her will is largely disconnected from her developing reason. But to help her become a person whose will is directed by reason, she must be dominated by the will of adults during the time of her development. She must be heteronomous in one sense in order to learn autonomy. Direction from the outside weakens as the internal force of reason develops to the point that it can overcome desire.

One of my claims in this chapter is that moral development should not be understood on the model of the development of the faculty of reason rather than the development of the dispositions and faculties in human beings that track value. That includes the disposition to admiration and the emotion dispositions that are components of individual virtues. A morally mature person will not be dominated by desire in Kant's sense, but she also will not be the same as the person who can trot out a series of reasons supporting moral judgment, an ability that is probably neither necessary nor sufficient for moral virtue. It is not necessary if the most morally admirable persons often act without the ability to give their justifying reasons beyond the simplest and most obvious. Again, think of Leopold Socha, popping up from the underground sewer into the Chigers' cellar, and later telling Paulina, "I knew at that moment I would save you." It is not sufficient because the people with the most developed powers of reason are often far from being the most admirable in their character and in their actions. Developing the right emotions is a different task from developing reason. The exemplars we have looked at in this book have varying degrees of a developed faculty of reason, but they all have a strong sense that they are not buffeted about by passing desire. They are directed by a force within them, and they are autonomous if autonomy means being directed by something within them with which they most closely identify upon reflection. There are many ways in which people acquire the ability to be directed in that way. But if I am right that exemplars help us in acquiring the internal resources to overcome contingent desire in Kant's sense, that means that taking direction from the outside can aid us in acquiring autonomy. If so, virtue education is not a paradox. Instilling virtue is no harder than instilling autonomy, and presumably can be done in a similar way.[23]

5. Conclusion

Wherever there are human communities, there are people who are admired by the community. Admirable persons may be part of the community's lore—exemplars from the distant past—or they might be moral leaders, or courageous heroes, or saints who are not skilled in leadership, but who are recognized for their superb compassion or humility or self-sacrificing generosity. It is probably not necessary for either theoretical or practical purposes that these exemplars be perfect. If we map a domain of moral concepts around these persons, we can safely ignore their imperfections. This is not hard to do as long as we can recognize their imperfections as imperfections, and we can do that if we can trust our emotion of admiration to distinguish the aspects of their psyche that are admirable

---

23. A different model of moral improvement is proposed in an interesting paper by Victoria McGeer (2008). McGeer argues that people who trust and hope in us reflect back to us an ideal image of ourselves, and we strive to live up to it. This makes our personal exemplar a version of ourselves. Notice that the objection from autonomy would not even arise for this kind of model.

from those that are not. Emulation of exemplars also does not require perfection in the admired exemplar for the purposes of moral development. Granted, young children cannot yet distinguish the truly admirable from the dis-admirable and will sometimes emulate the wrong persons or the wrong qualities of the right persons, but as the child's moral sense develops, in part under the influence of exemplars, and her disposition to admiration becomes more refined, she becomes able to distinguish traits or acts that are not deserving of emulation in those same exemplars.

This means that even if no pure exemplar exists, exemplars can still serve both theoretical and practical purposes. Daniel Russell (2009) makes a similar point when he argues that virtue is a model concept. The concept we express by "the virtuous person," like the concept we express by "the rational person," is a normative ideal. The virtuous person sets the top end of the scale of virtuousness and "calibrates" the scale so as to give meaning to the idea of being virtuous to a certain degree (123). In my view, the virtuous person need not literally set the top end of the scale, but we can tell where the top end is by observing the exemplar. For admirability or virtue to be real, it is not necessary that it exist unmixed, in a pure form like Plato's Idea of the Good, uncontaminated by mortal human life. It is enough that we see reflections of perfection in persons not so different from ourselves. We might even prefer to emulate the excellent but imperfect. Perhaps we like them more.

Are there limits to the virtues we can acquire through emulation? We have seen that in Aristotelian ethics the supreme virtue is *phronesis*, or practical wisdom. In Confucian ethics it is *ren*. In Christian ethics it is charity. It is highly doubtful that we can get all the way to *phronesis* by emulating a *phronimos*, and similarly for the emulation of a sage or a Christian saint. If I am right that we can acquire both moral and intellectual virtues through emulation, then we can get partway to the goal of becoming like exemplars through emulation. But I think that the fact that we cannot acquire *phronesis* or *ren* or saintly charity by emulation has two interesting consequences. First, it means that exemplars are not simply stand-ins for abstract virtues whom we can ignore once we learn the virtues. We need exemplars all the time. They show us how much further we can go morally. Second, it is fortunate that we cannot become exactly like the exemplars because we would not want to be, nor would they want us to be. Think about how different one exemplar is from another, even if both of them have practical wisdom or both of them are saintly. One of the most important things that exemplars do was revealed in the studies by Colby and Damon (1992) and Kristen Renwick Monroe (2004). Exemplars have an integrated self, a self that harmonizes all aspects of their psyche. That is to say, they have integrity.

Some parts of the human psyche, such as beliefs, aim to fit something external to the mind. Other parts of the psyche are expressive of one's internal being. I have argued that an emotion has an external object, and it aims to fit that object. But emotions are partly expressive of the person who has them. We may all hope for the same thing in some general sense, but each of us has particular hopes that express the person we are most deeply, and the same thing can be said for many of our other emotions. Each virtue looks somewhat different in each person who possesses it, and I think this point is magnified when we get to the supreme virtues that connect most directly with the self's direction of itself. At some point in our moral development, we will do less emulating and more self-reflective management. The process is the same as that used by exemplars. In fact, it is the same process used by any self. Exemplars are just persons who do an especially good job of directing the self. Emulation of an exemplar does not exhaust the creation of a moral self, and emulation is not sufficient to become morally virtuous in the highest degree. But it is a good thing if we never lose track of who the exemplars are.

6

A Good Life

1. Introduction

There are three classes of exemplars that are the focus of this book: the hero, the saint, and the sage. Earlier I mentioned briefly that there might be other kinds of exemplars, but I believe that these three have special importance in the moral life. It is interesting that Max Scheler ([1933] 1987) included the master in the art of living as a type of exemplar, along with the hero, the saint, the genius, and the leading mind of a civilization. But he thought of the master in the art of living as the lowest level exemplar because he interpreted such a person as one who has mastered a way of reducing the values of the other exemplars into objects of enjoyment (196). This is disappointing because I would have thought that the master in the art of living is a person who has succeeded in living well to an extraordinary degree. I do not know if we can call living well an art since living well is generally the outcome of practicing something else; we would not normally say that someone is "practicing life." But we do think that some people have managed to integrate the many desirable features of life into a life that others would want to live. It would be perverse to want to live a life that is just like someone else's life in its particulars, but we do find whole lives desirable and whole lives admirable, and there are models of both.

We want to have models of good lives for both practical and theoretical reasons. For practical reasons, we want to have an idea of the kind of life to which we can aspire, and the kinds of lives worthy of being the goal of people to whom we are connected by family or community, or whose lives are affected by our financial choices and our choice of political leaders. There is also a theoretical reason that is one of the issues for this chapter: What is the connection between a good life in the sense of an *admirable* life or a life of virtue, and a good life in the sense of a *desirable* life, or a life of happiness or flourishing? Mapping the moral domain requires giving some account of what a good life is in both senses.

The Stoics thought that virtue is both necessary and sufficient for a flourishing life. If you are virtuous, you can always find a way to flourish, no matter what your circumstances. Other philosophers have demurred. Even the optimistic Aristotle thought that in addition to acting virtuously, a person needs a measure of good fortune for a happy or flourishing life—a life of *eudaimonia* (*NE* I.8–9). At least you need health, adequate means, the company of friends, and a city that is not constantly at war. But notice that for Aristotle, living virtuously is nearly sufficient for happiness. All you need in addition is a bit of luck. Philosophers in the modern period have had a more pessimistic view. Notoriously, Kant thought that in this life there is little connection at all between moral goodness and happiness, and I suspect that many ordinary people would agree.[1]

Eudaimonism, or the position that virtue is closely connected with flourishing, is hard to defend if we think of a flourishing life as constituted by a combination of things we naturally desire such as health, material comforts, love and friendship, and interesting pursuits, and we then raise the question: How is living virtuously connected with a life that has these elements? Such a question is unfair to the position that virtue is as much an element of flourishing as health and friendship. If virtue is a component of a flourishing life, it does not have to be a means to some *other* component of flourishing. Nonetheless, there is a strong motive to find a necessary connection between virtue and flourishing in the sense that everyone naturally desires. My conjecture on the source of this motive is that success in closely tying virtue with flourishing would have the potential to solve two important problems in meta-ethics: the problem of what grounds the moral, and the why-be-moral problem.

Modern moral philosophers typically assume that the moral needs grounding, whereas flourishing does not. If flourishing can be analyzed in a way that includes only non-evaluative elements of a thriving human animal, and if in addition, it can be shown that living virtuously is a condition for flourishing in this naturalistic sense, many philosophers would take that to be an advance in our understanding of the moral realm. Of

---

1. Kant's idea of moral goodness is not the same as living virtuously, and his idea of happiness is not identical to flourishing or Aristotelian *eudaimonia*. Nonetheless, I interpret Kant as addressing the same issue I am addressing here: the relation between a life that is admirable and a life that is desirable.

course, ancient philosophers never thought that moral judgments have any greater need for justification than judgments about human biology, but we live in naturalistic times, and it is now thought to be an advantage if human morality can be shown to have a necessary or law-like connection to thriving in a way that can be determined by ordinary observation and empirical science. If morality can be grounded in this way, its objectivity is assured, or so it can be argued.

Another motive for claiming there is a necessary connection between virtue and flourishing is the why-be-moral problem. Here the idea is that we take for granted that everyone desires to flourish, but not everyone desires to be virtuous. If we can show that virtue is a necessary condition for flourishing, and if we can demonstrate that to the non-virtuous person, we will have given her a motive to be moral, or at least, we will have shown her that she will want to be moral if she is rational.

It is very difficult to use the alleged necessary connection between virtue and flourishing as a way to solve either problem, and I think that it is unlikely that virtue is a necessary condition for flourishing in the intended sense anyway, although I am willing to let that issue be settled by further investigation. But I think that there *is* a close connection between the two senses of a good life. I do not claim that a desirable life is identical to the life lived by admirable persons, nor do I claim that an admirable life is a necessary condition for a desirable life. Instead, I propose that a desirable life is a life desired by admirable persons. Exemplars show us what desirable lives are by showing us what they desire. I believe that my proposal on the connection between exemplars and the desirable life can solve both the grounding problem and the why-be-moral problem without requiring the acceptance of controversial claims about the desirability of the lives admirable persons actually live. But I will also argue that there is a complex connection between the exemplar's desires and her flourishing because the degree of flourishing of an admirable person is not simply a matter of luck.

I said in earlier chapters that an important thing that we learn from exemplars is the variety of lives that are admirable. I think also that we learn from them the variety of lives that are desirable. All three of the exemplars I discussed in Chapter 3 show us ways in which a desirable life can be lived. In fact, two of them show us ways in which a life that starts out undesirable can become desirable through the virtuous actions of oneself or others. I think that modern, educated persons often have an excessively narrow view of what it takes to flourish, and I address that issue later in this chapter. In the last section I look at aspects of exemplary lives that do not pertain directly to acting virtuously, and offer some conjectures about how the desires of admirable persons can show us features of desirable lives outside the domain of moral choice. Living morally vastly under-determines the way a life is lived. If exemplars can show us features of desirable lives that moral philosophers generally ignore, that would be an advantage of exemplarism over other theories.

2. The Desirability and Admirability of Lives

2.1. The Desirability of Admirable Lives

In the *Nicomachean Ethics*, Aristotle wrote: "Those things are both valuable and pleasant which are such to the good man" (1176b25). My application of that remark is to say that those things are desirable which are such to the good person. A desirable life is one that a good person would desire. Of course, there are many desirable lives that many good persons do not desire because they do not simultaneously desire every desirable life, and in any case, they have not even thought of the possibility of most such lives. But a desirable life is a life that would be desired by good persons in circumstances that would make such a life a live option for them. I propose, then, that we add the following definition to the list I proposed in Chapter 4:

> A *desirable life* is a life desired by an admirable person. It is a life desired by persons like that.

This addition makes exemplars the standard for both the admirable life and the desirable life. The life lived by an admirable person is admirable. The test that it is admirable is that we admire it on reflection and continue to admire it when we get additional information about the exemplar's life and the responses of others whom we trust. If a desirable life is a life worthy of desire, and if the exemplar is the standard for what is worthy of desire, then the life desired by the admirable person is desirable. If different exemplars desire different kinds of lives—which is quite obviously true, then there are different kinds of lives that are desirable. If an admirable life is not sufficient for a desirable life, that is because the life an admirable person lives is not the same as the one she desires.

It might seem reasonable to assume that if the life an admirable person lives differs from the life she desires, that must be due to luck, or circumstances beyond the exemplar's control. However, I think that that is too simple an inference. Often when a virtuous person lacks some uncontroversial feature of a flourishing life such as health and enjoyment, it really *is* within her power to have health and enjoyment if she is willing to give up other things she desires. Living virtuously sometimes puts the aspects of life we naturally desire at risk. In fact, that is one of the reasons we admire exemplars. We see that they find something more important than health, long life, and comfortable circumstances, and we find that uplifting. Some admirable lives are extreme precisely because they involve the sacrifice of goods we naturally desire—sacrifices the exemplar could have predicted in advance. This is not yet to say that their lives are not desirable, but it is reason to look at some examples of admirable lives that seem to lack basic features of a desirable life.

L'Arche caregivers give up an ordinary life with the relationships and enjoyments that ordinary life affords. Nelson Mandela spent twenty-seven years in prison. Holocaust rescuers were in constant danger, and some of them were caught and shot. Confucius wandered about, sometimes facing physical suffering and starvation. He lost his son and his favorite student. Although his students adored him, many others mocked him. He never received the recognition he deserved in his lifetime, and he failed to fulfill his ambition to influence state affairs by serving in government. Few exemplars have it all, but some seem to have less than the minimum we expect in a desirable life, if we judge a desirable life by what people naturally desire.

Christine Swanton (2003, 82–83) presents a good test case of a life that is admirable but appears to be undesirable. She describes an aid worker in the jungle who suffers repeatedly from malaria and dysentery, is often exhausted and discouraged, does not have the comfort of religious belief, and dies prematurely. Swanton judges that the aid worker's life is admirable, but it is not flourishing. I agree with her that the aid worker is admirable; indeed, she might even be an exemplar. But on the face of it, her life is not desirable. On the assumption that nobody wants to become discouraged and die young, it is not a life she desires, and so it is not desirable on my definition above. But the fact that the aid worker does not have the life she desires is not simply a matter of bad luck. She fails to flourish in part because of the virtues that led her to undertake the project that produced discouragement and an early death. It is partly due to her own choices that she does not have the life she desires. That tells us something about the way the elements we naturally desire in a life are integrated with the aid worker's desire to act virtuously.

I think we need to admit that the way the aid worker lives her life is what she is motivated to do, all things considered. She quite clearly makes sacrifices, and we call sacrifices "sacrifices" because certain goods are given up voluntarily. However, the aid worker does what she wants to do, given that she finds herself in circumstances in which she cannot have everything she would desire if she could write the script of her life herself. Holocaust rescuers interviewed by Kristin Monroe (2004) said the same thing. Many of them told her that they had to do what they did, given their circumstances. One way to look at their situation is to use Julia Annas's distinction between the living of a life and the circumstances of one's life (2011, 92–93). As Annas sees it, the virtuous living of a life is not an ingredient in flourishing in addition to goods of circumstance—health, wealth, enjoyment, and so on. One's circumstances are the backdrop against which we ask the question, "What is a life lived well in those circumstances?" There are always going to be better and worse circumstances, and it is not helpful to point out that one would have been better off if one's circumstances had been more propitious for flourishing. Instead, we should think of a good life as a life lived well *in* one's circumstances.

I think this point can illuminate my way of understanding a desirable life. In looking at a person's life as a whole, we may find it admirable, and we may assume that the admirable person desires to live the way she lives, given her circumstances. If so, it is desirable to live admirably. I assume also that the admirable person desires the ordinary things people desire in the circumstances of a life—health, comfort, friends, and all the rest. But living admirably and having the things we naturally desire are connected to a desirable life in two different ways. There is a difference between forgoing virtuous actions, and forgoing comforts and health. If the admirable person chooses to forgo her admirable work, then by her own choice she misses out on key elements of what she regards as a desirable life, whereas if she pursues her admirable work, she misses out on elements of a desirable life because of circumstances she did not choose. From her point of view, her life is as desirable as she can make it, given her circumstances. There is an indirect connection between her choices and her lack of flourishing, but she does not choose to be discouraged and die prematurely. In contrast, choosing to lose her life of virtue is the only way she can lose it.

My position does not take a definite line on the Stoic thesis that an admirable life is sufficient for a desirable life. The admirable life may not have everything the exemplar desires, but the admirable life is closer to the desirable life than a life that has the standard components of a desirable life but lacks admirability. The exemplar's own verdict on his life is relevant here, and Philippa Foot gives a good example of that. She mentions some courageous men who wrote letters home shortly before their executions for opposing the Nazis (2001, 94–95). In these letters, they expressed regret that they would never see their families again, but no regret for their actions. Foot argues that there was a sense in which they sacrificed their own happiness, but another sense in which they did not since from their point of view, their lives would have been worse if they had not opposed the Nazis. But she also goes on to say that happiness might not have been possible for them.

An important Nazi resister whom Foot does not mention is Dietrich Bonhoeffer, who was imprisoned for participating in the plot to kill Hitler and was executed one month before the Nazi surrender. As Damon and Colby point out (2015, 49), Bonhoeffer's beautiful letters from prison influenced anti-communist movements in Eastern Europe during the Cold War, the civil rights movement, and the anti-apartheid movement in South Africa. Of course he could not know the effect his writings would have on subsequent history, but it seems to me that the desirability of his life was greatly enhanced by subsequent events.[2]

Swanton does not say whether her imaginary aid worker dies with regret for the way she lived her life, but the answer could easily be no. The anti-Nazi conspirators Foot mentions did not regret their lives. I also suspect that if the Holocaust rescuers interviewed by Monroe had been caught, they would not then regret their actions. They knew very well the risks they were taking, and did what they did anyway. But even when one does not regret one's life, one does not necessarily regard it as happy. Nonetheless, it might be a life that others would desire to live. "I would like to be the one who lived like that."

---

2. Aristotle raises the question of whether the fortunes of one's descendants and friends can affect one's happiness after death (*NE* I, Chapter 11). His answer seems to be that they do have some effect, but not of such a kind as to make the happy person unhappy or the unhappy person happy (*NE* 1101b 5–9). Presumably, then, he would not think that subsequent historical events could make an undesirable life desirable or a desirable life undesirable.

When I said that admirable persons desire admirable lives, I did not mean that admirable persons aim at being admirable. They aim at doing what is, in fact, admirable, and which others admire on reflection. But aiming to be admired is not an admirable aim. In fact, it is probably a dis-admirable aim. An interesting example of the unworthiness of the desire to be an exemplar appears in Robert Bolt's (1966) play, *A Man for All Seasons*. Thomas More's daughter, Margaret, visits him in the Tower of London and tries to convince him to sign the oath of allegiance to Henry VIII against his conscience. She says,

> In a State that was half good, you would be raised up high, not here, for what you've done already. It's not your fault the State is three-quarters bad. Then if you elect to suffer for it, you elect yourself a hero.

More replies:

> That's very neat. But look now . . . If we lived in a State where virtue was profitable, common sense would make us good, and greed would make us saintly. And we'd live like animals or angels in the happy land that needs no heroes. But since in fact we see that avarice, anger, envy, pride, sloth, lust and stupidity commonly profit far beyond humility, charity, fortitude, justice, and thought, and have to choose, to be human at all . . . why then perhaps we must stand fast a little—even at the risk of being heroes. (81)

More does not relish the idea that people will call him heroic, and he certainly does not aim at being a hero, but he will put up with heroism if necessary in order to do what the rest of us admire. I surmise that we do not admire people who seek to do the admirable *as such* because that is the aim to get a certain response from other people rather than the aim to do what virtuous persons aim to do. But it would be interesting to see empirical studies on whether and why people want to avoid being admired. One might expect admirable persons to be neutral on that issue, but it does not appear to be so.

If More is not aiming at being admirable, what is he aiming at? Robert Bolt says in the Preface to his play that he sees More as "a hero of selfhood" (xiii). Bolt's explanation for his motive in writing the play reveals a way in which an admirable life that ends tragically is more desirable than the many kinds of lives that are designed to prevent tragedy. Bolt says,

> Why do I take as my hero a man who brings about his own death because he can't put his hand on an old black book and tell an ordinary lie?
>
> For this reason: A man takes an oath only when he wants to commit himself quite exceptionally to the statement, when he wants to make an identity between the truth of it and his own virtue; he offers himself as a guarantee. And it works. There is a special kind of shrug for the perjurer; we feel that the man has no self to commit, no guarantee to offer....[W]e would prefer most men to guarantee their statements with, say, cash rather than with themselves. We feel—we know—the self to be an equivocal commodity. There are fewer and fewer things which, as they say, we "cannot bring ourselves to do." (xii)

Most of us design our lives in a way that eliminates the possibility of having to make a tragic choice. The failure to be committed to anything (or anyone) far enough to possibly cause us misery is one way to do that. As Bolt sees it, such a person lacks a self. Lacking a self cannot be desirable, even if it means avoiding early death. If so, there is a way in which Thomas More's life was more desirable than the lives of most of the people of his day and ours. It is desirable to be admirable, and it can be more desirable to be admirable than to have life, health, and ordinary enjoyments. But More's story is a tragedy because he *was* deprived of a desirable life, and he did not deserve that.

2.2. The Admirability of Desirable Lives

I have mentioned some examples of lives that are admirable but not wholly desirable. What about lives that are desirable but not wholly admirable? If a life is lacking in admirability, does that reduce its desirability? My former elderly neighbor enjoyed excellent health until she reached an advanced age. She had many friends and a close family. She was financially comfortable. She had social activities, and was engaged in community and church projects that brought her a lot of satisfaction. She had a wonderful marriage until her husband's death at ninety. She had no desire to travel and no knowledge of history, although she enjoyed reading. Her range of experience was almost entirely limited to central Oklahoma and parts of Texas. Her satisfaction with life was very high. She was neighborly, generous with her time, honest, sincere, kind, and responsible. She was also racist. Her racism was rarely expressed, as far as I could tell, because she rarely interacted with persons of other races, but a few times I heard her make inflammatory remarks about Latinos, and I suspect she did not have a very positive attitude toward some other ethnic groups either. Ironically (but perhaps unsurprisingly), she was very close to a Hispanic neighbor whom she treated like a son, and she did not seem to notice any incongruity between her attitude toward him and her attitude toward Hispanics in general.

It seems to me that her life was less admirable than it would have been if she had not been biased against persons outside her own ethnic group. But did she live a flourishing life, a life that is desirable? If we say no, we would have to say that the lives of most of the people in the history of the world were undesirable, even if they had all the virtues necessary in small homogeneous communities in addition to health, friendship, and the other natural goods. Perhaps we should say that xenophobia does not reduce the desirability of one's life except in certain circumstances. If a person spends her entire life with people in her own ethnic group, any hostility toward outsiders never leads to conflict, at least not directly. Her own flourishing no doubt depends on the flourishing of her community, but it is also possible that nothing happens that reduces the flourishing of her community due to her attitudes and the attitudes of people around her. It would seem, then, that her life is flourishing. She has a desirable life, and the fact that her life is less admirable than it would be without her racist attitudes does not make it less desirable.

However, on my definition of a desirable life, her life *is* less desirable because the admirable is desirable. Since she lacked an element of admirability, she lacked an element of desirability. My neighbor was an admirable person in many ways, enough ways to apply to most of the conditions of her life, and she desired the life she led. So her life was desirable, but I think not completely so.

I am sure that different readers will have different reactions to my neighbor, but it seems to me that the type of eudaimonist philosopher who thinks that virtue is a means to the things we naturally desire in a life will have a hard time explaining why something desirable might be missing from my neighbor's life. Of course, some readers will say that nothing desirable is missing, but if something desirable *is* missing, that must be because the admirable is desirable. But it is hard to explain that if the desirable is determined in advance of the admirable. If instead, the admirable is determined in advance of the desirable, as I propose, it is easy to show why my elderly friend's life was missing something desirable.

In the *Summa Theologiae* Aquinas says, "The most complete good absolutely must be what one with well-disposed affections desires for his ultimate end" (*Treatise on Happiness* I-II, q. 1 a 7, corpus) (1983). What is completely desirable in a life is what is desired by a person with the right affections. I am happy with that definition, but I have made it more concrete by picking out a set of persons whom we have most reason to believe have the right affections—the exemplars. I am leaving the substance of what these persons desire open, although I assume that in addition to desiring to act virtuously, they desire the ordinary goods of life, with the qualifications I have given. Aquinas thought that our ultimate good is the Beatific Vision, and many exemplars are religious persons who desire an end beyond this life. Exemplarism can easily incorporate research into desire for the transcendent among admirable persons. Fortunately, there is work on that already in the wisdom research literature (e.g., Levinson et al. 2005). As I mentioned in Chapter 3, self-transcendence is one of the defining features of wisdom used in scales such as the Brief Wisdom Screening Scale (BWSS). Damon and Colby (2015, 175) say that the six moral leaders they investigated, like the twenty-three they examined in their earlier study, experienced their faith as a source of serenity and courage in the face of extreme circumstances, danger, and death. Their faith gave them a way to transform suffering into something more satisfying than they would have desired without the suffering. It is hard for someone on the outside to see what a life is like on the inside, which often includes inner joys as well as inner suffering, and the joys sometimes arise from the suffering. As Nelson Mandela said, "Indeed, the chains of the body are often wings to the spirit" (Damon and Colby 2015, 175).

3. The Grounding Problem

Philosophers following Aristotle have attempted to make flourishing or *eudaimonia*, the foundational concept in ethical theory, in relation to which we are to understand what a virtue is and what the individual virtues are. Aristotle says at the beginning of the *Nicomachean Ethics* that *eudaimonia* is the final end for human beings. Everyone desires it, but there is considerable controversy about the content of such a life. Neo-Aristotelians like Rosalind Hursthouse (1999) have attempted to fill out the idea of a flourishing human being in a way that makes an investigation of human flourishing a naturalistic project on a par with an investigation of the flourishing of plants and animals. If that can be done successfully, and if it can be shown that the traits on standard lists of the virtues are means to leading such a life, the virtues will have been justified. If, in addition, it can be shown that the right thing to do can be explained in terms of virtue or directly in terms of acts that lead to flourishing, morality will have been justified naturalistically. Hursthouse has done a remarkable job of exploring such a project and taking it as far as anyone else has. I am not opposed to a project like hers. As I have said, I think there is more than one good ethical theory anyway. But I think that making exemplars foundational permits a different kind of naturalistic approach to ethics that has advantages over making the foundation a desirable life.

There is a straightforward sense in which exemplarism is naturalistic given that all major moral concepts are grounded in a set of persons identified through a natural human emotion. The theory is also naturalistic in that most of its elements are determined by observation. However, I do not have any particular desire to defend naturalism in ethics and will leave it to others to discuss the naturalism of exemplarism. As I have said, a major advantage of the theory is that the foundation is not a concept. A foundational concept does not have to be explained, nor do any substantive issues about human nature, human flourishing, human desires, ends, rationality, or the particular virtues have to be settled in advance. Moral theories usually give an enormous amount of attention to some of these concepts before the theory gets to the level of addressing anything specific about human life and providing action guidance. The theory must do that because the theory is grounded in complex and controversial concepts. In contrast, the grounding problem has a straightforward solution if the features of exemplars can serve the purposes I am describing in this book.

Grounding morality in the admirable rather than the desirable may have another advantage. It seems to me that admiration is more trustworthy than desire. That is, there is a smaller gap between admiration and the admirable than between desire and the desirable. I argued in

Chapter 2 that the fact that we admire x and continue to do so on reflection is a reason to judge that x is admirable. The reason may subsequently be defeated, but admiration for x that survives reflection is
reason to judge that x is admirable. Admiration is responsive to reflection
about the object because admiration has cognitive content. In a state of
admiration we see the object *as admirable*. When we look more closely
at the object and discover something dis-admirable about it, the admiration either decreases or the intentional object changes. For instance,
I admire Oskar Schindler when I see him perform heroic acts, but when
I see some of his other behaviors, the object of my admiration narrows.
I either admire him less overall, or I admire him only in a certain respect.
So admiration is responsive to my further observations and reflections.
In contrast, desire is not very responsive to reflection and I suspect that
that is because the state of desire lacks the cognitive content of states of
emotion. So we often desire what we judge on reflection to be undesirable, and continue to desire it even while judging it as undesirable. We do
not think that the fact that we desire x is a very good reason to think that
x is desirable for us, whereas we do think that the fact that we admire x is
a reason to think that x is admirable.

Even if I am right about this point, it does not mean that it is not a
good idea to have a theory based on the desirable. But it means that our
way of telling what is desirable is not very close to our experience of desire.
The content of the desirable needs to be filled out with something else
that is the real ground of the theory, usually human nature. We do not
have to do something comparable with the admirable. If I am right that
reflectively endorsed admiration grounds our identification of the admirable, and if admirable persons can ground the network of ethical concepts
I have described, then admiration grounds morality without requiring
disputed claims about the necessary connection between living virtuously
and having a desirable life. Morality can be grounded in a natural human
emotion.

The sense in which admiration grounds morality in exemplarism differs from the sense in which Kant thinks that morality is grounded in the
rational will, or Mill thinks that morality is grounded in pleasure, and it
differs from the sense in which Aristotle thinks that morality is grounded
in human nature. When I say that admiration is a "ground" in the map
I am drawing, I mean that we can show that our moral beliefs and practices can be derived from admiration in the way I describe. I do not mean
that they *must* be derived in this way. As I see it, all the grounding problem

requires of us is to find at least one way in which we can justify morality from something non-moral that we take to be more basic. Exemplarism gives us a new way to do that.

4. Why Be Moral?

In the *Republic* (Book II), Plato poses the deepest of all moral problems: Why should I be moral? This problem is sometimes an embarrassment to philosophers because if there is a solution to it, it is not one that links knowledge of moral philosophy with the motive to be moral. Moral philosophers are not known for their fine moral lives; at least, they are no better than the average person who has never studied moral theory. Philosophers have an advantage in moral reasoning, and fortunately, that is something we can teach in ethics classes, but it is sometimes difficult to identify the point at which reasoning begins, and even when reasoning yields a clear moral judgment, there is still the problem that the motive to act on the judgment may be missing.

Exemplarism is a theory in which a motivating state is at the foundation of the theory. If a non-virtuous person admires an exemplar, she will feel an attraction that gives her a motive to imitate the virtuous life. There *is* a motive to be moral in the natural emotion of admiration, so the problem that morality does not hook onto our motivational structure has a solution if I am right that admiration grounds the moral and the object of admiration attracts us.

But exemplarism does not guarantee that admiration will make us want to be moral when doing so conflicts with obtaining such goods of life as friendship, health, long life, and freedom from suffering. Admiration gives a person the motive to be moral in the ordinary way, but what gives people the motive to be exceptionally virtuous like Jean Vanier, or the Holocaust rescuers, or Mother Teresa, or Swanton's aid worker? It is not enough to see that a life of sacrifice is desirable from the point of view of the exemplar since the real question for us is whether to adopt the point of view of the exemplar. I think this problem arises for Foot in her discussion of the men who were executed for opposing the Nazis. She proposes that there is a sense in which they were happy because they did not regret their actions, but the claim that they were happy depends on seeing their lives from their own point of view. Nelson Mandela spent many years in prison and tells us that the chains of the body can give wings to the spirit, but someone who reads these words might reasonably worry that if *his* body had chains, that would not give his spirit wings. Seeing that others are satisfied with lives we admire does not by itself give us a motive to imitate them. If their lives were happy only from a point of view we do not already have, then the natural response will be to say, "Well, I admire these people's ability to sacrifice their lives and not regret it, but I'm afraid that if *I* did what they did, I *would* regret it."

Emulation of superb virtue requires taking the point of view of the exemplar. Narratives permit us to adopt the viewpoint of others in imagination as a way to test how we would respond to incorporating elements of other lives into the narrative of our own lives. Each of us has a story that we can enhance by imaginatively adopting and discarding a multitude of other points of view. For most people, emulating exemplars is not likely to result in imitating their extraordinary moral achievements, but as long as the admirable qualities of exemplars admit of degree, emulating them can make us more virtuous than we would be otherwise. It is very hard to know our own moral capacities without models of supreme moral accomplishment, and admiration for the most admirable does motivate us to become more virtuous.

In this chapter I have brought up the why-be-moral problem because of its connection with the ancient and influential eudaimonist view that we can explain moral virtue in terms of its connection with living a flourishing life. Philosophers since the ancient Greeks have tried very hard to persuade themselves and others to live a virtuous life on the grounds that they would thereby gain, or have a good chance of gaining, what they desire in a life. I have argued here that even though I am sympathetic with that viewpoint, I find it hard to defend. If the primary motives for eudaimonism can be satisfied without the claim that living admirably leads to other things we desire, we need not try so hard to defend eudaimonism. Since I think we can get solutions to both the grounding problem and the why-be-moral problem in an exemplarist framework, it is not necessary to focus so much attention on debating the eudaimonist thesis. In any case, it seems to me that the obsession with eudaimonism has led to the neglect of other interesting issues about desirable lives that have nothing to do with their admirability. In particular, I think it is worth looking at the wide variety of desirable lives, and the many features of desirable lives that are not determined by their moral properties. If we set aside eudaimonism in our inquiry about desirable lives, there are many things we can discover about what makes a person flourish.

5. The Varieties of Desirable Lives

Who lives a flourishing life? There are people who spend their whole lives on a houseboat on the Yangtze River. Can they flourish? What about people who lived before the era of technology, modern medicine, and widespread education? Did none of them flourish? I am accustomed to living among people who think that it is very important to travel the world, to eat the best food any culture has ever produced, and to read the best literature. We pity the people who have never read Plato or listened to Beethoven, and whose lives mostly involve manual labor. We take for granted that every medical complaint can and should be treated immediately. We assume that we can communicate easily with anybody anywhere in the world. Since we are university professors, we champion a college education on the grounds that it enables our students to live a more flourishing life. Are we right to do all of that? I would not say we are wrong, but surely the kind of "good life" I have described is optional. Staying in one place enhances human relationships. Always eating food in the same cuisine fosters culture in a sense that most educated persons have given up. Education opens the mind, but it weakens attachment to one's origins. St. Benedict made stability one of the three central vows of his monastic communities. As an anonymous hermit in Egypt said long before Benedict, "A tree cannot bear fruit if it is often transplanted" (Ward 2003, 72).[3] Stability is necessary for spiritual growth. A life of movement is more adventuresome, but someone who travels out of restlessness lacks inner peace. There is more than one way to flourish. The Buddha probably led a more flourishing life because of his travels, but St. Benedict flourished because he stayed put. We sometimes romanticize the wanderer who has the kind of freedom that comes from lack of attachment, but unless the wandering ends, the story does not usually end well.

In the next four subsections I will look at some examples of lives that I think can be desirable even though they do not meet the usual expectations of a desirable life. In each case my hypothesis is that narratives and studies of exemplars aid the philosophical imagination by showing us the varieties of desirable lives.

---

3. In his Rule, St. Benedict criticizes the types of monks he calls Gyrovagues, who "spend their whole lives tramping from province to province, staying as guests in different monasteries for three or four days at a time. Always on the move, with no stability, they indulge their own wills" (Chapter 1). In contrast, Benedict says the best kinds of monks are Cenobites, who live in monasteries and serve under a rule and an abbot.

5.1. L'Arche: The Flourishing of Dependent Persons

Kevin Reimer writes that the disabled core members of the L'Arche communities he visited can have flourishing lives even though they lack some of the basic goods. Nobody thought that the men Jean Vanier took out of an institution to live in L'Arche were good for anything. They had all the normal human needs for health, friendship, enjoyments, interesting work and play, knowledge of the world as far as they could get it, and the development of their talents, but Vanier was virtually alone in his belief in their capacity to fulfill these needs, to grow and to mature into full adulthood, and to make a contribution to society. Vanier said, "If people with developmental disabilities are given a good human situation in which to live and are sustained by loving relationships, they are capable of progressing in an astonishing way on the psychological, human, and spiritual planes" (Clarke 2006, 40). With the help of outside professionals, volunteers in L'Arche communities train the core members to be responsible, and within their abilities, to develop virtues. L'Arche volunteers cannot make other persons happy, but they go a long way toward providing the conditions for their happiness.

The L'Arche communities exemplify Alasdair MacIntyre's point in *Dependent Rational Animals* (1999) that no one can live a flourishing life on his own. All of us are disabled in some ways, and L'Arche communities simply make this feature of all human lives especially vivid. The communities started by Jean Vanier are consciously based on interdependent relationships. For Aristotelians, flourishing requires actualizing the potentialities of the species, but it seems to me that the capacities of the human species take a different form in each individual that determines what flourishing is for each of us. If so, the mentally disabled can live flourishing lives. But clearly, our society is organized around people with normal abilities. It is very hard to get along in many places without abilities that disabled persons do not have, such as the ability to drive a car. The disabled cannot drive themselves to the store or to a party, but they need provisions and they can enjoy the party. We all need the help of others (I cannot drive myself around Rome either). Mentally disabled persons need friends and relationships as much as anyone else, but there needs to be a structure through which these relationships can be developed and sustained.

One of the most interesting observations Kevin Reimer makes from his L'Arche visits is the extent of the vulnerability of the caregivers. As

I mentioned in Chapter 3, Reimer found that long-term L'Arche assistants have often suffered in their own development and life experiences, and many battle depression. Since the disabled core members have suffered deeply, caregivers often told Reimer that a core member was a catalyst for a redemptive process by which the caregivers found meaning in their own lives. The relationship between the assistants and the core participants is a good example of networks of giving and receiving described by MacIntyre, and discussed in Chapter 4. Assistants take the lead in helping core members achieve a desirable life, and under the inspiration of the core members, the assistants are also able to achieve a more flourishing life. However, I think that Reimer's discoveries about L'Arche assistants show us another feature of a flourishing life. Sometimes aiming at flourishing for oneself is not the best way to achieve it. One of the many gifts we get from the L'Arche communities is a view of how a life can be desirable when the person living the life does not think about its level of desirability, and perhaps especially when he does not think about it. There is such a thing as excessive reflection on the desirability of one's own life, and I hope that this chapter does not contribute to a neurotic concern about one's level of flourishing. I mention the flourishing of the members of L'Arche communities as a way to suggest that the model of flourishing that dominates most of us in an educational environment in an advanced industrialized country is excessively narrow. If others are like me, I suspect that we need to loosen up our image of what is desirable in life. It is not only exemplars who can show us a desirable life, but also exemplary communities, like L'Arche, whose core members flourish because of the structure created by other persons. These communities might also serve as the basis for investigation of exemplary communities and lead to projects using exemplarism in social and political philosophy.

5.2. Confucius and the Life of the Sage

Confucius was a different kind of exemplar—blessed with high intelligence and competence, a natural leader, a master of the proprieties, the possessor of profound insight into the human condition. He was an exemplar for the ages. The *Analects* shows the pleasures of his life, his disappointments, his close companionship with others, his aesthetic sensibility, the wisdom of his advice, and many details of his life that allow us to see, as Olberding remarks, why he would desire the life he had even when it cost him much

(2012, 65). Confucius shows us a way in which a person can flourish, but Olberding argues that there is no evidence that the *Analects* intends to portray the life of Confucius as an image of *human* flourishing (59). Confucius flourishes in a quite different way from the hero or the saint, and in a very different way from the ordinary person, even the ordinary person of his day and place. But I think that the way Confucius flourished is very important for us to study because his life is another one that is much at odds with contemporary values.

Each of the exemplars I have chosen as special exhibits gives us a different model of flourishing. Leopold Socha shows us the importance of courage, steadfastness, and hope to remake one's life when it has gone wrong. Jean Vanier shows us the joy of self-giving, and the way our personal flourishing depends on communities of interdependence. But Confucius shows us the importance of intellectual competence, perceptiveness, a high aesthetic sense, and the lost virtue of civility. Confucius was one of those persons whose special form of charisma was the glow of serenity. Stephen Angle (2009) identifies harmony as the ideal we see in the sage, and he argues that the sage is a regulative ideal that needs to be recaptured. As I mentioned at the end of Chapter 3, the sage seems to be a disappearing species. There are so few wise persons around, we are even losing the concept of wisdom. I think that Angle is right that the harmonious life achieved by wise persons is one of the types of desirable lives that deserves more attention from scholars and ordinary people. It is true that narratives of sages are not generally entertaining enough to be made into popular movies, but it would be a great advantage if the sagely ideal was able to work its way into public consciousness.

I think there are many reasons that the sage has no recognition or standing in modern Western cultures. An obvious one is that our culture values youthfulness more than wisdom. An elderly person who still looks young is admired more than an elderly person who looks elderly and who also has a font of reflective life experience with the features of wisdom mentioned in Chapter 3. On the other hand, I identify with John Updike when he said, "Now that I am sixty, I see why the idea of elder wisdom has passed from currency" (*New Yorker*, November 1992). Age is no guarantee of wisdom, and it is particularly important to identify young people with wisdom because of their influence on their peers. This might mean that calling a wise person "a sage" is misleading. We need sages who remind us of Confucius, but we also need to identify many young wise persons. The wisdom nominees in the study by Glück et al. (2013) ranged in age from twenty-six to ninety-two. The purpose of that study was to identify the components of wisdom, not to study the lives of the nominees, but I think it would be helpful to see the many ways in which wise persons live their lives. I suspect that both the commonalities and the differences will be revealing.

5.3. Leopold Socha: Atonement as a Way to Flourish

Is flourishing always a possibility, or can it be irrevocably lost? Suppose a person committed a horrific crime, like Dostoyevsky's Raskolnikov? Can anything make his life good? What about a man like Leopold Socha, who for some years had been a petty thief, with little sense of responsibility and not much accomplishment? Ignacy Chiger wrote in his diary that Socha told them that hiding the Jews was his mission, that he was doing it to atone (Marshall 1990, 132). I do not know what atonement meant to him and what, exactly, he thought he was atoning *for*, but I propose that atonement is what a person who has sinned against someone needs for flourishing. His sin is offensive to the person he has wronged, and in traditional Christian theology, it is also offensive to God. Atonement puts him back into a good relationship with the wronged person. Having good relationships is critical for flourishing. The deeper the relationship and the more serious the offense, the greater the atonement must be.

Socha truly cared about the people he was hiding as persons, not only as victims of the Nazis. When one died, Socha and his friend buried him. When a woman secretly gave birth and smothered her child, Leopold buried the child. When there was a flash flood, Socha swam to the spot where he had left the people, terrified that they had perished. These acts of burying the dead with dignity and protecting the hidden Jews from anything that would threaten their safety are acts of love. For Socha, love was atoning and it gave his life purpose. His life is inspirational for us when we have taken a wrong turn in our own lives.

Flourishing has much to do with a sense of self in which there is a connection among one's life activities. We do not have a record of Socha's story of his own life, but he apparently thought that there was a connection between his previous life and the life he lived after he found the Jews. If Socha lived a desirable life, it is partly because it is desirable to be admirable, and it is partly because a desirable life has meaning that connects the parts into a single story whose best interpretation is seen from the inside. But if it was wholly from the inside, we would not be able to recognize its desirability.

In 1946, Socha was killed on the street by a Soviet truck, and the Chigers and others of the group who were still in Poland took the train to Gliwice for the funeral. Many friends and family gathered at the Socha home afterward. It was reported that during the gathering, someone shouted from the back of the crowded room, "This is God's retribution. This is what comes of helping the Jews" (Marshall 1990, 195; also mentioned in Chiger 2008). Most of us look at the story of Socha and see a heroic man who died tragically in harmony with himself and with God, but as long as there are people who see with vicious eyes, the story of a good life can sometimes be interpreted as the story of a bad life that deserves to end in violent death. There is no guarantee that telling the story is enough to get everyone to see the desirable.

A famous story that aims to show that there is always hope for a life until the very end is Tolstoy's *The Death of Ivan Ilych* (2014). Ilych's life lacks admirability, but in an ordinary way. He finally discovers what it is to love on his deathbed, and ends his life in joy. Does he have a desirable life? I find it hard to say so, although Tolstoy seems to suggest that his entire past life is rectified in the last moments. If so, a life can be almost totally lacking in admirability and still be desirable. It is hard for me to believe that an admirable person would desire to live Ivan Ilych's life, but almost anybody, admirable or not, would be happy to have his final moments.[4] In contrast, Leopold Socha did much more than end his life with the brief feeling of love. He spent fourteen months taking great personal risks for the sake of helping people whom he came to love for much longer than a fleeting moment. What makes Socha's story even more amazing is that he seems to have begun with the same knee-jerk anti-Semitic attitude of the people around him, and then, within a very short time, began to love those same people. In Socha's story we see a continuous evolution from a life of irresponsibility and petty crime to love and astonishing courage in protecting the very people he once would have despised. Socha's life is a triumph of the human ability to rise above the forces that weaken us morally. It seems to me, then, that even if Tolstoy is right that it is never too late to redeem a life, some redeemed lives are much better than others.

---

4. See Robert C. Roberts (2007, Chapter 5, "The Salvation of Ivan Ilych") for an interesting commentary on this story.

5.4. Flaubert's Félicité

In his masterful novella, *A Simple Heart* (2009), Gustave Flaubert tells us the story of Félicité, a poor woman with a simple mind and a simple heart, who spends her whole life working as a maid. Félicité loses everyone she loves. She is orphaned. The boy she loved in her youth marries another woman. Her adored nephew goes to sea and dies in a faraway land. She devotes herself to the son and daughter of her cold and distant mistress, but the little girl dies, and the son goes off and forgets her. The pet parrot of her old age, in whom she invests all the significance of her love of God, dies also. She does not even get ordinary human respect. Near the end of her life she goes deaf, and one day while walking along a road, she cannot hear the shouts of an approaching driver who whips her with his lash as he goes by because she obstructed his path. Her joys come from the simplest pleasures of domestic life and her religious observances. When she dies, her death goes unnoticed.

Flaubert puts Félicité in circumstances that seem insurmountable, and then does the seemingly impossible: he gives Félicité a good life. Part of what makes Félicité a happy person is that she never feels conflict. I believe that is because she does not have the knowledge of good and evil. She is redeemed, but she does not know what that means because she never knew a Fall from grace. It's as if Original Sin somehow passed her by. She does not know what sin is, and so she does not see sin in others. When she falls and is whipped by the passing driver, she is temporarily reminded of all the sorrows of her life, but she is not harmed by the experience. She suffers, but evil does not damage her. As I read the story, she is lifted above the experience of evil, floating in a world filled with grace. At death she sees a beautiful parrot with widespread wings, perhaps symbolizing the Holy Spirit.

It is because of Flaubert's genius that Félicité is a believable person,[5] but her happiness seems above the lot of natural life. Her goodness is also. She has ordinary virtues, but what is truly astonishing about her is the degree to which she has the virtues Aquinas says are supernaturally infused—faith, hope, and love (*ST* I–II q. 62). She is one of the purest cases I can think of in fact or fiction in which there is a clear and direct connection between her happiness and her virtues. But her kind of life is not imitable for the rest of us because to recognize Félicité as

---

5. Flaubert says he modeled Félicité on Julie, a housemaid his family had in his home when he was a child.

an exemplar, one must already be a different kind of person. Félicité is a true innocent, and to recognize innocence is to have already lost it. But although a reflective person cannot be like Félicité, understanding her helps us to appreciate that she is not pitiable, and the disabled persons in L'Arche communities are not pitiable either.

My conclusion from the last few sections of this chapter is that eudaimonism is not helpful in telling us how to live a desirable life. Even though I am neutral on the disputed claim that living virtuously gives us the best chance for living a desirable life, I do not think it is illuminating to insist on it, nor do I think that it is very important. In previous sections I argued that eudaimonism is not needed to solve either the grounding problem or the why-be-moral problem, and in this section I have argued that there are so many varieties of desirable lives that there is no single life at which we should aim if we want to flourish. I think it is also important that virtually none of the people who live flourishing lives aimed at flourishing for themselves. Aiming at living virtuously as a strategy for living a desirable life is not a good idea.

6. What Values Can We Learn from Exemplars?

Exemplars differ from each other in many ways. Some of the exemplars we have looked at are extreme in their style of life, but even if we consider only persons whose lives are admirable yet ordinary, like the many good people who are known only to a small number of family and friends, we see a wide variety of desirable lives. Each person has a design of life that dictates a particular balance of time spent on different activities, and there are many variations in those designs. Exemplary lives may be alike in being moral, but I don't think we should conclude that since there are lots of different desirable lives, it does not matter what we do in addition to being moral. It matters a lot. It matters because of the connection between what we do and a life plan in which personal values and goals are integrated with moral commitments. A person with no goals or personal values does not lead a desirable life.

This is another reason eudaimonism does not help us much if we want to live a desirable life. To be told to live admirably is to be told very little about how to design a life pattern. Even assuming that we understand how to act virtuously and are motivated to do so, acting virtuously is not a goal that tells us what to do today or this year. Narratives of exemplars reveal the pattern of their lives as well as features of these individuals that cannot be easily categorized as traits of character or virtuous acts. We find out what they care about; what, if anything, they worry about; how important money is to them; how they balance their time spent at home and at work; how many children they are willing to have; how important beauty is to them; whether they think it important to work hard for their health; how they cultivate friendships; whether they practice a religion; how they react to being given more than they deserve or less than they deserve; how they respond to illness; how they react when other people envy them, or show disrespect, or express gratitude toward them, or admire them. All of these features of a person ought to have a place in our map of the moral. These features may not be what ethicists usually consider core moral matters, but they make a big difference to the kind of life a person lives, and if ethics ought to address the features of a desirable life, ethics ought to give attention to these features.

One feature that appears repeatedly in narratives of the lives of exemplars is ego integrity. One sense of ego integrity is described by Eric Erickson (1959) in his well-known stages of psychosocial development. He lists "ego integrity" as the challenge for the last stage of life. People in that stage of life reflect on their lives and assess them. They may render a positive or a negative verdict, and the danger for that period of life is despair. The kind of ego integrity Erickson is talking about is important; however, there is another kind that is not a judgment on one's life that one makes in one's later years, but a desire to have a consistency and continuity of ego that consciously integrates one's past self into one's present and future self and where one's beliefs, desires, values, and overt behavior are harmonious. Exemplars exhibit that kind of integrity. To get it, exemplars often resist cultural forces that would push them along in ways determined by other people. It seems to me that there is an important way in which exemplars do not change (e.g., Confucius, Jean Vanier, Nelson Mandela, Dietrich Bonhoeffer), or if they change, they change in a way that is self-directed (e.g., Leopold Socha). In Chapter 3, I noted the open-mindedness of wise persons (e.g., Glück et al. 2013), which makes them flexible, yet they do not passively accept of the flow of contingent forces in their culture. I am not suggesting that exemplars are necessarily countercultural, although I understand why David Brooks says that to live a decent life these days we have to join a counterculture that resists the achievement ethos (2015, 260). In that book Brooks tells stories of a series of admirable persons who would be considered countercultural if they were alive today: Dorothy Day, Dwight Eisenhower, Dr. Samuel

Johnson, George Eliot, George Marshall, Michel de Montaigne, Frances Perkins, Franklin Roosevelt, and others. These people have a strong sense of self that continues throughout the circumstances of their lives, giving them "iron in their core" (xiii), as Brooks puts it. These exemplars and the others I have discussed show us particularly effective ways of achieving ego integrity, whether or not the surrounding culture is cooperative.[6]

The feature of ego integrity and the features of exemplars I mentioned in the previous paragraph are components of a desirable life, but they are not virtues, at least not in the traditional sense, and they do not fall into any of the standard categories of moral evaluation. They are features we discover through narratives of lives, including the lives of fictional characters.[7] Unfortunately, philosophical ethics has traditionally neglected the importance of one's life story, or alternatively, has in recent decades associated narrative ethics with "anti-theory."[8] I hope that my project shows that it is possible to construct a kind of theory that has an important place for narratives while remaining a theory in the traditional sense.

One of the most significant features of the lives of exemplars is their sense of purpose, something that may come to them gradually, as happened to Jean Vanier, or all at once, as apparently happened with Leopold Socha. Damon and Colby (2015) in particular focus on the way the exemplars they describe acquired a sense of purpose in their lives.[9] Most of them found purpose through their striving for something of ultimate

---

6. The theme of Brooks (2015) is that there are two sides of human nature. What he calls Adam I is a shrewd player of the economic game, aims at success and spends a lot of time cultivating professional skills, but without a clear sense of life's meaning. Adam II is the inner person of moral character, who develops humility and wisdom, and understands that to live a life with meaning is to live by moral logic, not the logic of economic man (Introduction, xi–xiv). Brooks's examples are all persons he calls Adam II.

7. A fictionalized example is Herman Hesse's *Siddhartha* (1951). His life is full of contradictory, seemingly mutually exclusive phases. He is an extreme ascetic and then a devoted apprentice to a voluptuary. He is poor for a time, and then highly successful in business. He is prominent in the community, and then later he is the provider of a humble service— ferrying people across a river. He sees all at once, at the end of his life, and we see with him, how these disparate chapters had a single organizing principle and fit together into one majestic life.

8. A prominent exponent of the narratively enriched anti-theory approach is Bernard Williams (1973). Many works on anti-theory followed.

9. William Damon (2009) has also done extensive research on how adolescents struggle to find purpose in life. In his recent work he is exploring ideas on purpose for their relevance to education, the understanding of human development, and the future of American society.

concern, such as a passionate commitment to moral principles like justice or compassion, and a vivid sense of unity with humanity, with nature, or with God.[10]

When we study exemplars, we can also discover what they value in civil society. An interesting possibility is that we might get a way to test Jonathan Haidt's thesis in *The Righteous Mind* (2012) that there are distinct modes of value that affect moral and political positions: loyalty/betrayal, authority/subversion, sanctity/degradation, fairness/cheating, liberty/oppression, in addition to care/harm, and equality/inequality. Most human beings are sensitive to all these evaluative dimensions, but Haidt argues that people he calls WEIRD (Western, educated, industrialized, rich, and democratic) think differently from most of the people in the world because they respond almost exclusively to the last two dimensions (96). Haidt's hypothesis is that conservatives and liberals have trouble talking to each other when conservatives are responding to values of sanctity or authority or liberty, whereas liberals are reacting only to the dimensions of harm and inequality. I do not know whether a difference in the response to these value dimensions is responsible for political disagreement, but it would be interesting to find out whether exemplars are sensitive to these values. Clearly, Confucius was sensitive to dimensions of loyalty/betrayal, sanctity/degradation, authority/subversion, and fairness/cheating, as well as the dimension of care/harm, but few persons before the modern era cared about equality/inequality, and the dimension of liberty/oppression went through a long evolution. I surmise that some modern exemplars are WEIRD, but some are not. Maybe people have become WEIRD because their exemplars are WEIRD, but perhaps instead, once people become WEIRD, they only recognize as exemplars persons who have WEIRD values. In any case, it would be illuminating to test responses to different value dimensions among the most admirable persons. These features of exemplars differ from their personal traits, but they are important in showing us what is valuable in civil society. It might also help to move a society in the direction of consensus. People are not likely to come to an agreement about values such as loyalty, authority, or reverence for the sacred by arguing it out. But we are moved by admirable persons and the values they cherish, especially as we see the way these values shape a plan of life and a vision for our collective lives.

---

10. See Emmons (1999), and the discussion of his research on ultimate concerns in Damon and Colby (2015, 156–160).

In this chapter I have drawn another piece of my map, linking an admirable life with a desirable life. My proposal is that a desirable life is a life desired by admirable persons. It may not coincide with the life an admirable person actually lives because of circumstances beyond the person's control, but even in dreadful circumstances, an admirable life is more desirable than a dis-admirable life in the same circumstances. There are many features of a desirable life that are not directly connected to morality in the usual sense of the moral, but these features are important if ethics includes the study of the kinds of lives that are worth living. I think also that the components of a desirable life are *good for* the person who lives it. Given what I have argued in this chapter, it is good for a person to have health and friendship, interesting work and other pursuits, freedom from suffering, the respect of others, and a long life. It is good for a person to develop her talents and to express them. It is good for a person to have a life plan. It is good for a person to have the virtues. When I say it is good for a person to be virtuous, I do not mean that virtue benefits a person in the sense that virtue is a means to other elements of a good life, although that may be true also. Virtue is an element of a desirable life because virtue is admirable, and it is desirable to be admirable.

7

Right, Wrong, and the Division of Moral Linguistic Labor

1. The Principle of the Division of Linguistic Labor

The descriptive theory of meaning maintained that understanding a word is being in a certain mental state, the content of which constitutes the meaning of the word. Frege had argued that meanings are public property, accessible to many different persons and the same person at different times, but that is because he thought that meanings are abstract entities—like numbers.[1] Putnam argued that meanings are public in a more significant way. They are not just public because anybody can grasp them. They are public because they are partially constituted by social networks causally linking the individual members of the community to the referent of the term. The contents of a user's thoughts about water or gold or tigers are determined outside the mind in two ways: (1) They are partly determined by the way the world is—what water, gold, and tigers are like; (2) what a user of a term like "water" or "gold" or "tiger" means is determined by the user's connection to a social linguistic network. In previous chapters I have used the first way in which a term can be externalist for the purposes of exemplarism. In this chapter I argue that moral terms are externalist in the second way. When we look at how users of moral terms connect with a social network, we see a significant difference between the semantic function of deontic terms like "wrong" and "duty," and the semantic function of value terms like "virtue," "good act," and "good life."

---

1. Putnam mentions this at the beginning of "Meaning and Reference," although he does not cite the source. Frege argues for this position in his classic paper, "Sense and Reference" (1892).

An important feature of a linguistic network according to Putnam (1975) is that certain individuals have the role of expert in identifying the objects in the extension of terms such as natural kind terms. We can all refer to diamonds and tigers and elm trees because some of us can do so, and the rest of us rely on the experts for our semantic success. Putnam called this the *Principle of the Division of Linguistic Labor*. The "labor" of referring to natural kinds is divided between experts and ordinary users. The ordinary users defer to the experts to tell them what a diamond really is and to distinguish real diamonds from fake diamonds, but ordinary users also have a role to play in using a term correctly. In order to know what "elm tree" or "diamond" means, it is not enough to speak English and to be willing to defer to experts in identifying diamonds and elm trees. There is a linguistic obligation to have a certain minimal competence in the use of the term in order to count as knowing what the word means. Roughly, we need to grasp what Putnam calls the "stereotype," a description that is usually vague but usually accurate. We need to know something about stereotypical tigers in order to know what "tiger" means. We need to know something about stereotypical elm trees in order to know what "elm tree" means, and so on (168). Interestingly, Putnam conjectures that it is linguistically obligatory to be able to tell tigers from leopards in order to know what "tiger" means, but it is not required that one be able to distinguish elm trees from beech trees in order to know what "elm tree" means.[2]

As far as I know, Putnam does not explain why the stereotype of a tiger distinguishes it from a leopard, yet the stereotype of an elm tree does not distinguish it from a beech tree. My view is that since a linguistic network links individual users with the extension of a term through other speakers, then pictures and descriptions produced by other speakers become part of the network, and if they are common enough, some of them become part of the stereotype that every competent user of the term is expected to grasp. A competent speaker should have seen many pictures of tigers or heard them described. That would explain why ordinary speakers who know what "tiger" means must know that tigers are striped. If they do not know that, they are not properly connected to the network with respect to

---

2. Since Putnam says it is preferable to speak of acquiring words rather than knowing what they mean (167), we can make the same point as follows: It is not necessary to be able to distinguish elm trees from beech trees in order to have acquired the word "elm tree," but it is necessary to be able to distinguish tigers from leopards in order to have acquired the word "tiger" (169).

that word. On the other hand, pictures of elm trees do not function the same way as pictures of tigers, at least not in the part of the world I live in. Some of us can point out elm trees, but we do not expect everyone learning English to remember what is distinctive about that species of tree. I could be wrong about that, of course, in which case maybe neither Putnam nor I has properly acquired the use of the word "elm tree." But even if "elm tree" is more like "tiger" after all, there are still words like "titanium," "oryx," "Christmas heliconia," and many other words which are such that only a small percentage of the language users can give any descriptive details about the designated kind or reliably identify its members.

I think that Putnam is right that an ordinary speaker can succeed in referring to the members of a kind with only the vaguest idea of what the kind is like, and I think he is right that a competent speaker must be properly connected to a linguistic network, and that that requires having a minimal competence in the use of the word. I think he is also right that the linguistic network privileges certain users, but I believe that for some terms, the privileged users need not be experts in the sense of being authorities in identifying the members of the extension of the term, and I say more about that below.

The causal connection to other speakers allows an individual user of a term to enhance her grasp of the stereotype under their influence. If a speaker has only a minimal grasp of the stereotype but she is properly connected to the linguistic network, she will be willing to adopt the richer descriptions of others in the network, and she will be willing to defer to others who are better than she is at identifying the objects to which the term refers. When appropriate, she recognizes experts who make the final determination of the extension of a term, but for the most part, she defers to anybody who knows more than she does about the kind in question. Few speakers are connected to experts directly or pay much attention to the experts.

I suspect that there are practical reasons that stereotypes of different kinds have different levels of richness and precision. Ordinary speakers need to be able to distinguish water from other clear liquids, but they do not need to have the same level of competence in identifying non-poisonous plant species. So we all need to be able to grasp a stereotype of water that allows us to reliably identify water sufficiently to drink the right liquid, but it does not matter if each of us can reliably identify the different species of orchids and distinguish one from another. I am suggesting that the network develops that way intentionally. Since there are important practical reasons for every speaker to be able to identify water, the network includes numerous pictures and a very large amount of information about water, which contributes to both a richer stereotype and a better grasp of the stereotype by individual members of the network. Anybody who does not grasp a reasonable part of that information is not properly connected to the network of speakers and does not know what "water" means. The function of experts in the network is to determine what it takes to be "really" water, and to make distinctions such as the difference between different isotopes of water, but ordinary speakers cannot simply hand over to the experts the job of identifying the water in their ordinary environment. A term like "tiger" also has a reasonably robust stereotype, but the reason is probably cultural. We enjoy stories and pictures of tigers, even though few of us will ever encounter a tiger outside of a zoo. But if we are properly connected to our linguistic network, we will know that tigers are striped.

Putnam says that although the stereotype typically is roughly correct, it is not a necessary truth that the stereotype accurately describes the members of the extension of a term. That is plausible, and it follows from the fact that the stereotype can change. Putnam thinks that it is part of the stereotype of gold that it is yellow (I think he means golden) in color, but if jewelry made of white gold, pink gold, and green gold became more common in the experience of the users in a linguistic community, I surmise that the stereotype could change without a change in referential intentions, and without any change in the meaning of "gold." So a stereotype can change because of a cultural accident without any change in what the experts believe.

We also like to think that as the experts find out more about the kinds they investigate, the stereotype of the kind that spreads throughout the community becomes more accurate. That assumes, of course, that the experts are good at their job and that communication through the network works well. Individual speakers succeed at referring to members of the kind partly because the experts do a good job, but partly because of the proper function of the network.

2. The Division of Moral Linguistic Labor

I believe that the division of linguistic labor applies to many terms other than natural kind terms; for instance, "mass spectrometer," "kilim rug," and "fuel injection system," and I think it applies to moral terms. Each user of the term "good person" needs to be able to grasp the stereotype of a good person. Virtue terms function as descriptors that are part of the stereotype of a good person, and they are important for communication among the members of a community, but they do not provide necessary and sufficient conditions for membership in the kind. So an ordinary speaker should be aware that good persons have certain traits like generosity, honesty, and humility, but it is not necessary that she can give an account of a good person or of a virtue or of the individual virtues in order to have properly acquired a virtue term or the term "good person." I also think that the stereotype of "good person" is not limited to a set of adjectives but is more likely to be expressed in narratives and pictures of virtuous actions. I have shown in this book how narratives can be components of a theory. They are not simply examples of a concept or a device for practical training. Here I want to say that narratives serve a critical semantic function in connecting the users of moral terms to a causal network linking them with the extension of the term. The stereotype associated with a virtue term or the term "good person" includes narratives about the virtues. No one knows what these terms mean without the ability to refer to such descriptions and narratives. The function of narratives in the stereotype means that an ordinary user of the term "good person" needs to be able to identify some good persons in order to count as having acquired the term "good person," and in this respect "good person" is more like "water" than "uranium."

The function of privileged users in the division of linguistic labor is different for moral terms than for scientific terms. We expect ordinary users of "diamond" or "gold" to be able to describe a stereotypical diamond or piece of gold, and perhaps pick out some examples, but we defer to the experts to tell us what is *really* gold or a diamond, and the experts are even more important for kinds that we do not regularly encounter in ordinary life, like cadmium or paphiopedilum orchids. In contrast, most of us probably think we are pretty good at identifying exemplars, probably as good as we are at identifying water, but as is the case with water, it would be a serious mistake to think that our community is irrelevant to our ability to identify exemplars and to convey to us the stereotype of a good person. The extension of "good person" is not determined privately, nor is it determined by democratic vote. Some members of the social linguistic network are linguistically privileged.

Specialized functions in the network of virtue terms do not necessarily involve authority. I have already mentioned the importance of narratives, and storytellers have the important linguistic function of filling out and transmitting stereotypes of virtues and other qualities of a good person. Empirical scientists have the role of finding out how widespread the extension of a virtue term is, how changeable the extension is (whether virtuous persons tend to remain virtuous), and whether there are any connections between the extension of one virtue term and another. I think that philosophers also have specialized functions that include making the functioning of the network clearer and pointing out inconsistencies in the stereotype, in addition to contributing their powers of abstract reasoning to the community. In Chapter 5 I conjectured that exemplars, like most ordinary people, do not typically engage in moral reasoning in the making of a moral decision. If that is true, we will be puzzled about the place of moral reasoning in our moral practices. Here I would like to offer the hypothesis that moral philosophers have the specialized function of providing the reasoning that justifies the judgments of exemplars. If that is the case, it would mean that it is not necessary that an ordinary person who is making a moral decision can display the reasoning justifying the decision any more than an ordinary person must be able to explain what makes something a diamond or an elm tree or a piece of titanium.

The people who deserve to be linguistically privileged are the people who are good at distinguishing true exemplars from the counterfeits, and who are good at spotting counterfeit virtues. Unfortunately, the people who have great influence in determining both the stereotype and the extension of moral terms often have that influence because of their political power or media presence rather than because of their wisdom. There are people who have a great deal of influence over the stereotype of a good person and the individual virtues, and their judgments affect the use of terms by the people in their community. If the opinion makers do not have good judgment, the result can be confusion about the meaning of these terms.

Imagine what it would be like to live in a community in which the acknowledged experts at identifying certain natural kinds start to misidentify the members of the kind, and put out to the public an inaccurate stereotype. The experts and ordinary users have the right semantic intentions, but they start to lose their causal connection to the extension of the term. The result would be semantic confusion. I think that this has happened in the use of moral terms when the opinion makers misidentify the persons, traits, or acts to which we refer in our moral vocabulary, thereby leading those they influence to misidentify the members of the extension of these terms, and leading to a change in the stereotype that makes it less accurate than it was previously. It should not be surprising that this can happen, given that what we admire is partly determined by what the people who influence us the most admire, and what those people admire may not be admirable.

A virtue term can go out of use when people no longer admire a person who fits the stereotype, and this often happens when the stereotype changes. I think that happened with the word "chastity." In Christian moral theology, chastity is the virtue that governs sexual desire and leads to appropriate sexual behavior. In that sense it is a virtue everyone needs. But many people identify chastity with sexual abstinence. Obviously, people are not going to think of sexual abstinence as a virtue for everybody, and if the stereotype of chastity is a person who does not engage in sexual acts, it is no wonder that the word has gone out of common use.

A virtue term can go out of use for another reason. When people say they have no use for the word "chastity," the reason does not necessarily have anything to do with a change in the descriptive stereotype of a chaste person. It may mean that people do not admire the chaste person as described in the original stereotype. Persons who do not have a negative emotional response (contempt, scorn, disgust) to the acts that fit the description of lewd acts do not use the word "lewd." Similarly, the word "chaste" is used only by persons who admire the acts that fit the description of chaste acts.[3] That suggests something very interesting about virtue and vice terms. Even when there is no change in the descriptive part of a stereotype, if the emotional reaction to the stereotype changes, the word no longer has any meaning. Admiration for virtue and contempt for vice are imbedded in the referential intentions of words for virtues and vices. Members of a linguistic network understand that. If a member of the network does not admire persons as described in the stereotype of a virtue term, that person will cease using the term except perhaps in an ironic way. If most members of the network cease to admire persons who fit the stereotype, the word goes out of use.

Sometimes new words need to be invented. Miranda Fricker (2009) has made an important contribution to social epistemology in her work on ways in which the use of language can be unjust. One kind of injustice she identifies is hermeneutical injustice, a type of injustice

---

3. See the exchange between Allan Gibbard and Simon Blackburn (1992) on whether there are thick concepts, and their discussion of the example of the word "lewd." See also Blackburn (2004).

in which a person's social experience is obscured from interpretation because the shared resources for interpretation are blind to that experience. An example is postpartum depression. Another is sexual harassment, an experience that can be invisible until someone invents a word for it. Fricker's point can be extended to a problem in the division of moral linguistic labor. The lack of an interpretive framework and the need to invent new words sometimes opposes the accepted division of linguistic labor. That is because the people with the greatest linguistic influence might be the same people who are ignoring the social experience of some members of the community. If so, I think that there can be a kind of injustice in the division of linguistic labor itself, which might be a different problem from the hermeneutical injustice already identified by Fricker.

Before words like "sexist" and "sexual harassment" were added to the general vocabulary, the stereotype of a good person did not include everything that expressed the full range of the value of respect for women. The stereotype changed for the better when these words became commonplace, and it is very difficult to see how that change could have happened without the change in vocabulary. If I am right that moral critique sometimes requires critique of a linguistic network, that will include critique of the claims of people who are most influential in the network. Fortunately, we are in a position to critique opinion makers as long as we become reflective about our emotions of admiration and contempt. It can be hard for a non-expert to know if someone is a climate expert or an expert economist, but we have ways to identify persons whose moral judgment is most trustworthy. We can do that through reflection on our moral emotions, and that can be used to critique moral discourse. When we do so, we may need to invent new words like "sexual harassment." We can also change a stereotype for the better without changing a word. For instance, we may want to eliminate the inclusion of vengeance in the stereotype of justice without eliminating the word "justice." These changes can be effected by extended reflection on what we admire as a community. A moral linguistic network can therefore change by internal critique, not just by the accident of political power and cultural influence.

Another way in which a linguistic community can change is by expanding under the influence of an encounter with other moral linguistic communities. A linguistic community expands as the causal connections between communities expand. In the case of moral communities, we get blended linguistic communities when one community's stories and literature about exemplars become available to another. Westerners who read the *Analects* are automatically causally connected to the Chinese readers (and writers) of the *Analects*. Obviously the connection is weak, but it exists. The same thing happens when Western readers read Viking tales or the *Bhagavad Gita*, and it is bound to happen if they spend any amount of time in a foreign country. The changes can be profound when especially admirable and influential persons change something in the stereotype they use for "good person" or a virtue term.

The acceptance of the Universal Declaration of Human Rights is an especially interesting example of the expansion of a moral linguistic community, especially when we look at the signatories that did not already have a word for "rights" in their linguistic community. One possibility is that they added a word to their vocabulary that was a translation of "rights," in which case their linguistic community expanded to include the linguistic community of persons using the term "rights" or one translated as "rights." It is more likely that they signed the document, not because they were willing to add a term to their vocabulary, but because they decided that what the drafters of the Declaration meant by "rights" was close enough to expressions already in use in their vocabulary that they could accept the Declaration. But even in that case it seems to me that the act of signing the Declaration put them into a causal network of the drafters of the Declaration and its other signatories, thereby expanding the linguistic community of which they were a part, and inevitably changing their use of certain moral terms.

I think that the expansion of causal linguistic networks is not only the best way to alter the usage of moral terms, but it is also the best way to get moral agreement. In fact, I think that such expansion is a necessary condition for agreement. There are examples of that in contemporary cross-cultural moral discourse. I have been told that one translation of "sexual harassment" in Arabic, التحرش الجنسي, would probably be unintelligible to most Arabic-speaking people other than intellectuals familiar with contemporary Western thinking.[4] This is a case in which Arabic speakers who are knowledgeable about Western views on sexual respect have a weaker connection with ordinary Arabic speakers in some part of their vocabulary than they have with most speakers of European languages. The Arabic speakers who have adopted terms for certain Western values are connected to a different linguistic network than ordinary speakers of Arabic. If that is right, we cannot expect to see a change in the views of ordinary Arabic

---

4. This is the view of Norman Stillman, a specialist in Arab-Jewish encounters in Arab lands (private correspondence).

speakers about sexual harassment without a network of Arabic speakers that more closely connects ordinary speakers with those who speak Arabic but who also use words for sexual harassment.[5]

I think this shows the importance of dialogue among morally admired persons in different communities. That kind of dialogue is an important impetus for linguistic expansion because of their effect on each other and their effect on their respective linguistic networks. That makes it all the more important that we solve the problem that admirable persons are often not the most influential. I think that when the wisest persons are sidelined in public discussion and non-admirable persons take center stage, that makes it difficult for us to even formulate the *thought* that certain good things are good and certain bad things are bad.

3. The Social Importance of Deontic Terms

I think that once we have the idea of a moral linguistic network, we can see the difference between the function of deontic terms like "wrong act" and "duty," and the value terms like "virtue" and "good life." There are different linguistic expectations for the deontic terms and the value terms, and the division of linguistic labor differs for the two sets of terms. We have a social obligation to know the members of the extension of the terms "wrong act" and "duty," and the linguistic community is much more demanding of competent users of those terms than of the value terms. The terms "wrong" and "duty" exist because no civil society can survive without agreement about a range of behavior that is critical to the basic functioning of the society. In particular, there are certain acts that we cannot tolerate, and it is crucial that we agree about what those acts are. A speaker who fails to recognize many wrong acts is deemed linguistically incompetent in the use of the word "wrong," and used to be called a sociopath. In theoretical ethics, moral terms are associated with concepts that are imbedded in complex and subtle theories, but it is not necessary that individuals have the same *concept* of wrong or duty. All that is necessary is that they agree that acts *like that* should not be done. It does not matter why they think that those acts should not be done. A well-functioning society

---

5. Stillman says that he often tells students that when reading some social or political thinker whose Arabic is hard to understand, they should try to go back to the European writer and language that that person must have been reading. In North Africa, most feminists and social scientists write in French, not Arabic, for that reason. Stillman says that there are many ideas that they cannot adequately express in Arabic.

cannot tolerate theft, but if you ask people why theft is wrong, it does not matter whether they give different answers or no answer. Furthermore, it does not matter whether their behavior is virtuously motivated as long as they refrain from stealing.

An intolerable act is an act that is wrong in the strongest sense of wrong. We demand that it not be done. The inverse of an intolerable act is a duty. A duty is what we demand of someone. So an act is intolerable if and only if it is a duty not to do it. In contemporary moral discourse, duties are often associated with human rights. The violation of a duty is a violation of someone's rights. But the idea of an intolerable act preceded the idea of a human right, and it probably also preceded the idea of a duty. The duty not to do an intolerable act is a negative duty. Assuming that there are certain acts that we demand of ourselves and others, then there are also positive duties.

There is more than one sense of a right act, but a right act in the sense I am using is the thing to do in a given set of circumstances. It is the act favored by the balance of reasons in the circumstances, where what I mean by a reason is any consideration that counts for or against the doing of an act. Sometimes wrong is treated as the complement of right, in which case we say that it is wrong to do anything else but the right act. This sense of wrong is weaker than the sense of an intolerable act since an act can fail to be the best supported by the balance of reasons in a set of circumstances without falling into the category of the intolerable or a violation of a duty. For instance, maybe the right thing for me to do is to take out the neighbors' trash when they are out of town even though I did not promise to do so, but failing to do so is not intolerable. It is not a violation of a duty, and it is not a violation of the neighbors' rights. For the most part, I will be using the term "wrong act" in the strong sense of the complement of "duty" rather than in the weaker sense of the complement of "right act."

I have said that it is critical that the terms "wrong" and "duty" are used correctly within a whole community. We must all agree that *those* acts are intolerable and that *those* acts are demanded. All societies include individuals with widely differing degrees of virtue and differing degrees of reflectiveness and understanding of morality. In addition, we cannot rely on the natural bonds of friendship, gratitude, and loyalty in a large, heterogeneous society, so the duties must be such that they can be done by the non-virtuous, and in interactions with strangers, and it is important that everybody can understand them. These reasons also apply to the term "right act" in the sense of an act that is best supported by the balance of reasons in the circumstances. Failing to do a right act in this sense is not intolerable, but we need a way to identify right acts that can be used by individuals with different levels of understanding, virtue, and attachment to the persons who will be affected by their acts.

I call the ideas of right, wrong, and duty "morality light." Doing the right thing does not go very far in giving an individual a life that is either desirable or admirable. Even if most people act rightly, that is not enough to make a society flourish, but it is enough to make a society functional, and it gives each individual in the society the necessary social conditions for the development of admirable and desirable lives. In the rest of this chapter I argue that thinking of a right act, a wrong (intolerable) act, and a duty by reference to exemplars will serve three important social functions:

(a) It permits us to identify morality light without reliance on complex or disputed concepts.
(b) It helps us get agreement about the acts that fall into each category.
(c) It motivates us to do the right thing and to avoid doing the wrong thing.

4. Wrong and Duty

In Chapter 1 I said that I think of a moral theory as a map that simplifies, systematizes, and justifies our moral beliefs and practices, most of which already exist. Beliefs about intolerable acts already exist, and for the most part, there is already common agreement about what they are. Our practices include reactive emotions such as indignation, anger, and feelings of guilt and blame, as well as admiration. In earlier work I proposed that duty can be defined by an exemplar's feeling of guilt if she does not do an act of a certain kind.[6] Generally, we think of a feeling of guilt as the appropriate response to the same kind of act for which we blame others, so the feeling of guilt is something like self-blame. I think now that there may be a difference between the exemplar's reactive attitude toward her own failure to do an act of a certain kind, and her response to the failure of others to do acts of that kind. There might be acts that are such that she would feel guilty if she did not do the act, but she would not blame others for not doing an act of that kind in similar

---

6. I proposed that a duty is an act the *phronimos* characteristically would do, and he would feel guilty if he did not do it (2004, 160).

circumstances. Interviews with Holocaust rescuers reveal reactions like that. Almost all of them say they would not blame others for not doing what they did, but many say they think they had no moral option (Monroe 2004, 7). As they see it, their act was the only option permitted to them. Some moral philosophers might want to say that nothing can be morally demanded of one person but not another in the same circumstances, but generally the Holocaust rescuers did not adopt that view. I was not inclined to think of this position as coherent until I read the interviews with some of these people. Now I think that we should take their reactions seriously, given that so many moral exemplars have that attitude toward their own act. An advantage of exemplarism is that it leaves theoretical space for a type of first personal duty that applies to the agent but may not apply to everyone in the same situation. So there might be acts such that it is appropriate for an agent who does not do such an act to feel guilty, but it is not appropriate for one person to blame another for not doing it. This hypothesis can, of course, be tested by examining the attitudes of exemplars, particularly those to whom we attribute practical wisdom. Exemplarism permits this variation of duty, and clever readers will probably think of other variations as well.[7]

I propose, then, that the basic sense of wrong is the intolerable; it is an act that we cannot tolerate as a society. Clearly, it is socially more important to identify acts that we cannot tolerate of others than to identify any first person duties. So I aim to define a wrong act in the sense of the intolerable. The semantical context in which I offer these definitions is the same as the one in which I offered the definitions of the value terms in Chapter 4, only in the case of the deontic terms, the inadequacy of the descriptivist theory of meaning is even more obvious. People not only *can* succeed in referring to wrong acts without a descriptive meaning in the head, but they are expected to identify these acts no matter what conceptual framework they adopt, and even if they have no conceptual framework at all. I think also that there is no descriptive stereotype associated with the terms "wrong" and "duty." But what we can do, and should do, is to point to these acts directly. *Those* acts are demanded. *Those* acts are intolerable. I think this means that even though stories can be useful in giving the extension of "wrong," wrong acts usually can be adequately identified in a list of prohibitions. In contrast, it takes a story to explain what loyalty

---

7. Not many philosophers have endorsed this kind of first person duty. An exception is Robert M. Adams in his discussion of vocation (2002, 307).

and disloyalty are. The value terms are part of a different kind of linguistic network from that of the deontic terms.

Most of us can find most of the intolerable acts, just as most of us can find most of the water. As I have said, the division of moral linguistic labor differs in some ways from the division of linguistic labor for natural kind terms. We do not rely on experts to tell us what the wrong acts really are, but I propose that what we cannot tolerate as a society can be determined by what exemplars cannot tolerate, particularly the subset of exemplars with *phronesis*, or practical wisdom. A wrong act is an act that is blamed by persons with practical wisdom, and such an act is blamewor-thy. A duty is an act the non-performance of which is blameworthy. What is blameworthy is what is blamed by persons with *phronesis*, those whose emotions are most likely to fit their objects. Assuming that feeling guilty is self-blame, a positive duty is an act which is such that a person with *phronesis* would feel guilty if she did not do it and would blame others for not doing it, and a negative duty is an act which is such that a person with *phronesis* would feel guilty if she did it, and would blame others for doing it.

So I suggest the following:

> A *duty* in some set of circumstances C is an act that persons with *ph-ronesis* (persons like that) would judge to be the only option in C. It is an act such that if they did not do it, they would feel guilty, and they would blame others if others did not do it.

I said above that a wrong act is an act such that it is a duty not to do it. That leads to the following definition of "wrong act":

> A *wrong act* in some set of circumstances C is an act that persons with *phronesis* (persons like that) would judge is not an option in C. They would feel guilty if they did it, and would blame others for doing it.

Let me reiterate that these definitions are not constructed to give the content of a concept. Like the definitions of Chapter 4, they are compara-ble to defining "water" as "stuff like that," where stuff like that is what the experts say it is. The existence of water does not depend on the existence of the experts. The existence of wrong acts and duties does not depend on the existence of exemplars of practical wisdom. What is wrong would be wrong even if persons with *phronesis* did not exist, or if they existed but did not have practical wisdom, or if they had practical wisdom, but on some occasion their reactive attitude of intolerance did not fit the object. Persons with *phronesis* are not infallible. Experts are not infallible either.

I hope it is also clear that when I define wrong and duty by reference to the emotional reactions of certain exemplars (those with *phronesis*), I am not offering a non-cognitivist analysis of wrongness and duty. When I say wrong acts are acts like that—acts that admirable persons of a certain kind cannot tolerate—I do not mean that the *property* of wrongness is identical with the property of not being tolerated by certain persons. As I said in previous chapters, my purpose is neither to give a conceptual analysis nor to give the nature of a virtue, a duty, a wrong act, and so on. My purpose is to map the terms "virtues," "duties," and "wrong acts" by finding the admirable persons—in particular, the persons admirable for their practical wisdom—and then looking at their reactions to certain classes of acts. An investigation of commonalities among the acts that admirable persons cannot tolerate will probably reveal properties that are essential conditions for the development of desirable personal and communal lives. If so, this would be a place in which exemplarism converges with neo-Aristotelian virtue theory.

How do we know that these definitions pick out the correct class of acts? Since the definitions are indexical—the judgment of *those persons*—the accuracy of the definitions depends on the reliability of our ability to pick out persons with *phronesis*. Of course, since a theory is a map of our moral practices and beliefs, we would not accept a definition unless it yielded a class of acts supported by our intuitions and common moral practices. Persons with practical wisdom would not be recognized for their practical wisdom if their judgments regularly deviated from the judgments of ordinary persons. The majority of their judgments coincide with our own, and they make judgments that we recognize as correct, at least in retrospect. But the acts identified by the above definition are not limited to the set of acts endorsed in common practice and ordinary intuition, nor would we would want them to be. The exemplars to whom we look for their practical wisdom can lead us to modify our responses, and they can lead whole communities to modify previous moral judgments. We modify those judgments in part because of our trust in the practical wisdom of moral exemplars. This is important,

I think, because there has to be reflective equilibrium between theory and the practices the theory explains and justifies. We would not accept an exemplar whose judgment conflicted with judgments strongly embedded in our moral practices which were themselves developed in part under the influence of previous exemplars. But we also know that we can be mistaken, and the shaping of our moral emotions and alterations in our moral reasoning can lead us to adopt the point of view of an exemplar over conventional wisdom.

5. A Right Act

"Virtuous act" is the link between the value terms and the deontic terms since it is both a value term and a term for act evaluation. It is not surprising, then, that the relationship between a virtuous act and a right act has received quite a bit of attention among virtue ethicists. The easiest way to define a right act using virtue terms is to identify a right act with a virtuous act, the strategy of Daniel Russell (2009), among others. Russell argues that we cannot get an account of right action without referring to all practical considerations (what he calls the "account constraint"), and an act is right only if it sufficiently meets all practical concerns (what he calls the "act constraint" (Russell, 44ff). An act is not right because it is virtuous in some respect, but only if it is virtuous overall or in all respects (141). Since *phronesis*, or excellence in practical deliberation, is a component of every virtue (139), a right act involves excellence in practical deliberation.

I agree with Russell that we need the idea of an act virtuous overall or in every respect, and I certainly agree about the importance of *phronesis*, but it seems to me a duplication of terminology to identify a right act with a virtuous act. As I see it, the terms "right act" and "virtuous act" have different roles in our moral practices and are connected to different kinds of linguistic networks. I have said that there are reasons we want to talk about an evaluative category of acts that is thinner than a virtuous act, and which does not rely on any particular theoretical background, nor does it rely on a particular personal history of the agent for its understanding. The respective roles of these terms in our moral linguistic network can be discovered by investigation, but my hypothesis is that the issue of what act is right arises in contexts in which we want a verdict on what to do in a given situation. In many circumstances it is too late to go back and develop the perceptions, motives, and inner strengths necessary to act the way a virtuous person acts in both external behavior and inner motives. We need a category of act that applies to anybody in any situation, and I think that "right act" best serves this function. When we ask "What should I do now?" the answer cannot be, "Care about X and then, because you care, do Y," nor can the answer be anything that requires that the past was different—I should have made different choices in the past, I should have acquired different emotion dispositions, I should have learned excellence in practical deliberation, I should have purified the mind, and so on. Since other people care that I know what is right and wrong, the criteria for a right act should be accessible to anybody. This leads to tying the idea of a right act to a kind of practical reasoning that can be used by many different kinds of persons, including persons who are not philosophers and who have little or no skill at moral reasoning, and who may not be virtuous. I think that this means that the term "right act," like the terms "wrong act" and "duty," needs to connect the users to the extension of the term through a linguistic network that makes minimal demands on the user, and the stereotype must be as thin as possible.

The idea of a right act dominates act-based theories but is not central in a virtue theory, and some virtue theorists prefer to ignore it. For instance, Julia Annas says (2011, 47) that doing the right thing is not a very helpful notion in an ethics that makes virtue central, and she refers to Elizabeth Anscombe (1958) and Iris Murdoch (1970, 42) for similar remarks (n. 36). Rosalind Hursthouse says she defines right act "under pressure" in order to maintain a fruitful dialogue with other contemporary ethicists (1999, 69). But if I am right that the deontic terms have an important social function that differs from the function of virtue terms, we ought to have a way to define a right act, and it seems to me that an exemplarist approach is well suited to doing so.

A good place to begin is with the well-known approach of Rosalind Hursthouse (1999). She identifies a right act with what a virtuous person would characteristically do in the same circumstances (28), and I proposed something similar in earlier work (1996, 235; 2004, 160). This way of thinking about a right act is not simply a theoretical move on the part of virtue ethicists because we see it in Zen Buddhism, where the disciples are set a problem: What would the master do? We also see it among Christians who ask themselves what Jesus would do. We see it among ordinary people who ask someone they morally trust, "What would you do if you were in my situation?"

A common objection to this definition is that there are cases in which exemplars would not be in my circumstances.[8] Maybe I am in my circumstances because of stupidity or past wrongdoing, so there is nothing an exemplar would do in my situation.[9] Daniel Russell handles this problem by distinguishing between a *right act* and what *ought to be done*. There are actions I ought to do to compensate for or to remedy past wrongdoing even though such actions are not right.[10] I find this response rather implausible, but even if we accept Russell's position, I think that it does not address the broader issue—that there can be many reasons that, given my past history, temperament, and moral development, I should not do what a moral exemplar would do in similar circumstances. I should not do what the exemplar would do if doing so would put me in the way of temptation that the exemplar could resist but I probably could not. Maybe if I said what the exemplar said to an opponent, then that would precipitate a response from the opponent that would make me angry, leading to an unhelpful altercation, although the exemplar would not get angry, or would handle the anger better than I would. There might also be promises I could not keep, although the exemplar could, or there are ways to express respect that would be appropriate for the exemplar but not for me. Furthermore, even when a person does what a saintly person would do, it can end up with no moral value if it is performed in a poorly constituted way, and the morally preferable action is not to do it at all. Martin Luther King Jr. made this point about people participating in sit-ins and marches, saying that the practice of non-violence requires both internal and external non-violence. If people are unable to abide by the totality of the non-violent

---

8. Johnson (2003) offers examples such as the habitual liar, who undertakes a program of self-improvement, which is completely uncharacteristic of the virtuous person (816–818), and an intemperate person, who ought to perform acts of self-control unnecessary for the virtuous. One of Johnson's main points is that defining a right act by what the virtuous person characteristically does is incompatible with the plausible view that self-improvement is morally right. In what follows, I define a right act in a way that can be used for self-improvement by the non-virtuous person.

9. Could a man with practical wisdom end up married to three women? In the Paul Mazursky film, *Enemies: A Love Story* (1989), based on the novel by Isaac Bashevis Singer, a man who survived the Holocaust marries the woman who hid him during the war, mistakenly thinking that his first wife had been killed, and then marries the woman he loves. When he has to face all three of them, he has a problem.

10. Russell argues that "ought" does not imply "right," and there can nonetheless be something morally praiseworthy about remedial action even though it does not qualify as a central case of moral excellence and so is not "right" (47–59).

approach to bus integration, they should stay off the bus and keep walking (King 2003, 459, rule 9). Similarly, Gandhi (1948) said that he would not reject self-defense, even to the point of bloodshed, for people who cannot master non-violence.[11] What the person who cannot master non-violence should do is not what the non-violent virtuous person would do.

This problem reveals something important that we want in the definition of deontic terms in a virtue theory. I think that the insight that the virtuous exemplar is primary is correct, but we want to recognize the fact that there are reasons the act that is right for one person cannot always be the same as what the exemplar would do in the same set of circumstances. My approach is to define a right act, not by what the exemplar does, but by what the exemplar judges there is most reason for some person to do in a given set of circumstances, which may be different for different persons. One of the advantages of this approach is that it preserves the link between right action and practical reasons, but without requiring that the agent is adept at identifying practical reasons. The determination of a right act is the judgment of the exemplar. We need not prejudge what is included in the exemplar's deliberation. As I said in Chapter 5, the exemplar might act on reasons or on emotion; the exemplar might engage in a process of practical reasoning in deliberation, or she may not. She might not even deliberate. But I propose that the exemplar's judgment determines what is right in that situation. It is not necessary that the exemplar actually be in the situation to make judgments about it.

Given these constraints, let me propose the following definition of "right act":

A *right act* for A in some set of circumstances C is what the person with *phronesis* (persons like that) would characteristically take to be most favored by the balance of reasons for A in circumstances C.

---

11. There are several places in which he makes remarks like this. Here are three of them: "If the capacity for non-violent self-defense is lacking, there need be no hesitation in using violent means" (Gandhi 1948, Vol. 1, 260). "It is better to be violent, if there is violence in our hearts, than to put on the cloak of non-violence to cover impotence. Violence is any day preferable to impotence. There is hope for a violent man to become nonviolent. There is no such hope for the impotent" (Vol. 1, 240). "No doubt the non-violent way is always the best, but where that does not come naturally, the violent way is both necessary and honorable. Inaction here is rank cowardice and unmanly. It must be shunned at all cost" (Vol. 1, 402) Many thanks to Guy Crain for showing me these passages.

I assume that the majority of the time there is no unique act favored by the balance of reasons. There may be a set of acts equally favored by the reasons, and many acts that are less favored. If I am right that in many situations a number of acts would be tied for the status of most favored by the reasons, that is an advantage of defining a right act by what the exemplar judges rather than by what the exemplar does. The exemplar can only do one act in any given situation, but the exemplar might judge that a number of other acts would have been equally well supported by the reasons. All of them would be right.

On this definition, a right act is something that anybody can do, whether or not she is virtuous, and anybody can find out what a right act is. The degree of practical reasoning demanded of the agent is minimal since all she need do is find exemplars. But there are demands on the agent's imagination because in most cases she is not in a position to consult an exemplar who fully understands her situation. But there are ways in which the exemplar's emotions and reasons can be learned, and I discussed that in Chapter 5. An exemplar can teach us how to think like he does, as Confucius does with his students.

It might seem that the above definition is trivially true and uninformative. If a right act for A in C is the act (or one of the acts) most favored by the balance of reasons for A in C, then the act most favored by the balance of reasons for A in C is the act a person with the best judgment would judge to be the act that is most favored by the balance of reasons for A in C. If *phronesis* is a property that is or includes the property of having the best judgment, it follows that the right act is the act judged to be the act most favored by the balance of reasons by the person with *phronesis*. Notice that the definition is not trivial if we make the assumption I have been making throughout this book that persons with *phronesis* are identifiable in advance of knowing what they do and what they judge in particular circumstances.

In Chapter 1 I mentioned the example of Simeon Stylites, who lived thirty-seven years on top of a pillar. Peter Brown (1971) describes him as a man of power who escaped to a high platform in an attempt to get away from the people who kept coming to him for advice. What is particularly interesting about him to me is that his wisdom led people to recognize him as an authority, and he reluctantly took on the role of a judge—mediating disputes, specifying interest rates one party should pay another, and so on. He is an example of the difference between the role of the wise exemplar and the role of the saint or hero. Saints or heroes are models for ourselves. Wise persons are authorities.

I know of one person who uses an imaginative method of determining a right act similar to the one I propose, only his method is much more elaborate and suggests a number of variations. Philosopher Charles Taliaferro tells me that when he faces a difficult decision, he imagines a discussion and verdict of the Council of the Wise in his imaginary alternative world, a world he first invented with his sister as a child. This world has at its center a Chair, selected by the Council of the Wise, the House, the Cathedral, several universities, and more, all populated by persons who are largely, but not always, based on persons taken from life or fiction. He borrows the neo-Freudian term "introjection" for his process of creating imaginary inhabitants of his world. His method for appropriating the virtues of those he admires is to "internalize the admired person (boots and all) and then have them play an imagined interaction with other characters." The characters in Taliaferro's imaginary world are not all exemplars, and it is important to him that they represent many different points of view. Taliaferro tells me that he thinks of the dialogues and personal interactions in his imaginary world as a cousin of the formal philosophical practice of displaying different positions in dialogue format. So he thinks it is not all that different from the dialogues of Plato, Anselm, Berkeley, or Hume.[12] This approach suggests that the "verdict" of the wise person is often a verdict we arrive at in our imagination.

In Chapter 5 I argued that a moral reason is whatever an exemplar takes to be relevant to moral judgment. If so, we should leave open the issue of what counts as a moral reason in our definition of "right act." A moral reason should include whatever persons with practical reason take to be relevant to the determination of what to do in a given situation. I argued that emotions can be reasons, and in other work (2012) I have gone further and argued that many psychic states can be reasons.[13] So if a right act is an act that a *phronimos* takes to be best supported by the

---

12. Taliaferro asks, "What if Hume really did have within him (so to speak) a Cleanthes and a Philo and a Demea? While the *Dialogues Concerning Natural Religion* was obviously written by Hume, what if he also listened to the dialogue? He might have imagined/introjected Cleanthes and Demea and Philo based on persons he knew. Most readers hold that Philo most resembles Hume, but it is possible that Hume was quite divided and he could see himself as either Cleanthes or Demea or Philo. This possibility is especially tempting in light of the new, non-traditional understanding of Hume as less skeptical than generally believed" (private correspondence).

13. As I mentioned in Chapter 5, I distinguish first person epistemic reasons from third person epistemic reasons in Zagzebski (2012), and argue that emotions are first person reasons. I argue this point also in Zagzebski (2013).

moral reasons in some situation, then that includes whatever the *phronimos* takes to be such that it supports a moral judgment about what to do.

By designating a right act for A in C as what a person with practical wisdom would judge A should do in C, I do not mean to identify a right act as what a *phronimos* would advise A to do in C. I think that many exemplars (and non-exemplars) are unwilling to give advice to others. It is difficult to fully grasp another person's situation, and advice giving is risky when one has a personal relationship with the person asking for advice. This is one of the advantages of learning what is right by reference to judgments about what a fictional or hypothetical person has most reason to do. There is no relationship at risk, and because the situation is artificially constructed, it is often transparent. This is one of the advantages of literature and film. Compare the way we treat a character in a Jane Austen novel with Sartre's famous example of the young man who asked Sartre's advice about whether he should join the Resistance, or instead stay home with his ailing mother. Sartre connected his unwillingness to give the student advice with his existentialist approach to morality, but it seems to me that many non-existentialists would be equally unwilling for the reasons I have mentioned. Yet those same people would not hesitate to say what a fictional character should do. The principle here is plain enough. The act best supported by the balance of reasons in some situation depends upon shareable features of the person and shareable features of the situation, so the right thing for person A to do in situation C is the same as what would be right for persons *like* A in situations *like* C.

This approach leaves us with a degree of indeterminacy about an actual concrete choice. One reason for the indeterminacy is straightforward: There will always be vagueness in the idea of one thing being like any other. There are indeterminate boundaries. But I want to leave open another possibility. There might be something essentially unique about each individual person that can render it impossible to say that what Ann should do in some set of circumstances C is what any person like Ann should do in C. If persons are unique in this way, that would be a problem that could not be solved by making what we mean by likeness to Ann more precise. The problem here is that it is possible that nobody is like Ann in all respects. It might even be metaphysically necessary that nobody is like Ann in all respects. For many of life's choices, Ann's differences from everyone else do not matter, and that is why we can often confidently say that the right thing for Ann to do is such-and-such. But as long as it is possible that Ann differs from all other persons in some ways, and as long as it is possible that those ways are relevant to moral choice, then it is possible that the right thing for Ann to do in some situation does not reduce to what anyone who fits Ann's description ought to do in situations of that kind.[14] If we press this idea far enough, we get the view that the right thing for A to do is what an idealized version of A would judge should be done, where the idealized version of A is A with *phronesis*. This approach makes it clear that the right way for A to learn what to do is not by merely following someone else's judgment, but involves an adaptation of the exemplar's process of making a moral judgment to her own particular circumstances, with due regard for the fact that there is something uniquely different about each person.[15]

I think that the uniqueness of persons explains the germ of truth in Sartre's view that only the young man who needed to choose whether or not to join the Resistance could know the right thing to him to do. But unlike Sartre, I think there are plenty of acts whose rightness can be determined for others by persons with the greatest insight into the morally relevant features of a situation, with appropriate recognition to variations in human ability and psychology. A person with *phronesis* is a person with such insight. As long as we can identify a *phronimos* in advance of judging that he or she makes the correct moral judgment, we have a way to determine the correct moral judgments. This way of identifying the right acts is obviously imprecise, but it seems to me that it is the best we can do, given human fallibility and the need to avoid false precision.

6. Practical Advantages of the Exemplarist Definitions

Defining the deontic terms in the way I have suggested has some important practical advantages. It can help us get agreement about the wrong acts and duties, and it also can help to motivate us to do our duty and to avoid doing the wrong thing. Getting agreement is aided by the fact that the definitions are not conceptual.

---

14. It is possible that there is some qualitative property that is necessarily unique to Ann, but it is more likely that if there is something about Ann that is necessarily unique to her, and if every qualitative property is such that it is possibly shared by some other being, then what is unique to Ann is not qualitative. I argued for the latter position in Zagzebski (2000). I argued for individual qualitative essences in Zagzebski (1988).

15. I explore the uniqueness of persons as the ground for human dignity in Zagzebski (2016), my APA Presidential Address, Central Division, March 4, 2016.

It might seem that we cannot get agreement on the class of duties and wrong acts unless we agree on the class of exemplars. Fortunately, that is not the case. People do not have to agree about the identity of every exemplar. In fact, it is possible to disagree about all of the exemplars as long as all the exemplars identified by the persons in a society agree about certain things. I am not denying that there is room for disagreement among exemplars—for instance, about the precise bounds of the duty of truth-telling—but it seems to me very likely that all the exemplars will agree that there is a duty of truth-telling, and they will agree about a wide range of cases in which it applies. I will have more to say about disagreement below, but I propose that these definitions are the best way to get agreement about the class of duties. In my opinion, getting agreement about duties within a pluralistic society is not very easily accomplished by argument. It is easier to get agreement by the agreement of exemplars who influence the beliefs of those who admire them. The exemplars need not even agree on the arguments. They need only agree in their responses to certain acts.

Jacques Maritain, one of the framers of the Universal Declaration of Human Rights, liked to tell the story of a visitor at one of their meetings who was astonished that adherents of such strongly opposed ideologies had been able to agree on a list of basic rights. The man was told, "Yes, we agree about the rights, but on condition that no one asks us why."[16] The UNESCO committee that prepared a draft of the declaration found that there was considerable commonality among widely differing cultures about basic moral wrongs even though not all of them expressed these moral positions in the vocabulary of rights. The committee began by sending a questionnaire asking for thoughts on human rights from the perspectives of Confucian, Hindu, Islamic, and contemporary American and European perspectives, and they considered the place of rights in the legal frameworks of different countries. Although the document was formulated in the Western vocabulary of rights, many respondents to the questionnaire from non-Western countries (e.g., China, India, Bengal) noted that the basic idea of human rights existed in their traditions.[17] Without using the *concept* of rights, respondents from these traditions thought that they could agree on the substance of the rights document because they agreed that there are certain classes of acts that any human being can

16. Maritain, "Introduction," in *Human Rights: Comments and Interpretations* (1949, 9).

17. See Glendon (2002, 73ff) for a discussion of this finding of the committee.

demand from others. As I interpret their responses, they could agree on the document because they agreed that *those* behaviors are intolerable. They did not agree on the theoretical background of the moral prohibitions they agreed upon, nor was it necessary.

On December 10, 1948, the United Nations General Assembly adopted the Universal Declaration of Human Rights without a single dissenting vote.[18] This historic achievement had to overcome many obstacles, and its success was due to the fortuitous convergence of the talents and diplomacy of many people, but perhaps most of all, to the enormous prestige of Eleanor Roosevelt, chairman of the commission. She was the leader in fact as well as in name. She had the political influence to keep the US State Department on board, and she had already earned great respect all over the world for her previous humanitarian projects. She helped in innumerable ways to get cooperation from representatives of many different countries, and she gave personal attention to each member of the commission, ensuring that each one felt that his view was respected. When the Declaration was adopted, E. J. Kahn wrote, "In an era conspicuous for the self-interest of both nations and individuals, she has become more and more widely recognized as a person of towering unselfishness" (Glendon 2002, 206). Kahn then quoted from "an unnamed source with impressive overseas connections":

> Mrs. Roosevelt never cares if there's nothing in it for herself. She has absolutely no pride of station and no personal ambition. What's more, many Americans who have neither the time, the energy, the contacts, nor the ability that she has look upon her efforts to improve the lives of her fellow-men as the kind of thing they would like to do themselves if only they were capable of it and could get around to it. To them—and I suspect there are an awful lot of them—she is the personification of the American conscience. (206; note 30, 266).

I do not know if Eleanor Roosevelt was a moral exemplar all things considered, but she must have been an exemplar of the qualities of selfless

---

18. The final tally was 48 in favor, 8 abstentions, and 0 opposed. Members of the Soviet bloc abstained. Saudi Arabia also abstained because of the article on religious freedom, although the other Muslim nations voted yes. South Africa abstained. Eleanor Roosevelt said that she believed that the Soviet abstention was mainly attributable to the one article that provides that everyone has the right to leave his country (Glendon 2002, 169–170). In almost every case of abstention, the objections were to a small number of articles in a long list of rights.

humanitarianism and sensitivity to competing viewpoints. Many people came to agree with the Declaration because of their admiration for her, and that arguably had a greater effect than the arguments of its writers.

This leads to a second advantage of the exemplarist approach to defining duty and wrong acts. Admiration for an exemplar is motivating. As the unnamed commentator said above, Eleanor Roosevelt represented a kind of ideal self to many Americans, who emulated her passion for universal rights, at least in their emotional responses. My hypothesis is that admiration for someone who reacts with intolerance (horror, indignation) toward acts of a certain kind tends to move us to react in the same way. If I trust my admiration for the exemplar in the relevant respect, I will trust the emotion I acquire through emulation of the exemplar, and will judge that acts of that kind are intolerable. I will both judge that they are intolerable and will be motivated not to do them. If I am right about that, admiration of exemplars can serve as a psychological force to (a) get agreement within a community about the identification of negative duties and any positive duties, and (b) motivate persons to act on their duty. This mechanism does not require that everybody admire the same exemplars as long as the exemplars cannot tolerate the same acts. If the exemplars admired within a society express a similar emotion toward similar behavior, we can get social agreement about the intolerable, as well as a widespread motive to avoid such behavior. I believe that this mechanism can be empirically investigated.

The process of getting agreement on the list of human rights in the Declaration continued to increase in the succeeding decades. By 2011, polls indicated a remarkable degree of consensus among individual persons on these rights, with majorities in the twenty-five nations polled agreeing. I would like to see research on the causes of this agreement. It is very unlikely that each person interviewed agreed because of a justifying argument. In fact, we know that they do not all possess the same concept of a right. My hypothesis is that a great number of people accept the rights in the document because of the influence of persons they admire. Even if they do not know who wrote the original document, I argued in Chapter 5 that it is justified to adopt the moral judgment of an admired person when we judge that that person is more likely to get the truth about the relevant issue than we are ourselves. The reasons for the exemplar's judgment may include emotions as well as a process of reasoning. If so, it can be justified to judge that an act is wrong because admirable persons cannot tolerate the act. If people naturally form moral beliefs about wrong acts through epistemic trust in persons they admire, then we have a defense of the epistemic justification of what people do naturally. That would give us a third advantage of defining wrong and duty by direct reference to exemplars: It connects a natural belief-forming mechanism for moral beliefs to the justification of those beliefs.

The practical advantages of defining "right act" by reference to exemplars are similar. It can aid us in getting agreement, and it can motivate us to do the right thing. However, using exemplars to get agreement on the right acts is more difficult than getting agreement on the intolerable acts and the duties because even though persons with *phronesis* are more likely to reach agreement than persons in the larger society, they are clearly less likely to agree with each other about the balance of reasons in particular situations than about the class of intolerable acts.

This raises the prior question of the importance of reaching agreement about the class of right acts. I have already mentioned that it is crucial for the members of a civil society to agree on the acts that are intolerable, but it is less important that they agree on the rightness of acts that do not directly affect the proper functioning of the society as a whole. I do not deny that even acts that are wrong in the weak sense of failing to be supported by the balance of reasons can make a society unhealthy, but I have hypothesized that we have a distinct category of duties and intolerable acts in order to set apart those acts that are critical to the functioning of a society from those that are less critical. Agreement about the former is highly important. Agreement about the latter is less so. It would be wonderful if we all agreed on what the balance of moral reasons indicates in every case, but it is not essential to a well-functioning society. In any case, given the state of human moral consciousness and the wide areas of disagreement, it is not likely that we will reach such a high level of agreement any time soon. We will need to live with disagreement about what is right and what is not. But if exemplars can be helpful in getting agreement, we will all be better off.

What are the conditions that would make agreement possible? In section 2 I mentioned the importance of linguistic expansion and dialogue among morally admired persons in different communities. That kind of dialogue is an important impetus for linguistic expansion because of the effect of these persons on each other and their effect on their respective linguistic networks, and I think that the expansion of linguistic networks is a necessary condition for agreement in those cases in which a network does not have a word for a particular social phenomenon, as I mentioned in the case of a term for sexual harassment in Arabic. In the case of the Declaration on human rights, I proposed that the act of signing the document put the signatories and the people they influenced in their own countries into a blended linguistic network that inevitably changed the meaning of words in use in their original networks. Agreement on a list of rights did not require a common adoption of the concept of a right, much less did it require the resolution of metaphysical issues on the nature of a human being or the place of humans in the universe. It only required agreement that *those* acts are demanded in any civil society. This document and its increasing acceptance in the decades since then is a triumph in the effort to get agreement about some essential aspects of human morality, partly due to the influence of Eleanor Roosevelt. Nonetheless, we need another approach to the task of cross-cultural moral discourse about the value terms. The Declaration continues to get objections from people who say that the vocabulary of rights shows a Western bias. Even people who accept the idea of a right will not accept a discourse that ignores their religion and particular historical experiences in service to the goal of getting agreement. The aim of getting agreement is laudatory, but it seems to me that the process of getting agreement should do no violence to the theoretical frameworks of the participants in a moral dialogue.

The moral richness of the narratives of exemplars in particular cultures and the conceptual depth of reflection on those stories are not extraneous features of a moral community and should not be ignored, even for the purpose of finding common ground. Human beings are enough alike that even the exemplars of a radically different culture are recognizable, and we have no trouble appreciating their admirable qualities. We can understand why both warrior heroes and pacifist saints have been greatly admired by different groups of people. We have by nature the ability and desire to fight for what we care about, as well as the desire to respect others and not bring them to harm. Different cultures and individuals emphasize one or the other. Over time as a species we have become less pugnacious and much readier to use non-violent means against enemies, but we can still understand why violent persons can be admired, and we can learn from them. Similarly, we have become much less ready to punish by execution persons who are threats to society, but we can also understand why heretics would be executed based on the belief that their continued life threatened the eternal souls of thousands. Many exemplars in past ages supported the death penalty for crimes less than murder, whereas that would be unusual today. I think these are examples of gradual change of opinion, and in Chapter 8 I discuss the possibility of a gradual change in the extension of the term "good person."

I believe that it is important that there be dialogue among persons who are especially wise and who recognize each other as wise, and that the dialogue be available for public view and discussion. It seems to me that a focused discussion between the exemplars of different cultures on their areas of agreement and disagreement can lead to an expansion of the areas of agreement, and the influence of exemplars on other people in their own communities can lead to agreement among ordinary people in different communities. But I want to stress that it is a mistake to think that the way to get agreement is to change our moral vocabulary into an alleged culture-neutral language within which we agree on certain judgments. That approach worked with the adoption of the Universal Declaration on Human Rights, but it is unlikely to work for any part of morality beyond the special class of duties and intolerable acts. I have proposed that the process of getting agreement on moral judgments is essentially connected with becoming part of the same moral linguistic network, and a linguistic community expands through the interactions between influential members of different communities, thereby gradually changing what moral terms *mean*. But there is a part of morality that contains terms we might not want to change because they are deeply imbedded in a particular cultural tradition. One of the things I hope we can learn from wise persons is when to push for agreement and a common vocabulary, and when it is best not to try.

Exemplarist Semantics and Meta-Ethics

1. Introduction

According to Putnam's externalism, the content of a user's thoughts about water or gold or tigers is determined both by the way the world is and by the user's connection to a linguistic network that privileges certain users. I have argued that both ways in which a term can be externalist apply to moral terms. First, what we are talking about when we use words like "good person," "virtue," "duty," and "good life" is determined by features of the world, in particular, features of exemplars. Second, I argued in the last chapter that there is a Division of Moral Linguistic Labor, modeled on Putnam's Principle of the Division of Linguistic Labor for scientific terms, but usually without commonly recognized "experts" in the use of the terms. In this chapter I return to the first way in which terms can be externalist.

The externalist semantics of direct reference had dramatic implications for the connection between the mind and the world. Putnam (1981) used it to produce a famous argument against radical skepticism, and Kripke (1980) used it to argue for the existence of necessary truths known a posteriori. I am not going to discuss skepticism, but I want to look more carefully at the way Kripke used direct reference to support a startling position on the connection between knowing by observation and necessary truths.

Kripke's claim that there are propositions that are necessary but known empirically threatened to unseat a truism of philosophy: that the metaphysical distinction between the necessary and the contingent coincides with the epistemological distinction between the a priori and the a posteriori. It seemed incoherent to suggest that we could find out by observation in the actual world something that is true in *other* possible worlds.

Yet that is what Kripke proposed. Given that I am using a semantics of direct reference for moral terms, it is intriguing to consider the possibility that there can be such truths in ethics. Traditionally, it has been held that basic moral truths are known a priori because of the assumptions that moral truths must be necessary, and that the realm of necessary truth is accessed through reason alone. I can understand the desire to protect the necessity of a core portion of morality, but I think that there is sufficient doubt about the position that necessary truths must be a priori to make the possibility that necessary moral truths can be known empirically well worth exploring.

In the next section I look at early work from Saul Kripke, Nathan Salmon, and Keith Donnellan as a model for an argument that there are necessary a posteriori moral truths. In section 3 I consider alternative approaches that allow for a weaker form of realism without a commitment to necessary a posteriori truths, including a suggestion on a way to borrow features of Richard Boyd's theory in an exemplarist framework. In section 4 I conclude by offering some thoughts on how to categorize exemplarism as a moral theory, and my hopes for the usefulness of my theory to scholars in many disciplines and of many philosophical persuasions, including both moral realists and moral non-realists.

2. Moral Terms and the Necessary a Posteriori

Kripke argued that natural kind terms, like proper names, are rigid designators, designating the same substance or biological species in all possible worlds. Using this feature of natural kind terms and a series of thought experiments, Kripke argued that there are necessary a posteriori truths. His claim had at least two important implications. First, it meant that we can get a metaphysical conclusion out of the theory of reference. The semantical theory of direct reference supports a strong form of scientific realism; indeed, he maintained that it supports essentialism. Second, it meant that the epistemological distinction between the a priori and the a posteriori does not line up with the metaphysical distinction between the necessary and the contingent, a conclusion that went against the assumption of centuries of philosophers.[1]

---

1. This led Keith Donnellan to explore the possibility of the contingent a priori as well as the necessary a posteriori in Donnellan (2012).

The process whereby Kripke and Putnam thought that we come to discover that it is necessary that water is H_2O was examined in detail by Keith Donnellan in his UCLA graduate seminars in the 1970s and in his unpublished work from that period. Donnellan's reconstruction of the mechanism was summarized by Nathan Salmon in his 1981 book, *Reference and Essence*. The general form of it is the following:

(1N) Necessarily, to be water is to be a sample of the same substance of which this stuff is a sample.[2]

(2N) To be a sample of the same substance as something consists in having the same deep physical structure.

(3N) The deep physical structure of this stuff is H_2O.

(4N) Therefore, necessarily, water is H_2O.[3]

The conclusion (4N) was intended to be read both *de dicto* and *de re*. Read *de dicto*, it says:

(4N)DD In any possible world, if something is water in that world, it is H_2O in that world.

This reading of (4N) follows from a reading of (1N) interpreted as the premise that anything is water in any possible world just in case it is a sample in that world of the same substance of which this stuff is a sample in the actual world. So in any world whatever, whatever is water in that world is H_2O in that world.

But presumably, any portion of water is in other possible worlds a sample of the same substance of which it is a sample in the actual world. That is to say, if some portion of stuff is water in some world, it is water in any other possible world in which it exists. It is essential to water that it is water. With this assumption, we get the *de re* reading of (4N):

(4N)DR If any portion of stuff is water in one world, it is H_2O in any world in which it exists.

That is to say, being H_2O is essential to any bit of water.

---

2. This wording is close to that used by Putnam (1975), and which I discussed in Chapter 1.

3. This form of the argument is informal but similar to the one given by Salmon (1981, 166–167). Note that I have reversed the order of the second and third premises from the versions most common in the literature. I find the order above clearer for the parallel I make for exemplarism.

The above argument is therefore doubly interesting. It is not only a mechanism for generating necessary a posteriori truths, but it is a mechanism intended to show that essentialism follows from the semantics of natural kind terms.[4]

Premise (1N) is contained in the theory of reference and is a priori. Premise (3N) is clearly a posteriori. The debate begun by Donnellan centered on versions of premise (2N). Donnellan's position was that it is known a posteriori, but Salmon disagreed, and surmised that we know it a priori (263). But Salmon's main purpose was not to defend the position that (2N) is known a priori but to argue that it contains a hidden essentialist assumption that does not come from semantics.[5] Notice that we get the conclusion that we know (4N) a posteriori either way, assuming that we know a proposition p a posteriori as long as observation is required for at least one step in the process leading to the knowledge of p. More recently, Scott Soames (2004) reconstructed Kripke's argument in a way that he says contains no controversial metaphysical or semantical assumptions. If the argument works under one of these reconstructions, we get support for scientific realism and essentialism. That is to say, there is something out there in the world to which we refer when we use natural kind terms that persists long before and long after we discover some of the properties that make it what it is. Furthermore, we get the interesting conclusion that there are necessary truths that are non-conceptual. They are not known by unpacking a concept but are revealed by following a process to which our referential intentions point us in using natural kind terms.

An argument for necessary a posteriori truths about moral kinds, parallel to the argument above, could go as follows:

(1E) Necessarily, to be a good person is to be the same in admirability as persons like that.

---

4. Kripke seems to have held that any portion of water is essentially water, but we do not get that assumption explicitly in Putnam. See Salmon (1981, 113–114) for a discussion of this point.

5. The hidden premise as constructed by Salmon is the following: "If x exists in w1 and y exists in w2, and if x is a sample in w1 of the same substance that y is a sample of in w2, then whatever chemical structure x has in w1, y has that same chemical structure in w2, and vice versa" (179–180). Salmon argues that this premise is essentialist. I argued in my dissertation, *Natural Kinds* (1979) that that is not where the essentialism lies. Although Salmon devotes most of his attention in the book to arguing that essentialism cannot be derived from the theory of reference, he is clearly sympathetic to the overall project of Kripke, Putnam, and Donnellan.

(2E) To be the same in admirability as persons like that consists in having the same deep psychological structure as they have.

(3E) The deep psychological structure of persons like that consists in the following traits: generosity, fairness, compassion, and others, the components of which include identifiable emotional and behavioral dispositions.

(4E) Therefore, necessarily, to be a good person is to have the traits listed under (3E) with their specific components.

There is a disanalogy between this argument and the parallel argument about natural kinds that should be noted immediately. As we have seen, the modal operator in (4N) is intended to be read both *de dicto* and *de re*. It says that being H_2O is necessary to being water, and it also says that it is necessary to any bit of water that it is H_2O. But unlike "water," the term "exemplar" is not a rigid designator of the objects to which it refers. "Water" rigidly designates what this stuff *is* in the most basic way, according to Kripke. In contrast, "exemplar" or "admirable person" designates something important about this person, but certainly no part of the essence of this person. The argument above has no essentialist premises or conclusions about individuals. It is intended to tell us what is necessary to being admirable. If the argument works, it gives us the conclusion that it is a necessary truth that anybody who has the admirability that Gandhi (Confucius, Mother Teresa, etc.) has in this world has the features of an exemplar in that world. Those features are discoverable a posteriori. The exemplarist argument does not say that these persons, the exemplars to whom we point, are good in all possible worlds in which they exist. That would be very implausible, and the above argument does not have that conclusion.[6]

We know (1E) a priori. I have said that it is a conceptual truth that what we mean by "good person" is what is admirable. We determine what is admirable by what we admire on reflection, but being admired, of course, is not what we mean by "admirable." Admirability is that which makes admiration fitting.

(3E) is known a posteriori, as I argued in Chapter 4, but what about (2E)? Like (2N), (2E) can be supported by the assumption that what makes someone admirable is the deeper causes in the person that explain her admirable behavior and other signs of her admirability, such as the fact that other

---

6. An exception in Christian theology would be the goodness of Jesus Christ. If Jesus is God and God is essentially good, then Jesus was essentially good.

persons trust her advice. That is parallel to the assumption that what makes water *water* is something in the deep physical structure of water that explains water's most salient features: being colorless, potable, boiling and freezing at certain temperatures, being necessary for life, and so on. So in the theory of natural kinds, we think that the deep structure both explains the salient features of water, and is what we take water to *be*. The issue is how we know that. Likewise, we think that the psychological structure of an exemplar both explains the easily observable features of a good person and is what we take a good person to be, qua good person. How do we find that out?

Let us look at Donnellan's defense of a premise like (2N). Donnellan's distinctive contribution to the debate about how a premise (2N) can be defended is his view that there are two a posteriori elements in the generation of a necessary a posteriori truth like (4N). Obviously, (3N) is a posteriori, but Donnellan maintained that (2N) is also. Donnellan says:

> I think we might say that "Water is H_2O," assuming the correctness of Putnam's account, is doubly exotic.[7] Involved in our knowledge of its truth, even though it is necessarily true, is not only the empirical discovery that the stuff we call "water" has the chemical structure, H_2O, but also the knowledge, if that is the right term, that we have, and the ancients did not have, that two liquids are the same only if they have the same chemical structure. And that also is not a priori knowledge. (Donnellan 1973 unpublished, 1974 unpublished, quoted in Salmon, 166)

One reason to think that (2N) is known at least partially by observation is that we find out by observation that the deep physical or chemical structure of certain kinds causally explains the superficial features that we use in ordinary life to identify members of the kind. There is a law-like connection between these deeper properties and the properties that make up the stereotype of the kind. But there is some flexibility in identifying these deep properties, and that led Donnellan in later work (2012, originally published 1983) to offer an interesting hypothesis about the latitude that scientists have in determining what counts as an essential difference between one kind and another. To say that it is chemical structure, or "important physical properties," as Putnam put it, allows for a degree of

---

7. Necessary truths known a posteriori were sometimes called "exotic necessary truths;" hence, the expression "doubly exotic" in this passage from Donnellan.

indeterminacy that permits scientists to specify the features that are the intended target in more than one way.

To illustrate this point, Donnellan presents a thought experiment that is modeled on Putnam's Twin Earth example. He imagines two cultures existing on Earth and Twin Earth. They inhabit almost identical planets and have exactly the same history up to some point in the twentieth century, including the development of atomic theory. He also imagines that on Twin Earth, not only do elements have several isotopes, but as a general rule, one of the isotopes of a particular element makes up the bulk of the element as it occurs in nature. (He says that for all he knows, this situation might occur on Earth.) Isotopes are individuated by the atomic number and combined number of protons and neutrons in the nucleus. The elements with a certain isotope number therefore comprise a subset of the elements with a certain atomic number. Donnellan then goes on to say this:

> Now with these suppositions and facts, it seems to me not psychologically implausible for my Twin-Earthlings to be more taken with, so to speak, the isotope number of a bit of substance rather than with its atomic number and also not implausible for them to diverge from our practice and to identify the substance designated by some of their vernacular natural kind terms not with a certain element, but with the isotope which makes up the bulk of what had been previously called by that term. Hence, for example, they identify gold, not with the element having atomic number 79, but with a certain isotope having a certain isotope number. The rare isotopes of the element having number 79 would then be dismissed as not "really" gold, although, to be sure, in various ways very much like gold. (Donnellan 2012, 197)

Donnellan then goes on to say that when he and his Twin Earth doppelganger ask their respective chemistry departments what gold is, he will be told that it is the element with atomic number 79, whereas his doppelganger will be told that it is the substance with such-and-such isotope number. Given the division of linguistic labor as described by Putnam, it follows that the extension of Donnellan's term "gold" differs somewhat from the extension of the Twin Earthian's term "gold." In this way, Donnellan says, there will be a difference in the truth value of sentences such as "Gold has isotope number x" on Earth and on Twin Earth (198).

Donnellan draws two conclusions from this example. First, he says that although the story does not show that Putnam has failed to describe the way natural kind terms function in the vernacular, the story does show that there is a certain slackness in the semantical machinery. We might have done things somewhat differently with the same linguistic base and the same scientific discoveries (2012, 199–200). We might have taken the route of the Twin Earthians. Second, he is strongly inclined to agree with Putnam that there is no change in meaning after a scientific discovery, so both the Earthians and Twin Earthians mean the same thing by "gold" as they did before, yet their terms "gold" differ in extension. He is also strongly inclined to agree with Putnam that something is not, strictly speaking, gold, unless it has the atomic number our scientists say it has (200). But suppose John Locke had a ring composed of the element with atomic number 79, but it was one of the rare isotopes that the Twin Earthians say is not gold. We Earthians say his ring was really gold, whereas the Twin Earthians would say it was not. But surely we do not want to say that the extension of "gold" in Locke's day was determined by "the psychological quirks of some people several centuries hence" (201). The most reasonable conclusion is that the extension of "gold" can change without any change of meaning. Meaning does not determine the extension, at least not precisely.[8] The extension of a term can change over time because of a scientific decision.[9] So premises 2N and 3N are both known a posteriori in Donnellan's version of the derivation of 4N.

Kripke thought that the extension of a natural kind term is fixed at the beginning. What is not fixed is the epistemic path connecting users to that extension. But according to Donnellan, the conjunction of the way

---

8. Recall that Putnam (1975) proposes that a meaning is an ordered pair, one of whose members is the extension. Of course, in that sense of meaning, the meaning determines the extension trivially. Donnellan does not say what sense of "meaning" he is using, but presumably it is the sense in which the meaning of "gold" is, roughly, "stuff like that."

9. I have been told that there might be a real-life example of a change in the extension of a natural kind term like that proposed by Donnellan in his imaginary gold isotope example. There is a new coral species identified in the Red Sea whose existence was previously known, but the differences between it and others that looked like it were not detected until it was examined through an electron microscope. It was only through a close study of its features that it was reclassified since its previously observable features made it look like another species. I do not know to what extent the change in species classification was the result of a decision as opposed to closer observation, but this case does suggest that reclassification can be partly determined by a decision about what features are "deep and important." See Sarant (2014). My thanks to Cody Weaver for this example.

the world is and our initial referential intentions under-determines the extension of a natural kind. It is not known a priori that what makes gold *gold* is its atomic number. That is the result of a combination of scientific observation and scientific decision. It *is* necessary on Donnellan's view that water is H_2O, and it is necessary that gold has atomic number 79. We come to understand that through a process that has more than one a posteriori step.

In a very stimulating and helpful discussion of Donnellan, Erin Eaker (2012) argues that Donnellan's approach gives a more promising avenue for the derivation of necessary a posteriori truths and a defense of a more moderate (and, she thinks, more plausible) scientific realism than that of Kripke.[10] According to Donnellan's account, there is a robust phenomenon out there that is tracked by the historical trajectory of our linguistic practices, but our linguistic intentions undergo an evolution as science progresses, sometimes resulting in changes in what counts as *really* gold or water or tigers. The necessity that is known a posteriori is not a mere conceptual necessity. "Gold is the element with atomic number 79" is not known by anyone who understands the sentence. But neither is it a fully metaphysical necessity independent of us. It is our practices, linguistic and scientific, that determine that there is no possible world in which "Gold is the element with atomic number 79" counts as false. Taking a cue from Donnellan, then, Eaker suggests that there is a type of necessity that is in between purely conceptual and purely metaphysical. In that sense

---

10. In a later work, "Why There Isn't a Ready-Made World" (1982), Putnam seems to adopt a weaker form of realism and essentialism than that of Kripke in the course of arguing that the theory of reference does not help the materialist:

> I have myself spoken of "essential properties" in a number of my articles.... It *is* a sort of essentialism, but not a sort which can help the materialist. For what I said in those articles was that it has long been our *intention* that a liquid should *count* as "water" only if it has the same composition as the paradigm examples of water (or as the majority of them). I claim that this was our intention even before we *knew* the ultimate composition of water. If I am right, then given those referential intentions, it was always impossible for a liquid other than H_2O to be water, even if it took empirical investigation to find it out. But the "essence" of water in this sense is the product of our use of the word, the kinds of referential intentions we have: this sort of *essence* is not "built into the world" in the way required by an *essentialist theory of reference* to get off the ground.... I conclude that however one takes Kripke's theories (or mine); whether one takes them metaphysically, as theories of objective "essences" which are somehow "out there", or one takes them as theories of our referential practice and intentions, they are of no help to the materialist. (Putnam 1982, 157)

of necessity we can say that necessarily, gold is the element with atomic number 79, a truth that can be known a posteriori.

This debate about the possibility of knowing necessary truths about natural kinds a posteriori is a rich source of reflection on the metaphysics of morals. In spite of disagreements about the precise status of necessary a posteriori truths and the process that generates them, Kripke, Putnam, Donnellan, and Salmon agree that these truths exist, that the necessity is not analytic, and that it is partly—even largely—determined by the way the world is. According to Putnam and Donnellan, the necessity is not fully metaphysical, and according to Donnellan it is partly linguistic. But all of them agree that there are necessary truths known a posteriori.

The key features of the semantics that enable them to get this conclusion are shared by exemplarist semantics. In exemplarism I have proposed that we have initial referential intentions applied to indexically identified objects—admirable persons or persons like *that*—and a historical trajectory in the use of the terms that connects everyone in the community to the extension via a network that privileges certain users. Moral practices develop in the attempt to find out what makes somebody *really* admirable in the same general way that practices develop in the attempt to find out what makes something really gold or really a tiger. There is a continuity of subject matter that leads us to say that what we mean by "good person" or "virtue" or "right act" does not change, even if the persons we call "good," the traits we call "virtues," and the acts we call "right" undergo a gradual change. There is nonetheless something there that we are talking about all along when we undertake theoretical moral discourse, or more frequently, tell stories. The continuity of subject matter is even more obvious in the case of good persons than in Donnellan's example of isotopes of gold because the historical trajectory Donnellan describes in discussing gold does not bring past users and past experts in conversation with current scientific experts. The trajectory moves forward, governed by a combination of new discoveries and theoretical decisions about those discoveries. In these cases it is the current experts who have primacy in determining the extension of a natural kind term. In contrast, we do not necessarily privilege living users of moral terms over past writers about exemplars, and fictional exemplars continue to shape our use of moral terms as long as works about them are read. So the continuity of subject matter is clear.

But are truths about exemplars necessary, and if so, what is the source of the necessity? The difference between Donnellan's position and that of

Kripke and Salmon focuses on (2N). As I have mentioned, Salmon says that (2N) is a hidden premise in Kripke's argument. Donnellan agrees that we know (2N), but argues that we know it a posteriori. It is a deliverance of the practice of science. A consequence is that the extension of a natural kind term like "gold" can change. The parallel question for exemplarism is how we know (2E), and whether, taking a Donnellan-inspired approach, we should say that the extension of "good person" changes over time.

Fortunately, I think the exemplarist case has an advantage over the case of natural kinds with respect to this issue. For natural kinds, we have to figure out how we can know that to be the same substance as something consists in having the same deep physical structure. But in the case of admirable persons, we know how to determine what being the same in admirability consists in. We know it by reflection on our emotion of admiration. As I argued in Chapter 4, we identify psychological structure as the bearer of admirability by observing a putatively admirable person and subjecting a variety of her acts and features to the test of reflective admiration. That permits us to explain how it is that we discover the truth of (2E), and it gives us a way to display the possible progression of discovery of the necessity of certain moral traits of a good person. So to return to the steps of the argument:

> (1E) Necessarily, to be a good person is to be the same in admirability as persons like that.

This is a deliverance of the semantics of direct reference applied to "good person." It does not entail that it is a necessary truth *de re* that these persons are admirable. But if these persons are admirable, it is necessary that to be a good (admirable) person is to be the same in admirability as these persons actually are.

> (2E) To be the same in admirability as persons like that consists in having the same deep psychological structure as they have.

This premise is known a posteriori since it depends on reflection on what we admire and our reflective attempt to connect what we admire on reflection and what is admirable (Chapter 2).

> (3E) The deep psychological structure of persons like that consists in the following traits: generosity, fairness, compassion, and others,

the components of which are identifiable emotional and behavioral dispositions.

This premise is known a posteriori in the way described in Chapters 3 and 4.

(4E) Therefore, necessarily, to be a good person is to have the traits listed under (3E)

If (4E) is true, it is a necessary truth because it tells us what is necessary to being admirable. Of course, (3E) could be false, and so (4E) would be false; (4E) could also be false if our reflective admiration does not reveal admirability, as we discussed in Chapter 2. But if (4E) is true, it is necessarily true. It is a truth we have discovered by the identification of what we admire on reflection.

The pattern I have suggested for generating necessary a posteriori moral truths raises the interesting possibility that the extension of "good person" can change as there are changes in what human beings reflectively admire, even though what we discover about good persons can be necessary. Donnellan's proposal that the extension of a natural kind term can change without change in meaning or referential intentions and without affecting its modal status is relevant here. Donnellan's proposal is that change in the extension of a natural kind term is partly due to the fact that the extension is under-determined by the scientific data and the initial referential intentions. That was the point of his example of the isotopes of gold. Yet the result of this theoretical decision can be a necessary truth. Donnellan's approach, like Kripke's, permits the derivation of necessary a posteriori truths about natural kinds, but it permits enough latitude in the extension of a natural kind term that the extension can change due to a change in scientific decisions. On this approach, the extension of a natural kind term is not fully determined by the nature of the world, although it is partly so determined. For this reason, Donnellan's scientific realism is weaker than that of Kripke, and the kind of necessity we get from this approach is not as robustly metaphysical as that of Kripke.[11]

Can the extension of moral terms change and yet truths about them still be necessary? Here is an example in our moral practices that makes a good test case of the Donnellan approach as applied to exemplarism. What should

---

11. Donnellan does not say that the necessity he supports is weaker than that of Kripke, although I agree with Eaker that that seems to follow.

we say about the fact that at some point in time racism eliminated a person as a candidate for an exemplar? If we follow a Donnellan-style approach, we could say that the extension of "good person" was not fully determined by our initial referential intentions and the way the world is, but it was determined by a change in linguistic usage, guided by a change in admiration, which was itself guided by collective reflection on beliefs, emotions, and practices. We now think that a racist is not an exemplar. Did the extension of "good person" change? Surely there were many racists who would have passed the test of reflective admiration in the past. In fact, it is likely that most of them were racist by contemporary standards. On a Donnellan model of natural kinds, we would say that the extension changed. Although the meaning of "good person" did not change, there were racist exemplars in the past, but racists are no longer in the extension of "good person."

But there is an important dis-analogy between "good person" and "gold." Donnellan's defense of a change of extension in his imaginary story about gold is that it would be unacceptable to claim that past users of a term were wrong because their use did not agree with the extension as used by future scientists. To do so would make the past users mistaken, not because of something about the world not yet discovered, but because of the "psychological quirks of future users" (Donnellan 2012, 201). However, we do not think that the change in our response to racism is a psychological quirk. We think that we have *improved* our sense of the admirable. The people we now admire are closer to those who are truly admirable than in the past. If so, that supports a stronger realism about the admirable than the more modest realism of Donnellan about natural kinds. If we take a Kripke-inspired approach, we should say that in the case of the admirable, the extension of "admirable person" *is* fixed by our initial referential intentions, in combination with what we find out about the world by reflecting on our disposition to admiration, which slowly evolves over time. We do not simply make a decision based on classificatory convenience, as in the gold example. What we take to be in the extension of "admirable person" can change, and in the case of a moral revolution, it can lead to a radical change, but that is because we think that we are getting closer and closer to the truth.

But strong realism about admirability has not yet won the day. There are problems with this approach. If we say that we were wrong about the class of exemplars for most of human history, and in fact, there were few, if any, exemplars during that period, we are on the verge of admitting that what we *mean* by "good person" has changed. The earlier referential intention of the human community in designating good persons was to pick out persons *like that*, and persons like that had many admirable qualities, but they were also what we now call racist. Furthermore, a case could be made that their racism was as much a part of their deep psychological structure as their honesty, compassion, generosity, and other traits. So if we meant to be designating persons *like that*, that meant persons who were racist as well as virtuous in other respects. When we change our minds about a part of the set of qualities that are admirable, we lose the meaning of "good person" we have been using all along unless we can give an account of the historical trajectory of the term that explains why we still refer to exemplars of the past as exemplars.

So far we have two options for modeling a strong form of moral realism on direct reference to natural kinds. The strongest version is closest to Kripke. On this version we could see the term "good person" as referring directly to an abstract object—good personhood or admirable personhood, a property that is invariant across possible worlds in the way the element gold, the substance water, and the species tiger are invariant across possible worlds. Although portions of water, individual tigers, and bits of gold differ from world to world and from time to time in the same world, when someone says "gold," or "water," or "tiger," they mean to be referring to the same thing in one world as another, and at one point of time as another, assuming that the same element or substance or species exists in different worlds. If we take this approach for exemplarism, the exercise of our capacity for reflective admiration rigidly designates good personhood, but we would have to accept the possibility that many of the exemplars to whom we point at any particular time are not actually exemplars, although they may be admirable in many ways. With natural substances and species, we are in the fortunate position of being able to rely on the cooperation of nature with our referential intentions, so even though we can make mistakes in designating bits of gold or portions of water, we can trust that these mistakes are few and easily corrected. In contrast, if we think of good personhood as designated through our disposition to admiration, we would need to accept the possibility of many more mistakes, mistakes that hopefully can be corrected in the course of time, but not at any given time or in any one culture.

If we continue the use of this model to the derivation of necessary a posteriori truths, we could think of a judgment like "A good person is generous" as necessary (*de dicto*, not *de re*), and discovered in a way that parallels the Kripke/Putnam account as modified by Salmon. We might make the case that (2E) is known a priori, a position that may seem implausible, but perhaps no more so than the view that (2N) is known a priori.

If we can know a priori that what makes something the same substance as something else is its deep physical structure, why couldn't we know a priori that what makes something the same in admirability as something else is its deep psychological structure? This approach is strongly realist and has a dramatic conclusion about the possibility of knowing a necessary moral truth a posteriori.

The second approach I have described in this section is also realist, but less so than the first. Modeling our account on Donnellan, we could say that "good person" does not refer to an abstract object but to something that is partly determined by the features of actual good persons and partly by theoretical decision. Since our practices of reflective admiration can change over time, the extension of "good person" can change, and along with it, the features of good persons can gradually change. A peculiarity of this approach is that a proposition like "Good persons do not respect persons of other races" can at one time in history be true and at another time in history be false, and in fact, necessarily false. It would be necessarily false because whereas once the exemplars of goodness failed to respect persons of other races, that is no longer the case. That would be comparable to the situation in which the classification of a species changes in such a way that what was formerly classified as a member of one species comes to be reclassified as not a member of the species. One way to interpret that is to say that the extension of the term "species X" changes, and although it was once true that certain individuals belonged to the species, after the change in classification it is false that they belong to the species, and in fact, it is necessarily false that they belong to the species.

Using this approach to the derivation of necessary a posteriori truths in exemplarism, the Donnellan approach would permit us to take the position that (2E) is known a posteriori while also explaining how the extension of "exemplar" or "admirable person" has changed. The necessity of moral propositions about the components of admirability and the moral realism that accompanies this position are weaker than the full metaphysical necessity Kripke wanted for science, but this approach is at least as plausible in the moral realm as in the scientific realm.

3. Moral Realism without Necessity

Moral realism does not require the boldness of the Kripke/Donnellan-inspired claims about necessary truth, and I have not assumed in this book that when we discover virtues and other psychological characteristics of exemplars, we are discovering necessities. We clearly are discovering something deep and important about admirable persons, but someone can adopt the exemplarist approach without taking on the position that what we discover are necessary features of exemplarity. It depends in part on precisely *what* we think we are referring to when we say "good person." If we have a Platonist bent, we might think we are referring to something that none of our exemplars expresses fully, but to which all of them point. We might then be comfortable with the position I outlined above modeled on Kripke's idea that a natural kind term refers to a substance or species.[12] Alternatively, we might think that we are referring to collections of concrete individuals who are alike in admirability, where we are looking at what actual persons share rather than that to which they aspire. The latter leaves more room for variability and change over time.

There are other approaches that use direct reference in a different way from the way I have used it in this book, but which could be adapted to a version of exemplarism. A particularly interesting approach is the well-known moral theory of Richard Boyd (1988), whose theory is realist, but without the position that there are necessary a posteriori truths. Boyd proposes that each moral term T rigidly designates natural properties that causally regulate the use of the term T. Reference is established by the right sort of causal connections between the use of a term and instances of its referent (321ff). Boyd argues that taking biological species as paradigms of natural kinds rather than chemical kinds like gold and water raises the possibility of thinking of natural kinds as defined by property clusters that contingently co-occur in nature but which conjointly have theoretically and practically important effects. According to Boyd, such a cluster F is homeostatic, meaning that some of the properties in F favor the presence of others, or there are underlying processes that tend to maintain the presence of the properties in F. A kind is defined by observation of the co-occurrence of these properties, and an individual is a member of the kind just in case it possesses a sufficient number of the properties in F. There is therefore a degree of indeterminacy in the extension of the term.

Boyd favors a form of consequentialism in which "good" refers to a homeostatic cluster of important physical, psychological, and social goods. Acts, policies, and traits are morally good to the extent that they

---

12. Perhaps Daniel Russell's (2009) view that virtue is a "model concept" is a theory in this vein. I am not suggesting that Russell is a Platonist, but someone who adopts his view about virtue might also find it congenial to think of "good person" as rigidly designating the abstract object *good personhood*.

foster the realization of these goods or develop and sustain the homeo-static mechanisms on which they depend.

If someone wanted to borrow features of Boyd's approach for the pur-poses of exemplarism, one option would be to think of the term "good person" as referring directly to clusters of contingently related proper-ties that causally regulate the term "good person" or "admirable person" through the disposition to admiration.[13] This approach might be used to resolve the tension between the intuition that we *do* mean the same thing by "moral exemplar" or "admirable person" now and in the past, yet the extension of moral exemplars has apparently changed. If we think of the extension of "moral exemplar" as defined by a homeostatic cluster of vir-tues and other psychological properties that are empirically discovered, and if we also say that membership in the kind requires only a sufficient number of these properties, we are led to the conclusion that exemplars need not have all of the virtues to function as exemplars for most theoreti-cal and practical purposes. The case of the racist exemplar is one in which the exemplar's lack of a feature of admirability was not noticed in the past because of historical circumstances that made racism invisible, but now that that feature has been noticed, we are forced to see the contingency of the relationship among the properties that make up admirability. A racist exemplar is an exemplar, but an exemplar can lack an admirable trait.

If we took this approach, we would still need an explanation for the fact that we can recognize racist exemplars of the past as exemplars, even though I surmise that the same racism today would preclude a person from being an exemplar. The idea that admirability is a homeostatic clus-ter of properties regulating our use of the term "good person" does not yet explain why we would deny that a racist living in modern Western societies has a sufficient number of admirable traits, whereas we would be willing to say that such a person in the past does have enough admirable traits to be an exemplar, and we would probably say the same thing about racists in some parts of the world today.

Here is one way a Boyd-inspired approach might be able to explain this. What is homeostatic at one time might not be homeostatic at a later time or in a different place. One of Boyd's ideas is that the presence of some of the properties in F favor the presence of others. That works well for clusters of virtues if we accept a weak unity of the virtues thesis. For

---

13. I thank Evan Schultz for discussion about ways that Boyd's approach is useful for the issues of this section.

instance, it is not unreasonable to think that the presence of compassion, kindness, and self-control favor the presence of generosity. We need not think that there is a necessary connection among the virtues to think that they are clustered in such a way that a person virtuous in many respects is more likely to be virtuous in other respects. So it seems to me that a person in former eras (and some places today) who was racist by contemporary standards could have most of the virtues. But that would not be the case for a person living in many societies today because once racism becomes recognized in a community, the community expands the range of persons who are thought to be proper objects of the exercise of *all* the virtues. It then becomes much harder than in times past for a racist to have virtues. If she is racist, she does not treat everyone justly, compassionately, and respectfully. If so, that would explain why a racist today would lack most of the virtues and hence could not be an exemplar, but a racist in the past could have been an exemplar because her racism would not preclude her from having most of the virtues.

A well-known objection to Boyd's theory is the moral Twin Earth argument of Horgan and Timmons (1992). They argue that it follows from Boyd's position that if moral terms are causally regulated on Twin Earth by natural properties that are different from those on Earth, the moral terms of the Twin Earthlings would not be inter-translatable with our terms, and that is the wrong result. For instance, on Earth moral terms might be causally regulated by consequentialist properties (Boyd's view), while on Twin Earth moral terms could be causally regulated by deontological properties. This is a problem, they say, because we want to say that the Earthians and the Twin Earthians have a substantive disagreement, not that they are talking about different things.

A Boyd-inspired version of exemplarism can be formulated in a way that avoids this issue. I have argued that admirable properties are the properties that make admiration fitting; they do not merely *cause* an emotional response. We have ways to reflect on our disposition to admiration to make it more fitting, and that is undoubtedly what happened when people came to recognize admiration of racists as unfitting. As I have said, there are different views on the nature of emotions, and it is possible to think of an emotion like admiration as no more than a feeling caused by circumstances, where our disposition to have the emotion has no moral significance. But I have argued that admiration reveals the admirable; it has a perceptual aspect. We can then unpack the content of the admirable by observation. Beings whose disposition to admiration is elicited by very different properties from the ones we admire would not be beings like us. Our inability to morally converse with them cannot be compared to the ability of consequentialists to converse with Kantians, where we clearly see a substantive debate about the same set of moral practices. I think, then, that if someone wanted to devise a theory that blends exemplarism with some of the elements of Richard Boyd's theory, I see no objection from this direction, but since I am not advocating this approach, I will not pursue it further here.

Clever readers will no doubt think of other theoretical variations of exemplarism, including non-realist versions. There is nothing about exemplarism per se that requires a realist view of moral goodness. For instance, a constructivist might see moral goodness as constructed out of our experience of admiration. A certain kind of anti-realist might believe that in an emotional state we project our internal emotions onto the world. On this approach, the admirable is a projection of our feeling of admiring, not a response to the admirable. We could then directly refer to the projections of our own internal states, and our moral discourse would be a system of beliefs and practices about those states. In this book I started with a view of the nature of emotion that I think is plausible, and I then developed the rest of the theory out of the set of exemplars to whom we refer through admiration. But readers who disagree about the objects of admiration need not reject the rest of the theory. Although I have given a realist interpretation based on my view of the nature of admiration, the theory can be modified to reflect a variety of positions on the metaphysical status of the admirable.

4. Conclusion: What Kind of Theory Is Exemplarism?

Alasdair MacIntyre argued in *After Virtue* that we have lost the sense of the human *telos*, and so our virtue terms and other moral terms are no longer intelligible. MacIntyre assumed that without a conception of *eudaimonia*, or human well-being, there is nothing to which we can attach our terms for the virtues. I have argued in this book that we do not need a common conception of human well-being or the human *telos* in order to make virtue terms and the other moral terms intelligible. We need shared narratives and shared emotions of admiration and contempt, together with the ability to rationally reflect on those emotions, and a desire to emulate exemplars. We do not need any particular conceptual framework to make sense of virtue terms. In fact, we do not need any conceptual framework at all. That is fortunate because very few people have such a framework, and I suspect that the number of people who do was always in the minority.

As a moral theory, it is natural to classify exemplarism as a virtue theory because it makes the virtues more central than deontic categories, but the deontic terms are not defined by reference to the virtues, and it is not *eudaimonist*. In exemplarism, virtues, right and wrong acts, and a good life are all defined by reference to what the exemplar is, judges, or desires. Is it a virtue theory? I can see why it might be regarded as a kind of theory that does not fit any traditional category. But this is probably not a very important question.

There are some ways in which exemplarism is unlike any other theory. Virtue ethics has always been broader in scope than moral theories with a modern origin, but exemplarism permits an even broader scope than traditional eudaimonist theories. Anything that is the object of admiration in the sense in which we admire courage, compassion, and generosity is an element of the theory I am proposing. I have said that that includes intellectual virtues like open-mindedness and intellectual humility, and it includes wisdom. The hero, the saint, and the sage are all exemplars in the sense I mean for moral theory, but the saint is spiritually as well as morally exemplary, and the insight of the sage is an intellectual excellence as well as a moral excellence. The hero's excellence is also not clearly limited to the moral, given that self-control is arguably a non-moral excellence.

Exemplarism broadens the range of the moral in another way. If the admirable person is the repository of admirable qualities, then there are many qualities that do not easily fit into traditional categories of moral classification. I have argued that what admirable persons hope for, what they dread, whether they have religious faith, how much they value beauty, how they resolve conflict, what gives structure to their lives, what goals they have for civil society—all of these things can be the object of reflective admiration, and exemplarism puts these features into philosophical moral discourse. I think that the broadening of the scope of the moral in exemplarism is an advantage of the theory. For too long we have lived with a theoretical view of the moral realm that ignores much of what is admirable, as well as much of what is desirable.

My map of the moral is not intended to supplant other theories that have different maps, at least not completely. The methodology is intended to be collaborative. In earlier chapters I proposed that it is crucial to investigate the psychology of exemplars, and that includes the way they engage in moral deliberation and the way emotions function in their judgments and actions. A theory must simplify and systematize our moral practices, and I said in Chapter 1 that I think that theories are part of the practices a theory must explain. That means that *other* theories should be explained by a good theory. This is especially important if a theory is common enough to be assimilated by a large number of people engaged in the practice. If there are practically wise persons who are Kantians, or consequentialists, or Aristotelians, exemplarism will incorporate their forms of moral reasoning and moral decision making into the theory. I doubt that we will find many exemplars whose moral judgment is fully and consistently explained by any standard theory, but it can be revealing to find out what sort of principles wise persons use and how they apply those principles, and whether they are driven by value insights that are not reducible to a set of principles. I proposed in the last chapter that the division of moral linguistic labor gives philosophers the special task of codifying the judgments of wise persons, and consequentialist and deontological theories are attempts at fitting the judgments of the wise onto a theoretical map. It is not necessary that wise persons actually use a philosophical theory themselves to make the theory useful, and I think that in this way other theoretical maps have a place on the map of exemplarism.

In exemplarism a little theory goes a long way because the map is intended to be filled in by other parts of our moral practices, with a special place for narratives and empirical studies. In this respect, exemplarism can be compared to the Stoic approach to ethics. Rachana Kamtekar (2013, 45) says that the Stoics liked to use metaphors for the relationship between one branch of human thought and another. Diogenes Laertius suggests that physics is the content-giver for ethics' otherwise formal statements about what is good, virtuous, appropriate, or correct. I have suggested something similar in exemplarism, except that the role played by physics in a Stoic like Diogenes Laertius is played by other empirical fields, as well as by narratives that enliven our sensibilities. The framework is simple, but the content is huge.

The content of exemplarism also includes practices of moral education. Moral education is neither a theory, nor a set of empirical studies, nor a set of narratives. It is a set of practices used by moral educators in the training of the young and by individuals for their personal moral improvement. I touched on some aspects of moral education in Chapter 5 on acquiring virtue by emulation of exemplars, but there are many aspects of learning how to be moral that can be organized around exemplars in ways that I think can be helpful to moral educators. For instance, I have not said anything about the significance of moral learning through friendship with exemplars,[14] nor have I said anything about the motive to be an exemplar for the young. I have also said very little about anti-exemplars—people we strongly desire *not* to emulate. Exemplars are motivating, and anti-exemplars are motivating in the contrary direction. This means that an examination of the emotion of contempt can be very revealing. I hope to see empirical and philosophical work on contempt and the contemptible as well as on admiration and the admirable.[15]

The fact that exemplarism includes the goals of admirable persons for civil society suggests that the theory could be expanded to include exemplarist political theory. I have not discussed the political and economic arrangements that would be justified by an exemplarist approach, but I think it would be very valuable to pursue the idea of using reflective admiration as a basis for evaluating different social and political structures. It is interesting that Alasdair MacIntyre claims in *After Virtue* (1984) that "characters" are the masks worn by moral philosophies (27). Characters provide the moral focus for a whole cluster of attitudes and activities and function as a cultural and moral ideal (28). MacIntyre's examples include the Public School Headmaster and the Professor in Germany. It is interesting to me that what MacIntyre means by a character is not a particular person, whether real or fictional, but is a construct out of values that have shaped the culture. How do we respond to the embodiment of the values of our age? One way we can respond—mentioned by MacIntyre almost immediately, is to reject it (29). The characters MacIntyre mentions become focal points of debate, and so the "manager" and the "therapist" are characters in a society that MacIntyre thought had become emotivist at the time he was writing.[16] MacIntyre's characters make an interesting comparison with exemplars. The character of the therapist takes on special importance in a society that is used to seeing the problems of life as mental health issues. So the therapist reveals what people care about, what

---

14. See Kristján Kristjánsson (2013), Chapter 6, "Dialogue and Aristotelian Character Education." See also Diana Hoyos-Valdes (unpublished).

15. See Bell (2013) for a valuable book on the moral importance of contempt, mentioned in note 1 of Chapter 2.

16. I think that MacIntyre exaggerated the dominance of emotivism in the 1980s, but that claim does not matter for my point about MacIntyre's hypothesis on the function of "characters" in a cultural milieu.

is constantly on their mind. But there are many things on their mind, and these things can be the object of collective attention. I am suggesting that a society can bring its shared habits of admiration to the forefront, and communities acquire distinctiveness partly by their habits of admiration, which is to say, by the exemplars they collectively recognize. Exemplars embody the qualities most admired in a community. We see our highest ideals in the face of our exemplars, and we can compare that with the highest ideals expressed by the exemplars of another society. I think that this approach to critiquing and improving a society is preferable to the approach of MacIntyre for the reasons I have given throughout this book.

I intend exemplarism to be a theory that is maximally useful for people with different philosophical proclivities. It is naturalistic in that it is based on a natural human emotion, the emotion of admiration, so it can be adopted by people who prefer a naturalistic approach to ethics. It permits many different forms for different communities, including faith communities, within a common framework, so it does not require particular communities to ignore their distinctive ideals when engaging in common moral discourse. It does not favor a priori reasoning in ethics over human experience, respecting the different kinds of experience of different groups of people, including minorities and the disadvantaged. And it engages a much wider range of cultural data and practices than those usually assigned to the philosopher's art.

Moral philosophers cannot be blamed for distinguishing theory from practice and concentrating on the former. As I have said, my position is that a theory aims at understanding and is not the same as a manual, and it is not necessary that it have anything in it that makes us want to use it. But, of course, we do not want to retreat to theory as an excuse for not engaging in the moral life. As Aristotle says "most people do not do these [temperate acts, just acts], but take refuge in theory and think they are being philosophers and will become good in this way, behaving somewhat like patients who listen attentively to their doctors, but do none of the things they are ordered to do. As the latter will not be made well in body by such a course of treatment, the former will not be made well in soul by such a course of philosophy" (*NE* 1105b). I do not know which philosophers Aristotle had in mind, but the philosophers I know have the same goals in life as everybody else. We know that being moral is more important than thinking well about morality, but I hope that exemplarist moral theory helps us with both.

For quite a long time philosophy has focused on topics that are deflating to the spirit or merely puzzling to the mind, and the results have often been uninspiring and tedious. Inspiring people do exist and have always existed in our literature, but they usually do not make their way into philosophical works except for the occasional example. Works about exemplars in the form of biographies or psychological studies are rich in content but rarely give us a sense of the precise features of them that elicit our admiration and the connections among those features. It is not an accident that what we admire in behavior is connected to what we admire in beliefs, motives, intentions, and aims, and it is not an accident that what we admire in one person is admirable in another. Our desire to understand and to navigate our moral practices and to occasionally revise them can only be satisfied by combining a systematic approach to the moral domain with the rich resources we share from our experience of the people who have led the best lives. As I have argued, admiration is both an uplifting emotion, and an emotion whose cognitive content can be used to draw a map of the moral domain.

Jean Vanier says in "The Wisdom of Tenderness," a 2007 interview with Krista Tippett, that an ethics of desire is good news for us at a time when we have become allergic to an ethics of law. He thinks of an ethics of desire as the ethics of Aristotle. Acting morally is pleasureful and the moral life should be joyful. Vanier has spent the greater part of his life centered on bringing love and joy to people who have it least. He is an exemplar of a joyful moral life. I have tried in this book to show a way that we can map the moral domain around people like him, while enjoying the process of making ourselves more like the exemplars who inspire us most.

Bibliography

Ackrill, John. (1980). "Aristotle on *Eudaimonia*." In *Essays on Aristotle's Ethics*, edited by A. O. Rorty, 15–33. Berkeley: University of California Press. Originally in *Proceedings of the British Academy* 60 (1974).

Adams, Robert Merrihew. (1984). "Saints." *Journal of Philosophy* 81(4): 392–401.

Adams, Robert Merrihew. (1999). *Finite and Infinite Goods: A Framework for Ethics*. New York: Oxford University Press.

Aikman, David. (2003). *Great Souls: Six Who Changed a Century*. Lanham, MD: Lexington Books.

Alfano, Mark. (2013). *Character as Moral Fiction*. Cambridge: Cambridge University Press.

Algoe, Sara B., and Jonathan Haidt. (2009). "Witnessing Excellence in Action: The 'Other Praising' Emotions of Elevation, Gratitude, and Admiration." *Journal of Positive Psychology* 4: 105–127.

Angle, Stephen C. (2009). *Sagehood*. New York: Oxford University Press.

Annas, Julia. (2011). *Intelligent Virtue*. Oxford: Oxford University Press.

Anscombe, G. E. M. (1958). "Moral Philosophy." *Philosophy* 33(4): 1–19.

Aquinas, Thomas. (1983). *Treatise on Happiness*. John A. Oesterle, translator. Notre Dame, IN: University of Notre Dame Press.

Aquinas, Thomas. (1972). *Summa Theologiae* Vol. 35, Thomas R. Heath, translator. London: Blackfriars.

Aquino, Karl, Brent McFerran, and Majorie Laven. (2011). "Moral Identity and the Experience of Moral Elevation in Response to Acts of Uncommon Goodness." *Journal of Personality and Social Psychology* 100(4): 703–718.

Ardelt, Monika. (2003). Empirical Assessment of a Three-Dimensional Wisdom Scale. *Research on Aging* 25: 275–324.

Aristotle. (1999). *Nicomachean Ethics*. Second edition, Terence Irwin, translator. Indianapolis, IN: Hackett.

Aristotle. (2006). *On Rhetoric: A Theory of Civic Discourse.* Second edition, George A. Kennedy, translator. New York: Oxford University Press.

Aurelius, Marcus. (1997). *Meditations.* George Long, translator. Mineola, NY: Dover.

Baehr, Jason. (2011). *The Inquiring Mind: Intellectual Virtues and Virtue Epistemology.* Oxford: Oxford University Press.

Balswick, Jack, and Bron Ingoldsby. (1982). "Heroes and Heroines among American Adolescents." *Sex Roles* 8(3): 243–249.

Baltes, P. B., and U. M. Staudinger. (2000). "Wisdom: A Metaheuristic (Pragmatic) to Orchestrate Mind and Virtue toward Excellence." *American Psychologist* 55: 122–136.

Bandura, Albert. (1977). *Social Learning Theory.* Englewood Cliffs, NJ: Prentice-Hall.

Bandura, Albert. (1986). *Social Foundations of Thought and Action.* Englewood Cliffs, NJ: Prentice-Hall.

Bandura, Albert, Dorothea Ross, and Shelia A. Ross. (1963). "Imitation of Film-Mediated Aggressive Models." *Journal of Abnormal and Social Psychology* 66(1): 3–11.

Bardsley, Nicholas, and Peter Moffat. (2007). "The Experiments of Public Goods: Inferring Motivations from Contributions." *Theory and Decision* 62(2): 161–193.

Becker, Bronwyn E., and Suniya S. Luthar. (2007). "Peer-Perceived Admiration and Social Preference: Contextual Correlates of Positive Peer Regard among Suburban and Urban Adolescents." *Journal of Research on Adolescence* 17(1): 117–144.

Bell, Macalester. (2013). *The Moral Psychology of Contempt.* Oxford: Oxford University Press.

Benedict of Nurcia. (2001). *The Rule of St. Benedict.* Trans by Leonard Doyle. Collegeville, MN: The Liturgical Press.

Berken, Kathleen. (2008). *Walking on the Rolling Deck: Life on the Ark.* Collegeville, MN: Liturgical Press.

Bilger, Burkhard. (2012). "The Strongest Man in the World." *New Yorker,* July 23.

Blackburn, Simon. (2004). *Lust: The Seven Deadly Sins.* New York: Oxford University Press.

Blackie, Laura E. R., William Fleeson, Erik Helzer, and Eranda Jayawickreme. "(Moral) Paragon Theory: Ethical Grounding, Life Guidance, and Identity through Paragon Emulation." (Under review). Winston-Salem, NC: Wake Forrest University.

Blake, P. R., T. C. Callaghan, J. Corbitt, and F. Warneken. (Under review). "Altruism, Fairness, and Social Learning: A Cross-Cultural Approach to Imitative Altruism." Boston: Boston University.

Bloom, Paul. 2013. *Just Babies: The Origins of Good and Evil.* New York: Broadway Books.

Bluck, Susan, and Judith Glück. (2005). "From the Inside Out": People's Implicit Theories of Wisdom." In *A Handbook of Wisdom: Psychological Perspectives,* edited by Robert J. Sternberg and Jennifer Jordan, 84–109. New York: Cambridge University Press.

Blum, Lawrence A. (1988). "Moral Exemplars: Reflections on Schindler, the Trocmes, and Others." *Midwest Studies in Philosophy* 13: 196–221.

Bolt, Robert. (1966). *A Man for All Seasons*. New York: Vintage Books.

Boyd, Richard. (1988). "How to Be a Moral Realist." In *Essays on Moral Realism*, edited by G. Sayre-McCord, 181–228. Ithaca, NY: Cornell University Press.

Brennan, Tad. (2005). *The Stoic Life: Emotions, Duties and Fate*. New York: Oxford University Press.

Brewer, Talbot. (2011). *The Retrieval of Ethics*. New York: Oxford University Press.

Brinner, W. M. (1987). "Prophet and Saint: The Two Exemplars of Islam." In *Saints and Virtues*, edited by J. S. Hawley, 36–51. Berkeley: University of California Press.

Brock, Peter. (1994). "Why Did St. Maximilian Refuse to Serve in the Roman Army?" *Journal of Ecclesiastical History* 45(2): 195–209.

Brooks, David. (2015). *The Road to Character*. New York: Random House.

Brown, Peter. (1971). "The Rise and Function of the Holy Man in Late Antiquity." *Journal of Roman Studies* 61: 80–101.

Brown, Peter. (1983). "The Saint as Exemplar in Late Antiquity." *Representations* 1(2): 1–25.

Brown, Warren S. et al. (2013). "Empirical Approaches to Virtue Science: Observing Exemplarity in the Lab." In *Theology and the Science of Moral Action: Virtue Ethics, Exemplarity, and Cognitive Neuroscience*, edited by James van Slyke et al., 11–26. New York: Routledge.

Bryan, James H., Joel Redfield, and Sandra Mader. (1971)."Words and Deeds about Altruism and the Subsequent Reinforcement Power of the Model." *Child Development* 42(5): 1501–1508.

Bryan, James H., and Walbek, Nancy, H. (1970). "Practicing and Preaching Generosity: Children's Actions and Reactions." *Child Development* 41(2): 329–353.

Bucher, Anton. (1998). "The Influence of Models in Forming Moral Identity." *International Journal of Educational Research* 27(7): 619–627.

Burns, Charlene. (2013). "Hardwired for Drama? Theological Speculations on Cognitive Science, Empathy, and Moral Exemplarity." In *Theology and the Science of Moral Action: Virtue Ethics, Exemplarity, and Cognitive Neuroscience*, edited by James van Slyke et al., 149–163. New York: Routledge.

Burnyeat, M. F. (1980). "Aristotle on Learning to Be Good." In *Essays on Aristotle's Ethics*, edited by A. O. Rorty, 69–92. Berkeley: University of California Press.

Carson, Thomas L. (2015). *Lincoln's Ethics*. Cambridge: Cambridge University Press.

Casebeer, William. (2003). "Natural Ethical Facts: Evolution, Connectionism, and Moral Cognition." Cambridge, MA: MIT Press.

Chiger, Krystyna, and Daniel Paisner. (2008). *The Girl in the Green Sweater: A Life in Holocaust's Shadow*. New York: St. Martin's Press.

Churchland, Paul. (1998). "Toward a Cognitive Neurobiology of the Moral Virtues." *Topoi* 17(2): 83–96.

Churchland, Patricia. (2003). "Braintrust: What Neuroscience Tells Us about Morality." Princeton, NJ: Princeton University Press.

Clairmont, David A. (2011). *Moral Struggle and Religious Ethics: On the Person as Classic in Comparative Theological Contexts.* Hoboken, NJ: Wiley-Blackwell.

Clark, P. M. (2014). "The Case for an Exemplarist Approach to Virtue in Catholic Moral Theology." *Journal of Moral Theology* 3(1): 54–82.

Clarke, Bill. (2006). *Enough Room for Joy: The Early Days of Jean Vanier's L'Arche.* New York: BlueBridge.

Confucius. (1997). *The Analects of Confucius: A Philosophical Translation.* Roger T. Ames and Henry Rosemont, translators. New York: Ballantine Books.

Colby, Anne, and William Damon. (1992). *Some Do Care: Contemporary Lives of Moral Commitment.* New York: Free Press.

Colby, Anne, and William Damon. (2015). *The Power of Ideals: The Real Story of Moral Choice.* Oxford: Oxford University Press.

Cua, A. S. (1978). *Dimensions of Moral Creativity: Paradigms, Principles, and Ideals.* University Park: Pennsylvania State University Press.

Curnow, T. (1999). *Wisdom, Intuition, and Ethics.* Aldershot: Ashgate.

Damon, William. (2009). *The Path to Purpose: How Young People Find Their Calling in Life.* New York: Free Press.

Damon, William, and Anne Colby. (2015). *The Power of Ideals: The Real Story of Moral Choice.* New York: Oxford University Press.

Donnellan, Keith. (1966). "Reference and Definite Descriptions." *Philosophical Review* 75(3): 281–304.

Donnellan, Keith. (1973). "Substances and Individuals." Unpublished. Delivered at the 1973 APA Eastern Division Symposium on Reference.

Donnellan, Keith. (1974). "Rigid Designators, Natural Kinds, and Individuals." Unpublished. Delivered at a UCLA Philosophy Colloquium, October.

Donnellan, Keith. (2012). *Essays on Reference, Language, and Mind,* edited by Joseph Almog and Paolo Leonardi. New York: Oxford University Press.

Donald, David Herbert. (1995). *Lincoln.* New York: Simon and Schuster.

Doris, John M. (2002). *Lack of Character: Personality and Moral Behavior.* Cambridge: Cambridge University Press.

Driver, Julia. (2001). *Uneasy Virtue.* Cambridge: Cambridge University Press.

Eaker, E. (2012) "Donnellan on the Necessary *a Posteriori.*" In *Having in Mind: The Philosophy of Keith Donnellan,* edited by Joseph Almog and Paolo Leonardi, 53–78. New York: Oxford University Press.

Emerson, Ralph Waldo. ([1841] 1903). "Self-Reliance." In *The Complete Works of Ralph Waldo Emerson* Vol. 2, 43–90. New York: Houghton Mifflin.

Emmons, Robert A. (1999). *The Psychology of Ultimate Concerns: Motivation and Spirituality in Personality.* New York: Guilford Press.

Enemies: A Love Story. (1989). Directed by Paul Mazursky. Los Angeles: Twentieth Century Fox Film Corporation.

Erikson, Erik H. (1959). *Identity and the Life Cycle.* New York: International Universities Press.

Erikson, Erik H. (1994). "Human Strength and the Cycle of Generations." Chapter 4 In *Insight and Responsibility: Lectures on the Ethical Implications of Psychoanalytic Insight.* 111–157. New York: W.W. Norton.

Finkelman, Paul. (1994). "Thomas Jefferson and Antislavery: The Myth Goes On." *Virginia Magazine of History and Biography* 102(2): 193–228.

Flaubert, Gustave. ([1877] 2009). "A Simple Heart." In *Three Tales,* A. J. Krailsheimer, translator. Oxford World's Classics. New York: Oxford University Press.

Fleeson, W., C. Miller, R. M. Furr, A. Knobel, E. Jayawickreme, and A. Hartley. (2016). *Beacon Project White Paper: What Are the Key Issues for the Study of the Morally Exceptional?* Winston-Salem, NC: Wake Forest University.

Flescher, Andrew. (2003). *Heroes, Saints, and Ordinary Morality.* Washington, DC: Georgetown University Press.

Foot, Philippa. (2001). *Natural Goodness.* Clarendon: Oxford University Press.

Fossheim, Hallavard J. (2006). "Habituation as Mimesis." In *Values and Virtues: Aristotelianism in Contemporary Ethics,* edited by Timothy Chappell, 105–117. Oxford: Oxford University Press.

Frege, Gottlob P. (1892). "Über Sinn und Bedeutung." *Zeitschrift für Philosophie und philosophische Kritik* 100: 25–50.

Fricker, Miranda. (2009). *Epistemic Injustice: Power and the Ethics of Knowing.* New York: Oxford University Press.

Frimer, Jeremy A., Lawrence Walker, Brenda H. Lee, Amanda Riches, and William Dunlop. (2012). "Hierarchical Integration of Agency and Communion: A Study of Influential Moral Figures." *Journal of Personality* 80(4): 1117–1145.

Gaita, Raimond. (2000). "Goodness beyond Virtue." In *A Common Humanity: Thinking about Love and Truth and Justice.* Second edition, 17–28. London: Routledge.

Gandhi. (1982). Directed by Richard Attenborough. Los Angeles: Columbia Pictures.

Gandhi, Mohandas K. (1948). *Non-violence in Peace and War,* Vol. 1, Ahmedabad, India: Navajivan Publishing House.

Garrels, Scott R. (2006). "Imitation, Mirror Neurons, and Mimetic Desire: Convergences between the Mimetic Theory of Rene Girard and the Empirical Research on Imitation." *Contagion: Journal of Violence, Mimesis, and Culture* 12(1): 47–86.

Gibbard, Allan, and Simon Blackburn. (1992). "Morality and Thick Concepts." *Aristotelian Society Supplementary Volumes* 66: 267–299.

Gilbert, D., and P. Malone. (1995). "The Correspondence Bias." *Psychological Bulletin* 117(1): 21–38.

Gill, M. G., D. Packer, and J. Van Bavel. (2013). "More to Morality than Mutualism: Consistent Contributors Exist and They Can Inspire Costly Generosity in Others." *Behavioral and Brain Sciences* 36(1): 90.

Glendon, Mary Ann. (2002). *A World Made New: Eleanor Roosevelt and the Universal Declaration of Human Rights*. New York: Random House.

Glück, J., S. König, K. Naschenweng, U. Redzanowski, L. Domer, I. Staßer, and W. Wiedermann. (2013). "How to Measure Wisdom: Content, Reliability, and Validity of Five Measures." *Frontiers of Psychology* 4(405): doi: 10.3389/fpsyg.2013.00405.

Goldman, Alvin I. (2008). *Simulating Minds: The Philosophy, Psychology, and Neuroscience of Mind-reading*. New York: Oxford University Press.

Goodwin, Doris Kearns. (2006). *Team of Rivals: The Political Genius of Abraham Lincoln*. New York: Simon and Schuster.

Haidt, J. (2001). "The Emotional Dog and Its Rational Tail: A Social Intuitionist Approach to Moral Judgment." *Psychological Review* 108(4): 814–834.

Haidt, J. (2003a). "Elevation and the Positive Psychology of Morality." In *Flourishing, Positive Psychology and the Life Well-Lived*, edited by C. L. M. Keyes and J. Haidt, 275–289. Washington, DC: *American Psychological Association*.

Haidt, J. (2003b). "The Moral Emotions." In *Handbook of Affective Sciences*, edited by R. J. Davidson, K. R. Scherer, and H. H. Goldsmith, 852–870. Oxford: Oxford University Press.

Haidt, J. (2007). "The New Synthesis in Moral Psychology." *Science* 316, 998–1002.

Haidt, J. (2012). *The Righteous Mind: Why Good People Are Divided by Politics and Religion*. New York: Vintage Books.

Haidt, J. S. Koller, and M. Dias. (1993). "Affect, Culture, and Morality, or Is It Wrong to Eat Your Dog?" *Journal of Personality and Social Psychology* 65(4): 613–628.

Haidt, J., and P. Seder. (2009). "Admiration and Awe." In *Oxford Companion to Affective Science*, edited by D. Sander and K. Scherer, 4–5. New York: Oxford University Press.

Hamlin, J. K., K. Wynn, and P. Bloom. (2007). "Social Evaluation by Preverbal Infants." *Nature* 450: 557–559.

Hamlin, J. K., K. Wynn, P. Bloom, and N. Mahajan. (2011). "How Infants and Toddlers React to Antisocial Others." *Proceedings of the National Academy of Sciences* 108(50): 19931–19936.

Harman, Gilbert. (1999). "Moral Philosophy Meets Social Psychology: Virtue Ethics and the Fundamental Attribution Error." *Proceedings of the Aristotelian Society* 99: 316–331.

Hart, D., and S. Fegley. (1995). "Prosocial Behavior and Caring in Adolescence: Relations to Self-Understanding and Social Judgment." *Child Development* 66(5): 1346–1359.

Hartshorne, H., and M. May. (1928). *Studies in the Nature of Character* (Vol. 1: *Studies in Deceit*). New York: Macmillan.

Hawley, J. S., ed. (1987). *Saints and Virtues*. Berkeley: University of California Press.

Herdt, Jennifer. (2008). "Aristotle and the Puzzles of Habituation." In *Putting on Virtue: The Legacy of the Splendid Vices*, 23–44. Chicago: University of Chicago Press.

Hesse, Hermann. (1951). *Siddhartha*. New York: New Directions.

Hills, Alison L. (2009). "Moral Testimony and Moral Epistemology." *Ethics* 120(1): 94–127.

Hills, Alison, David G. Rand, Martin A. Nowak, and Nicholas A. Christakis. (2010). "Emotions as Infectious Diseases in a Large Social Network: The Sisa Model." *Proceedings of the Royal Society, Biological Sciences* 277: 3827–3835.

Horgan, Terrance, and Mark Timmons. (1992). "Troubles on Moral Twin Earth: Moral Queerness Revived." *Synthese* 92 (2): 221–260.

Homer. (1991). *The Iliad*. Robert Fagles, translator. New York: Penguin Books.

Hoyos-Valdes, Diana. (2016). "Friendship and the Cultivation of Virtue." Unpublished. Presented at conference "Cultivating Virtues: Interdisciplinary Approaches," Oriel College, Oxford, January 7–9.

Huff, Chuck. (2014). "From Meaning Well to Doing Well: Ethical Expertise in the GIS Domain." *Journal of Geography in Higher Education* 38(4): 1–16.

Huff, Chuck, and Laura Barnard. (2009). "Good Computing: Moral Exemplars in the Computing Profession." *IEEE Technology and Society Magazine* (Fall): 47–54.

Huff, Chuck, and Almut Furchert. (2014). "Computing Ethics: Toward a Pedagogy of Ethical Practice." *Communications of the ACM* 57(7): 25–27.

Hurka, Thomas. (1987). "'Good' and 'Good For.'" *Mind* 96(381): 71–73.

Hurka, Thomas. (2001). *Virtue, Vice, and Value*. New York: Oxford University Press.

Hurka, Thomas. (2010). "Right Act, Virtuous Motive," In *Virtue and Vice: Moral and Epistemic*, edited by H. Battaly, 57–71. Oxford: Wiley-Blackwell.

Hursthouse, Rosalind. (1999). *On Virtue Ethics*. Oxford: Oxford University Press.

Iacoboni, M. (2008). *Mirroring People: The New Science of How We Connect with Others*. New York: Farrar, Straus and Giroux.

Immordino-Yang, Mary Helen et al. (2009). "Neural Correlates of Admiration and Compassion." *Proceedings of the National Academy of Sciences, U.S.A.* 106(19): 8021–8026.

In Darkness. (2011). Directed by Agnieszka Holland. Culver City, California: Sony Pictures Classics.

Irwin, T. H. (2015). "*Nil Admirari?* Uses and Abuses of Admiration." *Proceedings of the Aristotelian Society, Supplementary Volume* 89(1): 223–248.

Iyer, A., and C. W. Leach. (2008). "Emotion in Inter-Group Relations." *European Review of Social Psychology* 19: 86–125.

Jefferson, T. ([1771] 1975). "Letter to Robert Kipwith." In *The Portable Thomas Jefferson*, edited by M. D. Peterson, 349–352. New York: Penguin.

Johnson, Robert N. (2003). "Virtue and Right." *Ethics* 113(4): 810–834.

Kauppinen, A. (2007). "The Rise and Fall of Experimental Philosophy." *Philosophical Explorations* 10(2): 95–108.

Kahneman, Daniel. (2011). *Thinking, Fast and Slow*. New York: Farrar, Straus and Giroux.

Kamtekar, Rachana. (2013). "Ancient Virtue Ethics." In *The Cambridge Companion to Virtue Ethics*, edited by Daniel C. Russell, 29–48. New York: Cambridge University Press.

Kant, Immanuel. (1998). *Groundwork of the Metaphysics of Morals*, Mary Gregor, translator. Cambridge: Cambridge University Press.

Kawabata, Yasunari. 1996. *The Master of Go*. New York: Vintage Paperbacks.

Kierkegaard, Søren. (1962). *The Present Age*. Alexander Dru, translator. New York: Harper Perennial.

Kierkegaard, Søren. (1954). *Fear and Trembling and the Sickness unto Death*. Walter Lowrie, translator. New York: Doubleday Anchor Books.

King, Martin Luther Jr. (2003). "Stride toward Freedom." In *A Testament of Hope: The Essential Writings and Speeches of Martin Luther King, Jr.*, edited by James Melvin Washington, 417–490. New York: HarperCollins.

Kiser, J. (2003). *The Monks of Tibhurine: Faith, Love, and Terror in Algeria*. New York: St. Martin's Griffin.

Knobe, Joshua, and Shaun Nichols. (2008). *Experimental Philosophy*. New York: Oxford University Press.

Koonz, Claudia. (2003). *The Nazi Conscience*. Cambridge, MA: Harvard University Press.

Kotva, Joseph Jr. (1996). *The Christian Case for Virtue Ethics*. Washington, DC: Georgetown University Press.

Kraut, Richard. (1989). *Aristotle on the Human Good*. Princeton University Press.

Kraut, Richard. (2011). *Against Absolute Goodness*. New York: Oxford University Press.

Kraut, Richard. (2013). "Reply to Stroud, Thomson, and Crisp." *Philosophy and Phenomenological Research* 87(2): 483–488.

Kripke, Saul. (1980). *Naming and Necessity*. Oxford: Blackwell.

Kristjánsson, Kristján. (2006). "Emulation and the Use of Role Models in Moral Education." *Journal of Moral Education* 35(1): 37–49.

Kristjánsson, Kristján. (2013). *Virtues and Vices in Positive Psychology: A Philosophical Critique*. Cambridge: University Press.

Kristjánsson, Kristján. (2015). *Aristotelian Character Education*. Routledge.

Kristjánsson, Kristján. Unpublished. "Emotions Targeting Moral Exemplarity: Making Sense of the Logical Geography of Admiration, Emulation, and Elevation."

Kuhn, Thomas. (1970). *The Structure of Scientific Revolutions*. Second edition. Chicago: University of Chicago Press.

Lear, Jonathan. (2008). *Radical Hope: Ethics in the Face of Cultural Devastation*. Cambridge, MA: Harvard University Press.

LeBoeuf, R., and Z. Estes. (2004). "'Fortunately, I'm No Einstein': Comparison Relevance as a Determinant of Behavioral Assimilation and Contrast." *Social Cognition* 22(6): 607–636.

Ledyard, J. (1993). "Public Goods: A Survey of Experimental Research." In *The Handbook of Experimental Economics*, edited by J. Kagel and A. E. Roth. Princeton, NJ: Princeton University Press, 111–194.

Lee, Kang et al. (2014). "Can Classic Moral Stories Promote Honesty in Children?" *Psychological Science* 25(8): 1630–1636.

Lee, M., and Suk, K. (2010). "Disambiguating the Role of Ambiguity in Perceptual Assimilation and Contrast Effects." *Journal of Consumer Research* 36: 890–897.

Levenson, R., Jennings, P. A., Aldwin, C., and Shiraishi, R. W. (2005). "Self-Transcendence, Conceptualization and Measurement." *International Journal of Aging and Human Development* 60: 127–143.

Linderman, Frank B. (1962). *Plenty Coups: Chief of the Crows*. Lincoln: University of Nebraska Press.

Lockwood, P., and Z. Kunda. (1997). "Superstars and Me: Predicting the Impact of Role Models on the Self." *Journal of Personality and Social Psychology* 73(1): 91–103.

MacFarquhar, Larissa. (2015). *Strangers Drowning: Grappling with Impossible Idealism, Drastic Choices, and the Overpowering Urge to Help*. New York: Penguin Press.

MacIntyre, Alasdair. (1984). *After Virtue: A Study in Moral Theory*. Second edition. Notre Dame, IN: University of Notre Dame Press.

MacIntyre, Alasdair. (1990). *Three Rival Versions of Moral Inquiry*. Notre Dame, IN: University of Notre Dame Press.

MacIntyre, Alasdair. (1999). *Dependent Rational Animals: Why Human Beings Need the Virtues*. Chicago: Open Court Press.

A Man for All Seasons. (1966). Directed by Fred Zinnemann. Los Angeles: Columbia Pictures.

Maritain, Jacques. (1949). "Introduction." In *Human Rights: Comments and Interpretations*, edited by UNESCO, 9–17. New York: Columbia University Press.

Marshall, Robert. (1990). *In the Sewers of Lvov*. New York: HarperCollins.

Martijn, C., H. Alberts, H. Merckelbach, R. Havermans, A. Huijts, and N. De Vries. (2007). "Overcoming Ego Depletion: The Influence of Exemplar Priming on Self-Control Performance." *European Journal of Social Psychology* 37: 231–238.

Matsuba, M. K., and Walter, L. J. (2005). "Young Adult Moral Exemplars: The Making of Self through Stories." *Journal of Research on Adolescence* 15(3): 275–297.

McDowell, John. (1979). "Virtue and Reason." *Monist* 62(3): 331–350.

McGeer, Victoria. (2008). "Trust, Hope, and Empowerment." *Australasian Journal of Philosophy* 86(2): 237–254.

Mehl, M., S. Vazire, and J. M. Doris. (2013). "Eavesdropping on Character: Testing the Stability, Variability, and Changeability of Naturalistically Observed Daily Behavior." Presentation on conference on character, Wake Forest University, June 29.

Mehl, M., and T. S. Conner. (2012). *Handbook of Research Methods for Studying Daily Life*. New York: Guilford Press.

Mehl, M. R., J. W. Pennebaker, M. Crow, J. Dabbs, and J. Price. (2001). "The Electronically Activated Recorder (EAR): A Device for Sampling Naturalistic Daily Activities and Conversations." *Behavior Research Methods, Instruments, and Computers* 33: 517–523.

Melden, A. I. (1984). "Saints and Supererogation." In *Philosophy and Life: Essays on John Wisdom*, edited by Ilham Dilman, 61–79. The Hague: Kluwer Academics.

Meltzoff, A. N., and R. A. Williamson. (2010). "The Importance of Imitation for Theories of Social-Cognitive Development." In *Handbook of Infant Development*, second edition, edited by G. Bremner and T. Wachs, 345–364. Oxford: Wiley-Blackwell.

Mischel, Walter, and Yuichi Shoda. (1995). "A Cognitive-Affective System Theory of Personality: Reconceptualizing Situations, Dispositions, Dynamics, and Invariance in Personality Structure." *Psychological Review* 102(2): 246–268.

Miller, Christian B. (2014). *Character and Moral Psychology*. New York: Oxford University Press.

Miller, Christian B. (2013). *Moral Character*. New York: Oxford University Press.

Miller, Christian B. (2009). "Empathy, Social Psychology, and Global Helping Traits." *Philosophical Studies* 142(2): 247–275.

Moberg, D. J. (2000). "Role Models and Moral Exemplars: How Do Employees Acquire Virtues by Observing Others?" *Business Ethics Quarterly* 10(3): 675–696.

Monroe, Kristen R. (2004). *The Hand of Compassion: Portraits of Moral Choice during the Holocaust*. Princeton. NJ: Princeton University Press.

Murdoch, Iris. (1970). *The Sovereignty of Good*. London: Routledge.

Nagel, Thomas. (1979). "Moral Luck." *Mortal Questions*, 24–38. Cambridge: Cambridge University Press.

Nair, Remya et al. (2015). "'A Self for Others': Joint Self-Other Representation of Value during Morally Relevant Action." EuroAsianPacific Joint Conference on Cognitive Science, Turin, Italy, September.

Needham, R. (1985). *Exemplars*. Berkeley: University of California Press.

Nietzsche, Friedrich Wilhelm. (1967). "On the Genealogy of Morals, Ecce Homo." Walter Kaufmann and R. J. Hollingdale, translators. New York: Vintage Books.

Nussbaum, Martha. (2004). *Hiding from Humanity: Disgust, Shame, and the Law*. Princeton, NJ: Princeton University Press.

Nussbaum, Martha. (2011). *Creating Capabilities: The Human Development Approach*. Cambridge, MA: Harvard University Press.

Of Gods and Men. (2010). Directed by Xavier Beauvois. Culver City, California: Sony Pictures Classics.

Olberding, Amy. (2008). "Dreaming of the Duke of Zhou: Exemplarism and the Analects." *Journal of Chinese Philosophy* 35(4): 625–639.

Olberding, Amy. (2012). *Moral Exemplars in the Analects: The Good Person Is That*. New York: Routledge.

Oliner, Samuel P., and Pearl M. Oliner. (1988). *The Altruistic Personality: Rescuers of Jews in Nazi Europe*. New York: Free Press.

Oman, Doug, Crystal L. Park, Ralph W. Hood, Carl E. Thresen, Phillip R. Shaver, and Thomas G. Plante. (2012). "Spiritual Modeling Self-Efficacy." *Psychology of Religion and Spirituality* 4(3): 278–297.

Oman, Doug, and Carl E. Thoresen. (2003). "Spiritual Modeling: A Key to Spiritual and Religious Growth?" *International Journal for the Psychology of Religion* 13(3): 149–165.

Onu, Diana, Thomas Kessler, and Joanne R. Smith. (2016). "Admiration: A Conceptual Review." *Emotion Review*. Advanced online publication: doi:10.1177/1754073915610438.

Orwell, George. (1968). "Reflections on Gandhi." In *In Front of Your Nose, 1945–1950* (*The Collected Essays, Journalism and Letters of George Orwell*), Vol. 4, edited by Ian Angus and Sonia Orwell, 463–470. London: Martin Seeker and Warburg Limited. Originally published in *Partisan Review*, January 1949.

Palmer, Craig, Ryan Begley, and Kathryn Coe. (2013). "Saintly Sacrifice: The Traditional Transmission of Moral Elevation." *Zygon* 48(1): 107–127.

Peterson, Gregory. (2013). "Virtue, Science, and Exemplarity: An Overview." In *Theology and the Science of Moral Action: Virtue Ethics, Exemplarity, and Cognitive Neuroscience*, edited by James van Slyke et al., 27–46. New York: Routledge.

Peterson, Gregory et al. (2010). "The Rationality of Ultimate Concern: Moral Exemplars, Theological Ethics, and the Science of Moral Cognition." *Theology and Science* 8(2), 139–161.

Pinker, Steven. (2002). *The Blank Slate: The Modern Denial of Human Nature*. New York: Penguin Books.

Pinker, Steven. (2008). "The Moral Instinct." *New York Times*, January 13.

Polansky, Benjamin. (2014). *Admiration and Aporia: Contributions to Exemplarist Virtue Theory*. M.A. thesis, University of Oklahoma.

Polansky, Benjamin. Unpublished. *Moderation*.

Pury, C. L. S., R. Kowalski, and M. J. Spearman. (2007). "Distinctions between General and Personal Courage." *Journal of Positive Psychology* 2: 99–114.

Pury, C. L. S., and A. Hensel. (2010). "Are Courageous Actions Successful Actions?" *Journal of Positive Psychology* 5: 62–73.

Pury, C. L. S., and C. B. Starkey. (2010). "Is Courage an Accolade or a Process? A Fundamental Question for Courage." In *The Psychology of Courage: Modern Research on an Ancient Virtue*, edited by Shane J. Lopez and Cynthia L. S. Pury, 67–87. Washington, DC: American Psychological Association.

Putnam, Hilary. (1973). "Meaning and Reference." *The Journal of Philosophy* 70(19), Seventieth Annual Meeting of the American Philosophical Association Eastern Division. (November 8, 1973), 699–711.

Putnam, Hilary. (1975). "The Meaning of 'Meaning." *Minnesota Studies in the Philosophy of Science* 7, 131–193. Reprinted in *Mind, Language, and Reality* (*Philosophical Papers*), Vol. 2. Cambridge: Cambridge University Press, 1975.

Putnam, Hilary. (1981). "Brains in a Vat." In *Reason, Truth and History*. Cambridge: Cambridge University Press.

Putnam, Hilary. (1982). "Why There Isn't a Ready-Made World." *Synthese* 51(2): 141–167.

Railton, Peter. (2014). "The Affective Dog and Its Rational Tail." *Ethics* 124(4): 813–859.

Rebel without a Cause. (1955). Directed by Nicholas Ray. Los Angeles: Warner Bros.

Reeder, G. D. (2009). "Mindreading: Judgments about Intentionality and Motives in Dispositional Inference." *Psychological Inquiry* 20(1): 1–18.

Reimer, Kevin. (2009). *Living L'Arche: Stories of Compassion, Love and Disability.* New York: Bloomsbury/Continuum.

Reimer, K., C. Young, B. Birath, M. Spezio, G. Peterson, J. Van Slyke, and W. Brown. (2012). "Maturity Is Explicit: Self-Importance of Traits in Humanitarian Moral Identity." *Journal of Positive Psychology* 7(1): 36–44.

Rice, Marnie E., and Joan E. Grusec. (1975). "Saying and Doing: Effects on Observer Performance." *Journal of Personality and Social Psychology* 32: 584–593.

Roberts, R. C. (2013). *Emotions in the Moral Life.* Cambridge: Cambridge University Press.

Roberts, R. C. (2007). *Spiritual Emotions.* Grand Rapids, MI: Wm. B. Erdmans.

Rosner, S., and C. Todd. (2014). *Emotion and Value.* Oxford: Oxford University Press.

Ross, L. (1977). "The Intuitive Psychologist and His Shortcomings: Distortions in the Attribution Process." In *Advances in Experimental Social Psychology*, Vol. 10, edited by L. Berkowitz, 173–220. New York: Academic Press.

Royster, J. E. (1978). "Muhammad as Teacher and Exemplar." *Muslim World* 68(4): 235–258.

Rushton, Philippe, J. (1975). "Altruism and Cognitive Development in Children." *British Journal of Social and Clinical Psychology* 14: 341–349.

Rushton, J. Philippe. (1984). "The Altruistic Personality." In *Development and Maintenance of Prosocial Behavior: International Perspectives on Positive Morality*, edited by Ervin Staub, Daniel Bar-Tal, Jerzy Karylowski, and Janasz Reykowski, 271–290. New York: Plenum Press.

Rushton, J., and A. Campbell. (1977). "Modeling, Vicarious Reinforcement and Extraversion on Blood Donating in Adults: Immediate and Long-Term Effects." *European Journal of Social Psychology* 7(3): 297–306.

Russell, Daniel. (2009). *Practical Intelligence and the Virtues.* Clarendon: Oxford University Press.

Russell, Daniel. 2014. "Aristotelian Virtue Theory: After the Person-Situation Debate." *Revue Internationale de Philosophie* 1(267): 37–63.

Salmon, N. ([1981] 2005) *Reference and Essence.* Second edition. Amherst, NY: Prometheus Books.

Sanneh, L. (2005). "Saints and Exemplars." In *Blackwell Companion to Religious Ethics*, edited by W. Schweiker, 94–103. Oxford: Wiley-Blackwell.

Sarant, Louise. (2014). "New Coral Species in the Red Sea." *Nature Middle East* (September): http://www.natureasia.com/en/nmiddleeast/article/10.1038/nmid dleeast.2014.210.

Scheler, M. ([1933] 1987). "Exemplars of Person and Leaders." In *Person and Self-Value: Three Essays*. M. S. Frings, translator, 127–198. Dordrecht: Martinus Nijohff.

Scheler, M. (1994) *Ressentiment*. Second edition, William W. Holdheim, translator. Introduction by Manfred S. Frings. Milwaukee, WI: Marquette University Press.

Schindler, Ines. (2014). "Relations of Admiration and Adoration with Other Emotions and Well-Being." *Psychology of Well-Being: Theory, Research and Practice* 4(14): doi:10.1186/s13612-014-0014-7.

Schindler, Ines, Veronika Zink, Johannes Windrich, and Winfried Menninghaus. (2013). "Admiration and Adoration: Their Different Ways of Showing and Shaping Who We Are." *Cognition and Emotion* 27(1): 85–118.

Schindler's List. (1993). Directed by Stephen Spielberg. Universal City, California: Universal Pictures.

Schnall, S., J. Haidt, G. Clore, and A. Jordon. (2008). "Disgust as Embodied Moral Judgment." *Personality and Social Psychological Bulletin* 34: 1096–1109.

Schnall, S., J. Roper, and D. Fessler. (2010). "Elevation Leads to Altruistic Behavior." *Psychological Science* 21: 315–320.

Schneewind, J. B. (1990). "The Misfortunes of Virtue." *Ethics* 101(1): 42–63.

Schwarz, N., and H. Bles. (1992). "Scandals and the Public's Trust in Politicians: Assimilation and Contrast Effects." *Personality and Social Psychological Bulletin* 18: 574.

Segal, T. (2005). "Daniel Day-Lewis, Behaving Totally in Character; Oscar Winner Has Made Intensity His Hallmark." *Washington Post*, March 31.

Seroczynski, A. et al. "Reading for Life: A Narrative Character Education Intervention for First-Time Offending Juvenile Delinquents." Ongoing research project funded by the Science of Virtues initiative, Templeton Foundation.

Shanton, Karen, and Alvin Goldman. (2010). "Simulation Theory." *Wiley Interdisciplinary Reviews: Cognitive Science* 1: 527–538.

Shklar, Judith. (1985). *Ordinary Vices*. Cambridge, MA: Belknap Press.

Sidgwick, Henry. (1886). *Outlines of the History of Ethics* New York: Macmillan.

Smart, J. J. C., and Bernard Williams. (1973). *Utilitarianism: For and Against*. Cambridge: Cambridge University Press.

Smith, Adam. [1759] (1976). *The Theory of Moral Sentiments*. Edited by D. D. Raphael and A. I. Macfie. Oxford: Clarendon Press.

Smith, R. H. (2000). "Assimilative and Contrastive Emotional Reactions to Upward and Downward Social Comparisons." In *Handbook of Social Comparison: Theory and Research*, edited by J. M. Suls and R. L. Miller, 173–200. New York: Springer.

Smith, Richard H., and Sung Hee Kim. (2007). "Comprehending Envy." *Psychological Bulletin* 133(1): 46–64.

Smith, J. Warren. (2010). *Christian Grace and Pagan Virtues: The Theological Foundation of Ambrose's Ethics*. New York: Oxford University Press.

Snow, C. P. (1958) *The Search*. London: Macmillan.

Snow, Nancy. "Virtue Intelligence." (2014). Keynote address at conference of Jubilee Center on measuring virtue, Oxford University, January.

Soames, Scott. (2004). "Knowledge of Manifest Natural Kinds." *Facta Philosophica* 6: 159–181.

Soldier, Lydia Whirlwind. (1995). "Wancantognaka: the Continuing Lakota Custom of Generosity." *Tribal College* 7(3): 10–12.

Spezio, Michael, L. (2013). "Relating Political Theory and Virtue Science." In *Theology and the Science of Moral Action: Virtue Ethics, Exemplarity, and Cognitive Neuroscience*, edited by James van Slyke et al., 47–60. New York: Routledge.

Spink, Kathryn. (2006). *The Miracle, the Message, the Story: Jean Vanier and L'Arche*. Mahwah: Hidden Spring Press.

Spivey, C., and S. Prentice-Dunn. (1990). "Assessing the Individuality of Deindividuated Behavior: Effects of Deindividuation, Modeling, and Private Self-Consciousness on Aggressive and Prosocial Responses." *Basic and Applied Social Psychology* 11: 387–403.

Sreenivasan, Gopal. (2013). "The Situationist Critique of Virtue Ethics." In *The Cambridge Companion to Virtue Ethics*, edited by Daniel Russell, 290–314. Cambridge: Cambridge University Press.

Strauss, Leo. (1953). *Natural Right and History*. Chicago: University of Chicago Press.

Stocker, Michael. (1976). "The Schizophrenia of Modern Ethical Theories." *Journal of Philosophy* 73(14): 453–466.

Stroud, Sarah. (2013). "'Good For' Supra 'Good.'" *Philosophy and Phenomenological Research* 87(2): 459–466.

Stump, Eleanore. (2010). *Wandering in Darkness*. Clarendon: Oxford University Press.

Swanton, Christine. (2003). *Virtue Ethics: A Pluralistic View*. New York: Oxford.

Sweetman, Joseph, Russell Spears, Andrew G. Livingstone, and Antony S. R. Manstead. (2013). "Admiration Regulates Social Hierarchy: Antecedents, Dispositions, and Effects on Intergroup Behavior." *Journal of Experimental Social Psychology* 49(3): 534–542.

Thompson, Ross, A. (2006). "The Development of the Person: Social Understanding, Relationships, Self, Conscience." In *Handbook of Child Psychology*, Volume 3: *Social, Emotional, and Personality Development*. Sixth edition, edited by N. Eisenberg, 24–98. Hoboken, NJ: Wiley.

Tiberius, Valerie, and Jason Swartwood. (2011). "Wisdom Revisited: A Case Study in Normative Theorizing." *Philosophical Explorations* 14(3): 277–295.

Tolstoy, Leo. ([1886] 2014). *The Death of Ivan Ilych* and Confession. Peter Carson, translator. New York: Liveright.

Tweedt, Chris. "Fictional Exemplars." Unpublished. http://christweedt.com/Tweedt_FictionalExemplars.pdf.

Updike, John. (1992). "Hostile Haircuts." *New Yorker*, November 2.

Urmson. J. O. (1958). "Saints and Heroes." In *Essays in Moral Philosophy*, edited by A. Melden, 198–216. Seattle: Washington University Press.

Van de Ven, Niels, Marcel Zeelenberg, and Rik Pieters. (2011). "Why Envy Outperforms Admiration." *Personality and Social Psychology Bulletin* 37(6): 784–795.

Vanier, Jean. (1998). *Becoming Human*. New York: Paulist Press.

Vanier, Jean. (2007). "Wisdom of Tenderness." Interview by Krista Tippett, *On Being*, American Public Media, http://www.onbeing.org/program/wisdom-tenderness/234.

Van Slyke, James. (2013). "Naturalizing Moral Exemplars: Contemporary Science and Human Nature." In *Theology and the Science of Moral Action: Virtue Ethics, Exemplarity, and Cognitive Neuroscience*, edited by James van Slyke et al., 101–116. New York: Routledge.

Van Slyke, James, et al. (2013). *Theology and the Science of Moral Action: Virtue Ethics, Exemplarity, and Cognitive Neuroscience*. New York: Routledge.

Vasari, Giorgio (1991/1568). *The Lives of the Artists*. Julia Conaway Bondanella and Peter Bondanella, translators. New York: Oxford University Press.

Velleman, J. David. (2002). "Motivation by Ideal." *Philosophical Explorations* 5(2): 89–103. Reprinted in *Philosophy of Education: An Anthology*, edited by Randall Curren. Oxford: Wiley-Blackwell, 2006.

Vianello, Michelangelo, Elisa Marisa Gallani, and Jonathan Haidt (2010). "Elevation at Work: The Effects of Leaders' Moral Excellence." *Journal of Positive Psychology* 5: 390–411.

Walden, Tedra. (1991). "Infant Social Referencing." In *The Development of Emotion Regulation and Dysregulation*, edited by Judy Garber and Kenneth A. Dodge, 69–88. New York: Cambridge University Press.

Walker, L. J. (in press). "The moral character of heroes." In *Handbook of Heroism and Heroic Leadership*, edited by S. T. Allison, G. R. Goethals and R. M. Kramer. New York: Routledge.

Walker, L. J., and J. A. Frimer. (2007). "Moral Personality of Brave and Caring Exemplars." *Journal of Personality and Social Psychology* 93(5): 845–860.

Walker, L. J., and K. H. Henning. (2004). "Differing Conceptions of Moral Exemplarity: Just, Brave, and Caring." *Journal of Personality and Social Psychology* 86(4): 629–647.

Walker W., K. Diliberto-Macaluso, and J. Altarriba. (2011). "Priming and Assimilation Effects in the Automatic Activation of Religious Schema." *Psychology of Religion and Spirituality* 3(4): 308–319.

Wang, Shirley (2014). "Clues to Teaching Young Children to Tell the Truth." *Wall Street Journal*, June 30.

Ward, Benedicta. (2003). *The Desert Fathers: Sayings of the Early Christian Monks*. New York: Penguin Books.

Warnick, Bryan, R. (2008). *Imitation and Education*. Albany: SUNY Press.

Webster, J. D. (2007). "Measuring the Character Strength of Wisdom." *International Journal of Aging Human Development* 65: 163–183.

Weisberg, Deena Skolnick et al. (2008). "The Seductive Allure of Neuroscience Explanations." *Journal of Cognitive Neuroscience* 20(3): 470–477.

Weng, H. et al. (2013). "Compassion Training Alters Altruism and Neural Responses to Suffering." *Psychological Science* 24(7): 1171–1180.

Weststrate, Nic M., Michael Ferrari, and Monika Ardelt. (2016). "The Many Faces of Wisdom: An Investigation of Cultural-Historical Wisdom Exemplars Reveals Practical, Philosophical, and Benevolent Prototypes." *Personality and Social Psychology Bulletin* 42(5): 1–15.

Whitehead, Alfred North. (1929). "The Place of Classics in Education." In *The Aims of Education and Other Essays*, 61–76. New York: Free Press.

Wolf, Susan. (1982). "Moral Saints." *Journal of Philosophy* 79(8): 419–439.

Zagzebski, Linda. (1979). *Natural Kinds*. Dissertation, University of California, Los Angeles.

Zagzebski, Linda. (1988). "Individual Essence and the Creation." In *Divine and Human Action*, edited by Thomas V. Morris, 119–144. Ithaca, NY: Cornell University Press.

Zagzebski, Linda. (1996). *Virtues of the Mind: An Inquiry into the Nature of Virtue and the Ethical Foundations of Knowledge*. New York: Cambridge University Press.

Zagzebski, Linda. (2000). "The Uniqueness of Persons." *Journal of Religious Ethics* 29(3): 401–423.

Zagzebski, Linda. (2002). "The Incarnation and Virtue Ethics." In *The Incarnation*, edited by S. Davis, D. Kendall, and G. O'Collins, 401–423. New York: Oxford University Press.

Zagzebski, Linda. (2003). "Emotion and Moral Judgment." *Philosophy and Phenomenological Research* 66: 104–124.

Zagzebski, Linda. (2004). *Divine Motivation Theory*. Cambridge: Cambridge University Press.

Zagzebski, Linda. (2006). "The Admirable Life and the Desirable Life." In *Values and Virtues*, edited by Timothy Chappell, 53–66. Oxford: Oxford University Press.

Zagzebski, Linda. (2010). "Exemplarist Virtue Theory." *Metaphilosophy* 41: 41–57. Reprinted in *Virtue and Vice: Moral and Epistemic*, edited by Heather Battaly. Oxford: Wiley-Blackwell, 2010.

Zagzebski, Linda. (2012). *Epistemic Authority: A Theory of Trust, Authority, and Autonomy in Belief*. New York: Oxford University Press.

Zagzebski, Linda. (2013). "Powers and Reasons." In *Powers and Capacities in Philosophy*, edited by John Greco and Ruth Groff, 270–282. New York: Routledge.

Zagzebski, Linda. (2014). "Emotional Self-Trust." In *Emotion and Value*, edited by Sabine Rosner and Cain Todd, 169–182. Oxford: Oxford University Press.

Zagzebski, Linda. (2015). "Admiration and the Admirable." *Proceedings of the Aristotelian Society, Supplementary Volume* 89(1): 205–221.

Zagzebski, Linda. (2016). "The Dignity of Persons and the Value of Uniqueness." Presidential Address to the Central Division of the American Philosophical Association. In *Proceedings and Addresses of the American Philosophical Association*.

Index